Lecture Notes of the Institute for Computer Sciences, Social Informatics and Telecommunications Engineering   121

T0240556

Hua Qian   Kai Kang (Eds.)

Wireless Internet

7th International ICST Conference
WICON 2013
Shanghai, China, April 11-12, 2013
Revised Selected Papers

 Springer

Volume Editors

Hua Qian
Kai Kang
Shanghai Institute of Microsystem
and Information Technology
Chinese Academy of Sciences
Shanghai, China
E-mail: {hua.qian; kai.kang}@wico.sh

ISSN 1867-8211   e-ISSN 1867-822X
ISBN 978-3-642-41772-6   e-ISBN 978-3-642-41773-3
DOI 10.1007/978-3-642-41773-3
Springer Heidelberg New York Dordrecht London

Library of Congress Control Number: 2013951362

CR Subject Classification (1998): C.2, H.4, H.3, F.2, K.6.5

Typesetting: Camera-ready by author, data conversion by Scientific Publishing Services, Chennai, India

Printed on acid-free paper

Springer is part of Springer Science+Business Media (www.springer.com)

Preface

On behalf of the Organizing Committee, I would like to welcome you to the proceedings of the 7th International ICST Wireless Internet Conference (WICON 2013) held in Shanghai, China. Shanghai, "Paris of the Orient," is one of the most prosperous Chinese cities. The featured architecture, cloud-capped skyscrapers, and large-scale shopping malls are a perfect combination of Chinese and Western cultures.

In co-sponsorship with the IEEE Computer Society, the goal of the conference is to bring together technical experts and researchers from around world to discuss and exchange novel ideas in the field of future Internet, wireless, mobile, and vehicular technology.

I would like to sincerely thank everyone who performed reviews for papers or helped to manage the review process.

It is fitting to express here our deepest appreciation for the commitment and hard work of all who were involved in making this conference a success, including the EAI, the IEEE, the Organizing and Technical Program Committees.

April 2013   Hua Qian

Organization

String Committee

Xudong Wang   Shanghai Jiao Tong University
Hsiao-Hwa Chen   National Cheng Kung University

General Chairs

Hua Qian   Shanghai Institute of Microsystem and Information Technology, Chinese Academy of Sciences

Tao Zhou   Shanghai Research Institute, China Telecom

Panels and Keynotes Chair

Yang Yang   Shanghai Institute of Microsystem and Information Technology, Chinese Academy of Sciences

Publicity Chair

Zhaofeng Zhang   Shanghai Advanced Research Institute, Chinese Academy of Sciences

Local Chair

Fan Zhang   Shanghai Institute of Microsystem and Information Technology, Chinese Academy of Sciences

Website Chair

Kai Kang   Shanghai Research Center for Wireless Communications

Table of Contents

Vehicular Communications and Heterogeneous Networks

Cognitive Radio and Multi-antenna Systems

3G Networks and Beyond

Ad Hoc and Mesh Networks

Pilots Aided Channel Estimation for Doubly Selective Fading Channel in Vehicular Environment

Sunzeng Cai[1,2], Haiping Jiang[3], Hua Qian[4], and Weidong Xiang[5]

[1] Shanghai Institute of Microsystem and Information Technology, CAS
[2] Key Laboratory of Wireless Sensor Network and Communication, CAS
[3] Shanghai Research Center for Wireless Communications
[4] Shanghai Internet of Things Co., Ltd.
[5] Department of ECE, University of Michigan-Dearborn
{sunzeng.cai,haiping.jiang,hua.qian}@shrcwc.org, xwd@umd.umich.edu

Abstract. In vehicle communications, channel characteristic experiences time and frequency selective fading due to high velocity of vehicle and rapid changes of surrounding scatters. The packet format for IEEE 802.11p standard limits the choice of channel estimation algorithms. Conventional channel estimation algorithms perform the channel estimation based on the long preamble training sequence, then applies the estimated channel response to compensate for the entire packet. These algorithms are not optimal for a doubly selective channel in vehicle communications. In this paper, to overcome the effect of doubly selective channel, we propose a novel pilot insertion scheme that covers all subcarriers in both the time and frequency domains simultaneously. Adaptive channel estimation and equalization algorithms are then developed based on the new system architecture. Simulations show significant improvements comparing to other exiting methods.

1 Introduction

In recent years, road construction is not an economic solution to improve the traffic condition any more. The Vehicle-to-vehicle (V2V) and vehicle-to-infrastructure (V2I) communication systems can help to improve the traffic, provide vehicle information service and safety enhancement, as well as deliver the vehicle entertainment service. Wireless access for vehicle environment (WAVE) is launched recently to realize the vehicle communications. Among all candidate technologies, the orthogonal Frequency Division Multiplexing (OFDM) based IEEE 802.11p [1], which is published in 2010 by extending the IEEE 802.11 standard [2], is the most promising one.

In V2V and V2I communications, the signal may be shadowed by building, scattered and diffracted by vehicle and roadside infrastructure. In these situations, the frequency selectivity of the received signal can be worse than that for the indoor scenarios. In addition, the movement of vehicle leads to different doppler shift in each path, which causes the doppler spread in frequency. The

H. Qian and K. Kang (Eds.): WICON 2013, LNICST 121, pp. 1–13, 2013.
© Institute for Computer Sciences, Social Informatics and Telecommunications Engineering 2013

received signal is also selective in time domain. The wireless channel is doubly selective in high velocity vehicle communications. The wireless channel estimation
and equalization are critical for the receiver performance.

Traditional Wi-Fi is targeting at stationary and indoor environment. In
IEEE802.11 standard, two long preamble sequences are included. The location
of the known preamble and pilots of the IEEE802.11 standard is shown in Fig.
1(a). The channel estimation is applied based on the long preambles. Since the
channel for a stationary and indoor environment does not change over time, the
channel estimation based on the preambles can be applied to the entire packet.
The pilots inserted in the subsequent OFDM symbols are not designed for the
channel estimation purpose. While in V2V and V2I communications, the channel
coherence time is short, the channel estimation results obtained by the preamble
is not valid for the entire packet. The channel response must be estimated and
updated in corresponding to the changes of the environment.

In [3], a dynamic channel equalization scheme is proposed, which exploits data
subcarriers aided channel estimation method. This method, on the other hand,
may lead to error propagation in low Single-to-Noise Ratio(SNR) region. In [4], a
system enhancement algorithm is used to update the channel response. However,
the convergence velocity of the coefficients estimation cannot track the channel
changes. Pseudo-Random-Postfix OFDM (PRPOFDM), which inserts additional
pseudo-random sequences before guard intervals, has been proposed in [5] [6].
However, adding additional training sequence sacrifices the data rate. In [7] [8],
it proposed a method that insert training sequence for block transmissions over
doubly selective wireless fading channels, this will not only change the structure
of the frame, but also reduce the data rate. In [9], a pseudo-pilot scheme is
proposed. The pilot location is shown in Fig. 1(b). This scheme overcomes the
shortcomings of the original IEEE802.11a standard by substituting pilots in
selected data slots for channel equalization. On the other hand, this algorithm
does not take into consideration of the channel coherence time, thus may not be
appropriate when the vehicle velocity changes.

In this paper, we propose a new pilots aid channel equalization method. The
conventional fixed pilots in the symbol are replaced with shifted pilots as shown
in Fig. 1(c) and Fig. 1(d). The pilot shifts are determined based on coherence
time and coherence frequency bandwidth defined in [10]. The channel estimation and equalization is updated adaptively for the data symbols based on the
shifted pilots. The rest of this paper is organized as follows: in section 2, OFDM
system model in IEEE802.11p standard is described. In section 3, we present
the proposed channel estimation method. Section 4 shows the simulation results
and compare the system performance with other channel estimation algorithms.
Finally, conclusion is drawn in section 5.

2   Conventional IEEE802.11p System

For the IEEE802.11p standard, the OFDM is applied in physical (PHY) layer.
The norminal channel bandwidth is divided into 64 subcarriers, with 48 data

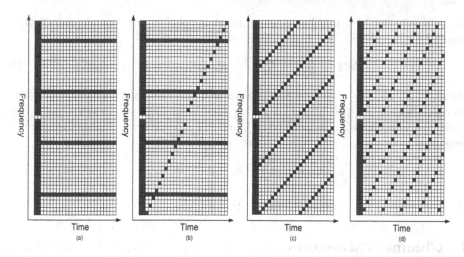

Fig. 1. IEEE802.11p standard pilot structure and the proposed pilot structure

subcarriers, 4 dedicated pilot subcarriers and zeros for other subcarriers. The system is operating at 5.9GHz frequency.

The transmitter components and configuration for IEEE802.11p standard are shown in Fig. 2. The information bits are firstly scrambled by a length 127 frame-synchronous scrambler. A convolutional code is applied to the scrambled data. To protect against burst errors, a block interleaver is applied. The modulator is applied to the interleaved sequence to get the data subcarriers. With additional inserted pilot subcarriers and zero subcarriers, the frequency domain OFDM symbol is constructed. The time domain transmitter output is obtained by performing the inverse fast Fourier transform (IFFT) to the OFDM symbol and appending cyclic prefix before each OFDM symbol.

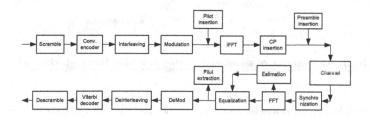

Fig. 2. The transceiver structure in IEEE 802.11p standard

The transmitted signal propagates to the receiver after passing through the channel response, mixing with thermal noise and possible interferences. At the receiver, the cyclic prefix can be removed from the receive data after synchronization. Denoting the OFDM symbol index by M and the subcarriers number by k ($k \in \{0, 1, ..., 63\}$), the received data at the kth subcarriers of the Mth transmitted OFDM symbol can be obtained by performing fast Fourier Transform(FFT) to the received time-domain signal:

$$FFT\{r_{n,M}\} = R_{k,M} = H_{k,M}S_{k,M} + Z_{k,M},\tag{1}$$

where $R_{k,M}$ and $S_{k,M}$ denote the receive and the transmit signals at the kth subcarriers of Mth transmitted OFDM symbol in frequency domain, $Z_{k,M}$ is the additive white Gaussian noise(AWGN), and $H_{k,M}$ represents channel frequency response

$$H_{k,M} = \sum_{l=0}^{l=L-1} h_{n,M}e^{j2\pi nkl/K},\tag{2}$$

where L denotes the number of multipath components.

3   Channel Estimation

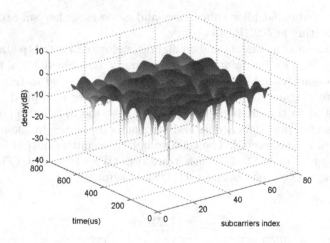

Fig. 3. An example of simulated doubly selective Rayleigh channel

In the vehicle communications environment, the channel response is selective in both time domain and frequency domain. An example of the channel response is shown in Fig. 3.

The conventional approach for channel estimation is to estimate the channel response with a training sequence. For IEEE802.11p standard, the 2 long preambles can be applied for channel estimation. Zero-forcing(ZF), minimum mean-square error (MMSE) [11], and maximum likelihood (ML) [12] channel estimation are typical for channel estimation. The MMSE channel estimation algorithm, which provides a satisfactory trade-off between the complexity and the performance, is selected in our study. MMSE channel estimation method [13] is to minimize the mean square error (MSE) of the estimated channel responses, which is given by

$$E[e^2[k, M]] = E[\|S_{k,M} - \hat{H}_{k,M}^* R_{k,M}\|^2].$$ (3)

To minimize the MSE, we have

$$\frac{\partial [e^2[k, M]]}{\partial \hat{H}_{k,M}} = 0$$

$$E[(S_{k,M} - \hat{H}_{k,M}^* R_{k,M}) \cdot R_{k,M}] = 0.$$ (4)

The solution to (4) is [13]

$$\hat{H}_{MMSE} = \Phi(\Phi + \frac{\beta}{SNR} I)^{-1} \frac{R_{k,M}}{S_{k,M}},$$ (5)

where Φ is the covariance matrix and the (k_1, k_2) element is given by

$$\Phi(k_1, k_2) = \sum_{i=0}^{N-1} \alpha_i \exp[\frac{-j2\pi(k_1 - k_2)i}{N}],$$ (6)

β is a constant value based on the modulation type,

$$\beta = E[|S_{k,M}|^2] E[|\frac{1}{S_{k,M}}|^2], k = 0, 1, ..., 63,$$ (7)

SNR is the signal-to-noise ratio and I is an $N_k \times N_k$ identity matrix.

With the preamble training sequences, the channel can be estimated. However, given the doubly selectivity of the channel characteristics, the initial channel estimation results are not suitable for the entire packet. Moreover, since the coherence frequency bandwidth of the channel is limited, the channel responses for the data subcarriers cannot be interpolated from the dedicated pilot tones in the subsequent OFDM symbols. The traditional IEEE802.11p packet structure may not be suitable for the doubly selective channel.

From [10], we know that the coherence frequency bandwidth can be calculated as

$$B_c \approx \frac{1}{50\sigma_\tau},$$ (8)

or

$$B_c \approx \frac{1}{5\sigma_\tau},$$ (9)

where σ_τ denotes root mean square (rms) delay spread, B_c denotes the coherence frequency bandwidth. Eq. (8) is valid when frequency coherence function is above 0.9, and eq. (9) is valid when frequency coherence function is above 0.5. In a typical open space multi-path Rayleigh channel [14], the rms delay spread can be $\sigma_\tau = 250$ ns. The coherence frequency bandwidth is only $B_c = 80$ kHz from eq. (8), or $B_c = 800$ kHz from eq. (9). In contrast, the tone spacing for the IEEE802.11p subcarriers is 156.25kHz. If the tone spacing is larger than the coherence frequency bandwidth, the correlation between subcarriers is limited. In this case, all data and pilot subcarriers are uncorrelated in the sense of strict coherence frequency bandwidth of 80 kHz. In IEEE802.11p standard, the 4 dedicated pilot subcarriers are separated apart by 1.875 MHz. Interpolating the channel response for data subcarriers from pilot subcarriers is not feasible.

The coherence time can be calculated as [10]

$$T_c \approx \frac{9}{16\pi f_m},\tag{10}$$

where f_m is the Doppler spread given by $f_m = v/\lambda = v f_c/c$.

The number of coherent OFDM symbols N_{OFDM} can be calculated from

$$N_{OFDM} = \frac{T_c}{T_{OFDM}} = \frac{9c}{16\pi v f_c T_{OFDM}}.\tag{11}$$

Given the length of one OFDM symbol T_{OFDM} of 8.0us, we can infer that $N_{OFDM} = 41$ for 100 km/h velocity and $N_{OFDM} = 20$ for 200 km/h velocity.

For the traditional IEEE802.11 structure, the channel is estimated by two preamble symbols. The 4 dedicated pilot tones in the subsequent symbols are used to calibrate the frequency drift or the common phase error. This approach does not apply to the IEEE802.11p when doubly selective channel exists. An example is shown in Fig. 5. Given a NLOS (Non-Line-of-Sight) channel with rms delay spread of 100 ns, the original channel estimation method can only support the velocity upto 30 km/h. The channel response must be updated timely with pilot tones or midambles. However, the four dedicated pilot subcarriers in IEEE802.11p standard are not enough to achieve satisfied performance as the correlation among subcarriers is limited.

To improve the channel estimation in subsequent OFDM symbols, a pseudo-pilot scheme that scrambles the location of the pseudo pilot is proposed [9]. As shown in Fig. 1(b), this pilot structure takes in to consideration of the frequency diversity. However, this scheme does not consider the channel coherence time, thus may not be efficient when the vehicle moves in high velocity.

To compensate for the doubly selective channel, we need to take into consideration the limitation of both coherence frequency bandwidth and coherence time. Therefore, we propose a new pilot subcarriers structure, assuming that we can manipulate the position of the two dedicated pilots. The position of the pilot subcarriers are determined by the coherence time T_c and coherence frequency bandwidth B_c. When the velocity of the vehicle is less than 100 km/h, the coherence time T_c is approximately 41 T_{OFDM} long. We may shift the pilot subcarriers by one in each OFDM symbols as shown in Fig. 1(c). The pilot subcarriers traverse all 52 subcarrier locations. The channel frequency response of current OFDM symbol can be obtained by updating the history frequency response with the pilot information from adjacent 12 OFDM symbols. In this case, regardless the coherence frequency bandwidth B_c, the channel frequency can be obtained.

When the vehicle moves faster than 100km/h, the coherence time T_c is less than 41 OFDM symbols, shifting the 4 subcarriers by one subcarrier in each OFDM symbol cannot cover the entire frequency band. Shifting by two or more subcarriers is needed to meet the coherence time constraint. The coherence frequency bandwidth B_c needs to be verified in order to interpolate the frequency response of data subcarriers from adjacent pilot subcarriers. For example, if velocity of the vehicle is 200 km/h, the coherence time $T_c \approx 6 * T_{OFDM}$ and coherence frequency bandwidth is $B_c = 800kHz$ by eq. (9) for the NLOS channel with rms delay of 250 ns. The pilot insertion scheme is shown in Fig. 1(d). At each OFDM symbol, the frequency response of the pilot subcarriers can be obtained directly. The frequency response of adjacent 4 data subcarriers can be updated by linearly interpolating the channel response of the pilot subcarriers in current and previous OFDM symbols. The overall channel response can then be obtained by combining the history channel response from the previous 5 OFDM symbols.

In summary, the proposed channel estimation algorithm with pseudo pilots is given by:

Step 1 Initialization. The initial channel estimation is given by the two long preamble training sequences. For example, if we choose the MMSE channel estimator, $H_{k,0}$ is given by (5), where $H_{k,M}$ denotes the channel estimation at the kth subcarrier and the Mth data symbol. Furthermore, denote by $H_{k_p,M}$ the channel estimate of pilot subcarriers and $H_{k_d,M}$ the channel estimate of data subcarriers.

Step 2 Pilot subcarrier estimation. For $M > 0$, the channel estimate of the pilot subcarriers $H_{k_p,M}$ can be obtained similarly by (5).

Step 3 Data subcarrier extrapolation. For the data subcarriers adjacent to the pilot subcarriers, the channel estimate can be obtained by interpolating the pilot subcarriers. When $|k_p - k_d| \leq \lfloor B_c/(156.25kHz) \rfloor$, the correlation between subcarriers exists. The channel estimate updating equation is given by

$$H_{k_d,M} = \sum_i \omega_i H_{k_{p_i},M},$$ (12)

where the pilot subcarrier k_{p_i} is chosen such that $|k_{p_i} - k_d| \leq \lfloor B_c/(156.25kHz) \rfloor$, and $\sum_i \omega_i = 1$.

If k_d is not correlated to any pilot subcarriers, we may reuse the channel update from previous iteration, i.e.,

$$H_{k_d,M} = H_{k_d,M-1},$$ (13)

Step 4 Coherence in time. To consider the channel coherence in time, the current channel estimate can be updated from the previous estimate by

$$H_{k,M} = (1 - \alpha)H_{k,M-1} + \alpha H_{k,M},$$ (14)

where α is determined by the channel coherence time [10], or

$$(1 - \alpha)^N_{OFDM} = 0.5.$$ (15)

In reality, α may be changed to account for the noise in the estimation.

To understand the above channel estimation procedure, an example is provided. We assume that velocity of the vehicle is 200 km/h, which gives the coherence time $T_c \approx 20 * T_{OFDM}$. For a NLOS channel rms delay of 100 ns [14], the coherence frequency bandwidth is $B_c = 200$ kHz by eq. (8). In this case, the channel response of data subcarriers right next to the pilot subcarriers can be inferred from the pilot channel estimate. In this case, $i = 1$ and $\omega_i = 1$. To consider the correlation in time, we know that $\alpha = 0.11$ from eq. (15).

With the proposed algorithm, we may apply the pilot structure shown in Fig. 1(c) to the IEEE802.11p system in low velocity. In this case, we do not need the data interpolation as shown in eq. (12), and only need to update the current OFDM symbol one by one to track the variable channel response. In general cases when the vehicle velocity is unknown, we may apply the pilot structure as shown in Fig. 1(d), channel response in data subcarriers can be linear interpolated by the adjacent pseudo pilot subcarriers.

The standard symbol architecture for IEEE802.11p does not guarantee a robust reception in doubly selective channels. The proposed algorithm changes 4 fixed pilot tones in the existing standard to 4 cyclically shifted pilot tones as shown in Fig. 1(c) or Fig. 1(d). The changes only occur when assemble and disassemble the OFDM symbol. The data rate and other OFDM parameters are not affected. In addition, the cyclically shifted pilot subcarriers can still be used to track the frequency drift or the common phase error as the 4 fixed pilots in the standard.

4   Simulation Result

In order to show the performance of the proposed pilot structures, we compare the system performance in terms of packet error rate (PER) for the four cases shown in Fig. 1: (a) the standard IEEE802.11p pilot structure, (b) the scrambled pilot structure proposed by [9], (c) the proposed pilot structure for low velocity scenario, (d) the proposed pilot structure for high velocity scenario. In simulation, we chose 10 MHz frequency bandwidth mode for the IEEE802.11p standard, the carrier frequency is set to be 5.9 GHz. The length of each transmitted OFDM symbol is 8.0 us, including 1.6 us-long cyclic prefix. The modulation scheme is BPSK and the coding method is rate-1/2 convolutional code. The structure of the simulation system is shown in Fig. 2. 300 Byte packet length (100 OFDM symbols) for different pilot structures, the only changes in the architecture exist in the pilot insertion block and the pilot extraction block. The channel applied in the simulation is a time-varying TGn 802.11n channel model B [14] which is an open-space channel model for NLOS conditions with average rms delay spread 100 ns. The mathematical model is given by

$$h(t;\tau) = \sum_{l=0}^{L} \alpha_l(t) e^{j\theta_l(t)} \delta(t - \tau_l), \tag{16}$$

where L denotes the number of multipath components, τ_l denotes the delay for the lth path, $\alpha_l(t)$ denotes time-varying amplitude and $\theta_l(t)$ denotes time-varying phase. The normalized delay power profile for this channel is shown in Fig. 4.

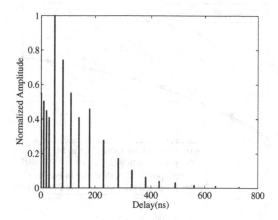

Fig. 4. The normalized delay power profile for the time-varying TGn 802.11n channel model B for NLOS condition with 100ns rms delay spread

In the first experiment, we study the system performance in terms of PER at different velocities varying from 0 km/h to 200 km/h with 30 dB SNR in Fig. 5. From top to bottom, the blue dash-dotted line shows the PER performance using conventional channel estimation method with the pilot structure in Fig. 1(a); the green dotted line shows the PER performance using channel estimation method with the pilot structure in Fig. 1(b); the red dashed line shows the PER performance using channel estimation method with the pilot structure in Fig. 1(c); the black solid line shows the PER performance using channel estimation method with the pilot structure in Fig. 1(d). From Fig. 5, we observe that for a doubly selective channel shown in Fig. 4, the conventional channel estimation method that just utilize the preamble of the IEEE802.11p standard does not perform well. To meet a standard 10% PER requirement, the highest velocity that the conventional channel estimation method can support is only 27 km/h. The channel estimation method utilizing the pilot insertion scheme shown in Fig. 1(b) provides better performance than the conventional approach at a cost of additional inserted pilots. On the other hand, this method can only support a vehicle velocity of 82 km/h at the 10% PER threshold. Considering a typical vehicle velocity of 120 km/h, this method is not satisfactory. In contrast, channel estimation methods with the proposed pilot insertion schemes achieve better performance than the above two algorithms. The channel estimation algorithm based on the pilot insertion scheme shown in Fig. 1(c) can support a vehicle velocity of 126 km/h at 10% PER, while the other works at a vehicle velocity of 150 km/h. The pilot insertion scheme in Fig. 1(d) is slightly better than that in Fig. 1(c) at high velocity as the pilot insertion scheme in Fig. 1(d) provides additional correlation in frequency among different OFDM symbols.

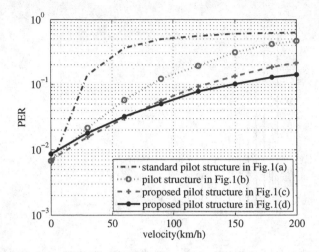

Fig. 5. Channel estimation method for standard pilot structure in Fig. 1(a), pilot structure Fig. 1(b), proposed pilot structure in Fig. 1(c), proposed pilot structure in Fig. 1(d) with different velocity (doppler spread) in 30dB SNR

In the next examples, we study the system performance in terms of PER at different SNR when velocity of the vehicle is fixed at 30 km/h, 90 km/h and 120 km/h, respectively. When velocity of the vehicle is 30 km/h, the system performance is shown in Fig. 6. We observe that the conventional channel estimation method experiences a PER floor and cannot meet the 10% PER requirement at 30 dB SNR. The rest three channel estimation methods work well in this case. We also notice that the pilot insertion scheme in Fig. 1(c) is slightly better than that in Fig. 1(d). At low velocity, the coherence time is relatively long, both pilot insertion scheme in Fig. 1(c) and pilot insertion scheme in Fig. 1(d) provides enough protection in channel coherence time. The pilot insertion scheme in Fig. 1(c) does not need to extrapolate the channel response from the know pilot subcarriers, which delivers better performance and the pilot insertion scheme in Fig. 1(d) that requires extrapolation of the channel response. When velocity of the vehicle is 90 km/h, the system performance is shown in Fig. 7. We observe that in addition to the conventional channel estimation method, the pilot insertion scheme in Fig. 1(b) cannot meet the 10% PER requirement at 30 dB SNR. This result show that the channel estimation method [9] cannot work well when the coherence time constraint becomes dominate. In this case, our proposed channel estimation methods can work well. When velocity of the vehicle is 150 km/h, the system performance is shown in Fig. 8. We observe similar trend that only the channel estimation method using the pilot insertion scheme in Fig. 1(d) can meet the 10% PER requirement at 30 dB SNR.

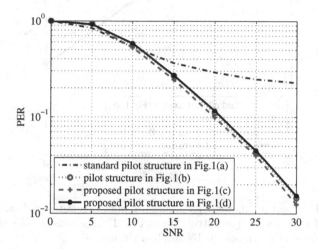

Fig. 6. Channel estimation method for standard pilot structure in Fig. 1(a), pilot structure Fig. 1(b), proposed pilot structure in Fig. 1(c), proposed pilot structure in Fig. 1(d) with 100OFDM symbols in 30km/h environment

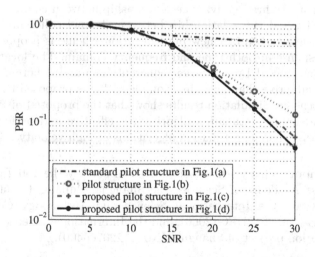

Fig. 7. Channel estimation method for standard pilot structure in Fig. 1(a), pilot structure Fig. 1(b), proposed pilot structure in Fig. 1(c), proposed pilot structure in Fig. 1(d) with 100OFDM symbols in 90km/h environment

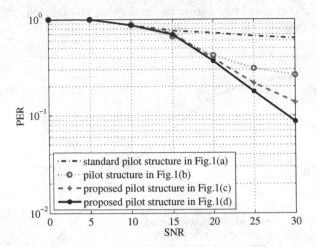

Fig. 8. Channel estimation method for standard pilot structure in Fig. 1(a), pilot structure Fig. 1(b), proposed pilot structure in Fig. 1(c), proposed pilot structure in Fig. 1(d) with 100OFDM symbols in 150km/h environment

5   Conclusion

The rich scatters and fast velocity in vehicle wireless communication make the channel doubly selective in the course of a packet transmission. An adaptive channel estimation is critical to track the channel variation to guarantee robust data transmission. We first analyze the relationship between channel coherence time and velocity, and the relationship between channel coherence frequency bandwidth and delay spread. A new pilot insertion scheme is proposed to provide channel response in both time and frequency domain. The location of the pilots can be determined by the target coherent time and coherent frequency bandwidth. An adaptive channel estimation algorithm is proposed based on the pilot insertion scheme. Simulation results show that the proposed pilot insertion scheme and the channel estimation algorithm is effective and performs better than other existing channel estimation algorithms at high velocity.

Acknowledgment. This work was supported in part by the 100 Talents Program of Chinese Academy of Sciences, the Shanghai Pujiang Talent Program (No. 11PJ1408700), the International Science and Technology Cooperation project of China (No. 2012DFG12060), and the International Science and Technology Cooperation project of Shanghai (No. 11220705400).

References

1. IEEE Std 802.11p: Part 11: wireless LAN medium access control (MAC) and physical layer (PHY) specifications. Amendment 6: Wireless Access in Vehicle Environment (July 2010)

2. IEEE Std 802.11-2007: IEEE Standard for Information Technology-Telecommunications and Information Exchange between Systems-Local and Metropolitan Area Networks-Specific Requirements Part 11: Wireless LAN Medium Access Control (MAC) and Physical Layer (PHY) Specifications (June 2007)
3. Fernandez, J., Borries, K., Cheng, L., Kumar, B., Stancil, D., Bai, F.: Performance of the 802.11 p physical layer in vehicle-to-vehicle environments. IEEE Transactions on Vehicular Technology 61(1), 3–14 (2012)
4. Abdulhamid, H., Abdel-Raheem, E., Tepe, K.: Channel estimation for 5.9 ghz dedicated shortrange communications receiver in wireless access vehicular environments. IET Communications 1(6), 1274–1279 (2007)
5. Muck, M., De Courville, M., Debbah, M., Duhamel, P.: A pseudo random postfix ofdm modulator and inherent channel estimation techniques. In: IEEE Global Telecommunications Conference, GLOBECOM 2003, vol. 4, pp. 2380–2384. IEEE (2003)
6. Lin, C., Lin, J.: Novel channel estimation techniques in ieee 802.11 p environments. In: 2010 IEEE 71st Vehicular Technology Conference (VTC 2010-Spring), pp. 1–5. IEEE (2010)
7. Ma, X., Giannakis, G., Ohno, S.: Optimal training for block transmissions over doubly selective wireless fading channels. IEEE Transactions on Signal Processing 51(5), 1351–1366 (2003)
8. Schniter, P.: Low-complexity equalization of ofdm in doubly selective channels. IEEE Transactions on Signal Processing 52(4), 1002–1011 (2004)
9. Sibecas, S., Corral, C., Emami, S., Stratis, G., Rasor, G.: Pseudo-pilot ofdm scheme for 802.11 a and p in dsrc applications. In: 2003 IEEE 58th Vehicular Technology Conference, VTC 2003-Fall, vol. 2, pp. 1234–1237. IEEE (2003)
10. Rappaport, T.: Wireless communications: principles and practice. IEEE Press (1996)
11. Hosseinnezhad, M., Ganji, F.: Low complexity mmse based channel estimation algorithm in frequency domain for fixed broadband wireless access system. In: IEEE 10th Annual Wireless and Microwave Technology Conference, WAMICON 2009, pp. 1–3. IEEE (2009)
12. Chen, P., Kobayashi, H.: Maximum likelihood channel estimation and signal detection for OFDM systems. In: IEEE International Conference on Communications, ICC 2002, vol. 3, pp. 1640–1645. IEEE (2002)
13. Van de Beek, J., Edfors, O., Sandell, M., Wilson, S., Borjesson, P.: On channel estimation in OFDM systems. In: 1995 IEEE 45th Vehicular Technology Conference, vol. 2, pp. 815–819. IEEE (1995)
14. Erceg, V.: TGn channel models, IEEE 802.11 - 03/940r4 (2004)

Dynamic Channel Estimation over Fast Time-varying Channel for Vehicle Wireless Communications

Haiping Jiang[1,2], Sunzeng Cai[2,3], Weidong Xiang[4], and Hua Qian[5]

[1] Shanghai Research Center for Wireless Communications
[2] Shanghai Institute of Microsystem and Information Technology, CAS
[3] Key Laboratory of Wireless Sensor Network and Communication, CAS
[4] Department of ECE, University of Michigan-Dearborn
[5] Shanghai Internet of Things Co., Ltd.
{haiping.jiang,sunzeng.cai,hua.qian}@shrcwc.org, xwd@umd.umich.edu

Abstract. In vehicle wireless communications, channel characteristics vary rapidly due to the high velocity of the vehicle and rich surrounding scatters. To guarantee a reliable transmission, dynamic channel estimation needs to track the channel changes in the duration of a packet. Within the framework of IEEE802.11p standard, we propose a new channel estimation algorithm that combines data subcarriers and pilot subcarriers to equalize channel response in both frequency domain and time domain. Depending on the changes of the channel, the channel response can be further dynamically equalized by combining the channel response of previous OFDM symbols. Simulations show significant improvement in terms of packet error rate (PER) comparing to the existing methods with little additional computation.

1 Introduction

Wireless Access for Vehicle Environment (WAVE) [1,2] is launched in recent years to realize both vehicle-to-infrastructure (V2I) and vehicle-to-vehicle (V2V) telematics services. Reliable and low-latency data transmission plays a key role in fast varying vehicle communication environment. The Orthogonal Frequency Division Multiplexing (OFDM) based IEEE802.11p [3] technique was published in 2010 by extending the IEEE802.11a mechanisms, which was originally designed for indoor scenarios, to the outdoor.

In mobile vehicle environment, the propagation of wireless signal can be shadowed, scattered and diffracted by other vehicles, trees or buildings on the roadside. This condition leads to Doppler shift, short channel coherence time [4,5]. Long delay spread is not a significant problem affecting wireless access by IEEE802.11p based on the previous measurements [4,6], and therefore our attention is focused on other channel impairments. Generally, channel state can not be regarded as a constant over the course of one packet transmission. Therefore, an efficient channel estimator to track the channel variation in such fast varying environment is important.

H. Qian and K. Kang (Eds.): WICON 2013, LNICST 121, pp. 14–24, 2013.
© Institute for Computer Sciences, Social Informatics and Telecommunications Engineering 2013

A lot of research [7,10,11,8,12,9,13,14] has been done on channel estimation and equalization for OFDM signals, some of which is independent of any given standard. Here, we focus on the channel estimation based on IEEE802.11p system. Conventional channel estimation methods in IEEE802.11p system only adopt two long preambles at the beginning of packet as the guided method in the standard. The performance of channel estimators with only preambles is not guarantied in fast moving environment. In [8], a dynamic channel equalization scheme is proposed, which exploits data subcarriers to aid the channel estimation update. The packet error rate (PER) of data transmissions is significantly improved. However, it does not consider equalizing multiple OFDM symbols in time domain when the channel is fast time-varying. In [9], a modified channel estimation scheme for intelligent packet communication systems adopts additionally the short training OFDM preambles in time domain to improve channel estimation capability, however the scheme only enhances the channel estimation for part of subcarriers position. An iterative reduced-rank channel estimator [10], which is based on generalized discrete prolate spheroidal sequence, obtains the same frame error rate as that with perfect channel state information with additional computational complexity. To reduce the number of implementation iterations, an improved pilot structure is designed by appending OFDM pilot symbol as postamble to the OFDM frame. For OFDM system with carrier frequency offset and phase noise, channel frequency response and phase noise are estimated jointly by employing the maximum *a posteriori* (MAP) criterion in [15].

In this paper, we focus only on receiver-centric improvements, and propose a dynamic channel estimation method based on IEEE802.11p systems over fast time-varying channel by jointly exploiting pilot subcarriers and data subcarriers. Especially, in fast time-varying environment, the relationship between the velocity of vehicle and channel coherence time motivates us to consider that channel frequency response in current OFDM symbol can be further equalized by the channel response of previous correlated OFDM symbols.

The rest of the paper is organized as follows: in section 2, OFDM system model in IEEE802.11p system is described and the problem of channel estimation is stated. Section 3 presents a new channel estimation algorithm for IEEE802.11p system, and the complexity of the presented algorithm is analyzed in Section 4. Section 5 shows simulation results and validates the performance improvement in terms of PER. At last, a conclusion is drawn in Section 6.

2   System Model

The IEEE802.11p standard defines an OFDM-based physical layer to operate in the 5.9 GHz frequency band. An OFDM symbol in frequency domain contains k_d data subcarriers and k_p fixed pilot subcarriers originally designated for frequency offset and phase noise correction, where $k_d = 48$, $k_p = 4$. At the beginning of packet, two long preambles are used to estimate the frequency offset and channel response. The time-frequency structure of the transmitted signal can be described in Fig. 1, where the shadowed tones contain known information.

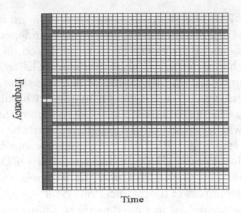

Fig. 1. IEEE802.11p time-frequency frame structure

We consider a packet with N consecutive OFDM symbols, which is transmitted via channel coding, interleaving, modulation and mapping. Denote by $H(i,k)$ the channel frequency response in the ith OFDM data symbol and kth subcarrier, $S(i,k)$ the transmitted frequency signal, $N(i,k)$ the additive white Gaussian noise (AWGN) at the (i,k)th OFDM symbol.

The OFDM signal in time domain can be obtained by performing Inverse Fast Fourrier Transform (IFFT) to the frequency domain symbol:

$$s(i,m) = IFFT\{S(i,k)\} = \sum_{k=0}^{K-1} S(i,k)e^{j2\pi mk/K}, \tag{1}$$

where m is the sampling index in time domain, $K = 64$ is to perform IFFT efficiently. The guard interval is inserted to the output of IFFT operation. The transmitter components and configurations are shown in Fig. 2. In the fast moving scenario, the channel suffers from time varying multipath fading with uncorrelated 2-dimensional isotropic scattering. Denote by $h(i,l)$ the channel impulse response for the lth complex path in the ith OFDM symbol. Channel frequency response $H(i,k)$ can be expressed as,

$$H(i,k) = \sum_{l=0}^{L-1} h(i,l)e^{-j2\pi kl/K}, \tag{2}$$

where $h(i,l) = \sum_{l=0}^{L-1} a_l e^{j\phi_l}\delta(iT_s - t_l)$, L is the number of paths, a_l is complex attenuation coefficient of lth path, ϕ_l is the phase of lth path, and T_s is the duration of an OFDM symbol. The received symbol $R(i,k)$ in frequency domain is

$$R(i,k) = S(i,k) \cdot H(i,k) + N(i,k), \tag{3}$$

where $i = 1, 2, \cdots, N$, and $k = 1, 2, \cdots, K$.

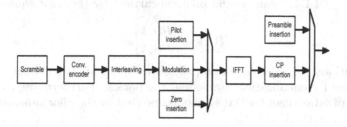

Fig. 2. Transmitter structure of IEEE802.11p physical layer

In the framework of IEEE802.11p standard, the channel can be assumed to be constant over an OFDM symbol, however the channel can change over a packet. In this case, the OFDM symbol duration T_{OFDM} is 8 μs for 10 MHz frequency bandwidth. The central wave length $\lambda = c/f_c$, where $c = 3 \times 10^8$ m/s is the speed of electric and magnetic wave. Assume that the relative velocity of two vehicles is v, and the channel frequency response is essentially invariant over the motion distance of $9\lambda/16\pi$ [16]. The coherence time τ_c over which the time correlation function is above 0.5 is given by

$$\tau_c = \frac{9c}{16\pi v \cdot f_c}. \tag{4}$$

In other words, the number of correlated OFDM symbols is

$$\gamma = \frac{\tau_c}{T_{OFDM}} = \frac{9c}{16\pi v \cdot T_{OFDM} \cdot f_c}. \tag{5}$$

In the vehicle communication case, the relative velocity can be as high as 240 km/h, we know that from eq. (5) the number of correlated OFDM symbols is approximately 16 for 10MHz frequency bandwidth, and the maximum Doppler shift is 1.09 kHz from eq.(6).

$$f_d = \frac{v}{\lambda} = \frac{v \cdot f_c}{c}. \tag{6}$$

When the system operates with the bandwidth 10 MHz, the subcarrier spacing for 64 subcarriers is as high as 156 kHz. The Doppler shift is generally less than 0.6% of the subcarrier spacing. Consequently, the inter-carrier interference is not significant for IEEE802.11p system. The short coherence time, on the other hand, can be a primary source of performance degradation, and this leads to the need of dynamic channel estimation. In the next section, we propose a new algorithm to dynamically update the channel response over the course of one packet to combat for the short coherence time.

3   Channel Estimation

For simplicity, we omit the noise item in this section. It is straightforward to estimate the channel response using known transmitted data, i.e. the short and long training OFDM symbols and pilot subcarriers by the least-square channel estimate

$$\hat{H}(i,k) = \frac{R(i,k)}{S(i,k)}. \tag{7}$$

For conventional channel estimation algorithms, the above channel estimation result is used for equalization throughout the packet. Furthermore, the channel estimation of subsequent OFDM symbol is updated by the pilot subcarriers using interpolation method.

When channel is not fast varying, the initial channel estimation obtained by preambles can be adopted to the following symbols. When the vehicle moves fast, channel correlations between OFDM symbols become small. The initial channel estimation can be outdated after the first few symbols. On the other hand, when the packet undergos multipath fading and delay spread, the pilots are not spaced closely enough to sample the channel variations in the frequency domain. The performance of conventional channel estimation algorithms is not satisfactory. Consequently, in V2V and V2I scenarios, an effective channel estimator must dynamically track the channel variation in both frequency and time domain.

To combat the fact that there are not enough pilot subcarriers, data subcarriers can be used to aid channel estimation. The noise in each subcarrier can be regarded as independent, the channel estimation accuracy can be improved by utilizing the correlation of channel response in subchannels. For example, in [8], several data subcarriers are exploited to make a single measurement at the given kth subcarrier.

With the received signal at the kth subcarrier and the ith data symbol $R(i,k)$, the transmitted signal can be recovered using the channel estimation of the $(i-1)$th symbol:

$$\hat{S}(i,k) = \frac{R(i,k)}{H(i-1,k)}. \tag{8}$$

When a decision of the received data is made, the channel estimation of ith symbol at kth subcarrier is updated by

$$H(i,k) = \frac{R(i,k)}{X(i,k)}, \tag{9}$$

where $X(i,k)$ is the estimated data after decision.

Since the estimation result (9) is suffering from measurement noise, combining adjacent subcarriers into the given subcarrier can help to reduce the effect of a single channel measurement noise. The linear combination of channel estimation in frequency domain for a given (i,k) OFDM symbol is expressed as

$$H_F(i,k) = \sum_{\iota=-\alpha}^{\alpha} w_\iota H(i,k+\iota), \tag{10}$$

where α is the number of adjacent subcarriers on one side for average, and w_ι is the weight of each subcarrier, and $\sum_{\iota=-\alpha}^{\alpha} w_\iota = 1$. The weight of subcarriers closer to the pilot subcarriers can be assigned a bigger value, because the channel estimation for these subcarriers has better performance.

To average the channel estimation, the channel needs to be extended for the first and last subcarrier, and the whole channel response is constructed for the ith symbol as $[H(i, \alpha+1), \cdots, H(i, 2), H(i, 1), \cdots, H(i, K), H(i, K-1), \cdots, H(i, K-\alpha)]$. Since the zero subcarrier is not used to data transmission, so the value of $H(i, 27)$ is replaced by $(H(i, 26) + H(i, 28))/2$.

Considering the fast variation of channel state, we should iteratively update the channel estimation depending on the changes of the channel. The combination of several channel estimation algorithms in the coherence time makes the channel estimation of current symbol more reliable.

$$H_T(i, k) = \sum_{\kappa=1}^{\gamma} \frac{p^{\gamma-\kappa}}{\sum_{\kappa=1}^{\gamma} p^{\kappa}} H(i - \kappa, k), \tag{11}$$

where γ can be chosen according to eq. (5) and is related to the velocity of vehicle, and p is the weight factor for each OFDM symbol in the coherence time (a large p implies more weight for the previous OFDM symbols which are closer to the current OFDM symbol). Note that γ maybe a rough estimaiton in the case with high velocity. The more precise threshold for the coherence time can be defined, and the number of correlated OFDM symbols can be chosen. Therefore, eq. (11) shows that the channel estimation update rate can be adjusted according to the change of the channel. It facilitates to dynamically track channel state and is expected to improve the performance. When the channel estimation is averaged in frequency and time domain respectively, we consider the final channel estimation as follows,

$$H(i, k) = (1 - \frac{1}{\beta})H_T + \frac{1}{\beta}H_F. \tag{12}$$

where β is determined by getting a balance between time dimension and frequency dimension.

To start the iterative procedure, the initial channel estimation $H(0, k)$ is calculated from the preamble symbols. The channel response of subsequent OFDM symbols are obtained from (12). The procedure is repeated until all OFDM symbols are processed.

4   Complexity Analysis

The proposed iterative channel estimation algorithm is complied to operate in IEEE802.11p system. The complexity of the presented method is determined by two steps:

1. Initial estimation
   This process includes the estimation of channel response by the direct decision of the received data. By eq.(8) and (9), the initial estimation involves $2NK$ complex divisions for all OFDM symbols in each subcarriers.

2. Iterative estimation

The channel estimation in frequency dimension combines the adjacent sub-carriers. The execution includes $(2\alpha + 1)$ multiplications and $(2\alpha + 1)$ additions, where α has generally small value.

The dominant factor in the computational complexity is iterative channel estimation in time dimension. From eq.(11), the algorithm involves γ^2 multiplications and $2(\gamma - 1)$ additions to obtain the estimation of each OFDM symbol.

In total, the complexity of the presented algorithm in term of floating point operations is $(\gamma^2 + 2\gamma + 4\alpha + 7)NK$. Comparing to other iterative channel estimation algorithms, e.g., see [10], our channel estimation method achieves good channel response without increasing the computational load.

5   Simulation Results

In this section, we study the performance of the proposed channel estimation method. In the simulation, we consider an uncoded input that is modulated by the QPSK modulation. Without loss of generality, the results can be easily extended to other modulations. The PER is determined based on the transmission of 10^6 packets, and the parameters α, β, p in (10), (12) and (11) are chosen to be 2, 2, and 3, respectively. In each simulation, we only model narrowband fading, where all multipath components are received within a single symbol period. The channel model is given by $h(i, l)$ in eq.(2). Fig. 3 is an example of channel response variation of the normalized fading power envelope. The signal is transmitted at a bandwidth of 10 MHz with central frequency band of 5.9 GHz.

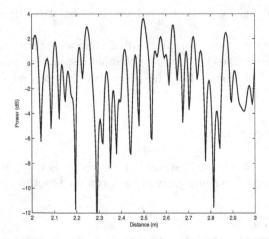

Fig. 3. Example of channel response variation of the normalized fading power envelope, where the vehicles travel relatively at 100 km/h

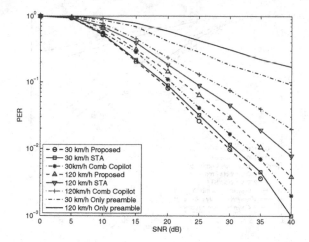

Fig. 4. PER comparison of the proposed algorithm, STA algorithm and Comb Copilot algorithm for velocities 30, 120 km/h, corresponding to maximum Doppler shift 164, 656Hz with fixed packet length 100 symbols

In the first simulation, PERs are shown in the cases with different velocities for STA (Spectral Temporal Average) channel estimation method [8], comb co-pilot interpolation (Comb Copilot) method [12], only preamble method, and our proposed method. In the simulation, we fix packet length to 100 OFDM data symbols, and choose two velocities 30 and 120 km/h, corresponding to Doppler shift values of $f_d = 164, 656$ Hz, respectively. Fig. 4 shows that the performance degrades for all algorithms with the increase of velocity. However, our algorithm always obtains lower PER than other algorithms. In comb copilot scheme, several data subcarriers are used as pilots to perform a linear combination in different data subcarriers. From eq. (5), we know that the channel responses of the less number of correlation OFDM symbols are averaged when the vehicle moves at a larger velocity. Therefore, when a single channel response is obtained with measurement error, it will lead to a smaller probability that the channel response is correctly estimated by averaging multiple measurements, and further affects the equalization to recover the transmitted data.

Next, we analyze the system performance for the proposed channel estimation algorithm with different packet length. From Fig. 5, we find that increasing the packet length degrades the PER performance for all algorithms. That is because the short coherence time in fast varying environment, the channel estimation by the known preambles is quickly outdated. However, our algorithm keeps a significant improvement (2 − 10dB) for all packet length values compared to STA algorithm and Comb Copilot algorithm.

In the last experiment, since the channel coherence time is related to the velocity of the vehicle, it is interesting to evaluate PER performance of three algorithms in terms of the velocity. In the simulation, packet length is fixed to 120 and the value of SNR is set to 30 dB. From Fig. 6, we see that PER

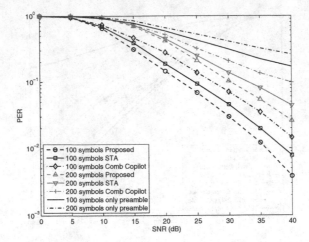

Fig. 5. PER comparison of the proposed algorithm, STA algorithm and Comb Copilot algorithm for different packet length in the case where the vehicles travel relatively at the fixed velocity of 120 km/h

is improved by our proposed algorithm in the cases with different velocities comparing to STA algorithm and Comb Copilot algorithm.

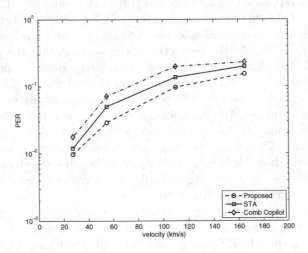

Fig. 6. PER comparison of the proposed algorithm, STA algorithm and Comb Copilot algorithm in terms of velocity for fixed packet length 120 symbols and SNR=30 dB

6   Conclusion

In vehicle wireless communications, the rich scatters and high mobility make the channel vary fast over the course of one packet transmission. The change of channel leads to the need of a channel estimator that can track the channel variation in such environment. In this paper, we first analyze the relationship between channel coherence time and vehicle velocity, which further determines the length of averaged channel response in time domain during the channel estimation. To reduce the effect of the noise in the channel estimation, we combine the data subcarriers and pilot subcarriers and average the channel response in frequency domain. In addition, channel response in subsequent OFDM symbols is iteratively equalized. Simulation results obtained in different scenarios prove the effectiveness of the proposed method.

Acknowledgment. This work was supported in part by the 100 Talents Program of Chinese Academy of Sciences, the Shanghai Pujiang Talent Program (No. 11PJ1408700), the International Science and Technology Cooperation project of China (No. 2012DFG12060), and the International Science and Technology Cooperation project of Shanghai (No. 11220705400).

References

1. Jiang, D., Taliwal, V., Meier, A., Holfelder, W., Herrtwich, R.: Design of 5.9 GHz DSRC-based vehicular safety communication. IEEE Wireless Communications 13(5), 36–43 (2006)
2. Xiang, W.D., Gozalvez, J., Niu, Z.S., Altintas, O., Ekici, E.: Wireless Access in Vehicular Environments. EURASIP Journal Wireless Communication and Networking 2009, Article ID 576217, 2 pages (2009)
3. IEEE P802.11p: Part 11: Wireless LAN Medium Access Control (MAC) and Physical Layer (PHY) Specifications: Amendment 6: Wireless Access in Vehicular Environments (July 2010)
4. Mecklenbräuker, C., Molisch, A.F., Karedal, J., Tufvesson, F., Paier, A., Bernad, L., Zemen, T., Klemp, O., Czink, N.: Vehicular channel characterization and its implications for wireless system design and performance. Proceedings of the IEEE 99(7), 1189–1212 (2011)
5. Cheng, L., Henty, B.E., Stancil, D.D., Bai, F., Mudalige, P.: Mobile vehicle-to-vehicle narrow-band channel measurement and characterization of the 5.9 GHz dedicated short range communication (DSRC) frequency band. IEEE Journal on Selected Areas in Communications 25(8), 1501–1516 (2007)
6. Alexander, P., Haley, D., Grant, A.: Cooperative intelligent transport systems: 5.9-ghz field trials. Proceedings of the IEEE 99(7), 1213–1235 (2011)
7. Letzepis, N., Grant, A., Alexander, P., Haley, D.: Joint estimation of multipath parameters from OFDM signals in mobile channels. In: 2011 Australian Communications Theory Workshop, January 31-February 3, pp. 106–111 (2011)
8. Fernandez, J.A., Borries, K., Cheng, L., Vijaya Kumar, B.V.K., Stancil, D.D., Bai, F.: Performance of the 802.11p Physical Layer in Vehicle-to-Vehicle Environments. IEEE Transactions on Vehicular Technology 61(1), 3–14 (2012)
9. Kwak, J., Cho, S., Lim, K., Park, P., Shin, D., Choi, J.: Intelligent modified channel and frequency offset estimation schemes in future generation OFDM-based packet communication systems. EURASIP Journal on Wireless Communications and Networking 2008, 1–11 (2008)

10. Zemen, T., Bernado, L., Czink, N., Molisch, A.F.: Iterative Time-Variant Channel Estimation for 802.11 p Using Generalized Discrete Prolate Spheroidal Sequences. IEEE Transactions on Vehicular Technology (2012) (to be published)
11. Lin, C.S., Lin, J.C.: Novel channel estimation techniques in IEEE802.11p Environments. In: IEEE 71st Vehicular Technology Conference (VTC-Spring), pp. 1–5 (2010)
12. Fernandez, J.A., Stancil, D.D., Bai, F.: Dynamic channel equalization for IEEE802.11p waveforms in the vehicle-to-vehicle channel. In: Forty-Eighth Annual Allerton Conference, September 29-October 1, pp. 542–551 (2010)
13. Zhao, M., Shi, Z., Reed, M.: Iterative turbo channel estimation for OFDM system over rapid dispersive fading channel. IEEE Transactions on Wireless Communications 7(8), 3174–3184 (2008)
14. Bourdoux, A., Cappelle, H., Dejonghe, A.: Channel tracking for fast time-varying channels in IEEE802.11p systems. In: IEEE Global Telecommunications Conference, pp. 1–6 (2011)
15. Tao, J., Wu, J.X., Xiao, C.S.: Estimation of channel transfer function and carrier frequency offset for OFDM systems with phase noise. IEEE Transactions on Vehicular Technology 58(8), 4380–4387 (2009)
16. Rappaport, T.S.: Wireless Communications: Principles and Practice, 2nd edn. Prentice Hall, New Jersey (2002)

The Android Intelligent Terminal-Based Implementation for Vertical Handover between Carrier-Grade WLAN and CDMA Networks

Zhou Tao, Shao Zhen, Shen Xiao, Liu Chen, and Xu Zhengfeng

Shanghai Research Institute of China Telecom, South Pudong Road,
Shanghai 200122, P.R. China
{zhoutao,shaozhen,shenxiao,liuchen,xuzf}@sttri.com.cn

Abstract. The popularizing of intelligent terminals and the advent of mobile internet give rise to significant data demand increase upon the mobile networks, even causing data alarm of particular areas. At the same time, the WLAN feature is becoming the standard configuration of these intelligent terminals, which gives opportunity to offload the data flow from cellular networks to WLAN. Therefore, it attracts great research interests from industries to design efficient handover between cellular networks and WLAN. In this paper, we propose a carrier-grade vertical handover scheme based on the Android operation system of intelligent terminals, which will help to inter-system handover without the awareness of users.

Keywords: WLAN, CDMA, WAG, Android, handover.

1   Introduction

There are mainly two types of vertical handover implementation for heterogeneous networks, software-based method and hardware-based method, Media Independent Handover and mobile IP for example. The former is implemented by software, and the continuity of service cannot be guaranteed in this implementation, making the user experience worse. However, if the mobile IP method is applied, the carrier cannot make use of its invested assets. It costs too much for the deployment, especially when the mobiles are large in quantity. In this paper, we propose an vertical handover method applied to WLAN and CDMA networks based on the android intelligent terminals. It makes the terminals handover smoothly without the awareness of users. Particularly, this method does not require any modification for the existing networks. It is some software-based method, but must base on the network deployment of operator.

2   The Converged Architecture for Carrier-Grade WLAN and CDMA Networking

In order to implement the handover operation between WLAN and CDMA networks, it is required that users can pass the authentication of different access networks, such as

H. Qian and K. Kang (Eds.): WICON 2013, LNICST 121, pp. 25–33, 2013.
© Institute for Computer Sciences, Social Informatics and Telecommunications Engineering 2013

CDMA 1x PS, CDMA CDMA and WLAN, and access to core networks. Therefore, China Telecom has developed a new network element to complete the carrier-grade converged networking for WLAN and CDMA, realizing the unified authentication procedure of CDMA/WLAN interworking.

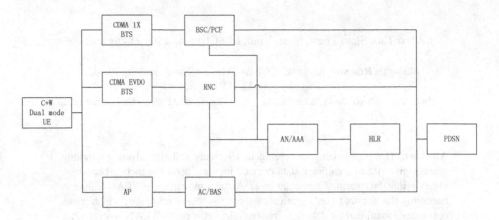

Fig. 1. The interworking architecture for carrier-grade WLAN and CDMA

The interworking architecture of carrier-grade WLAN and CDMA network is presented in Fig. 1. It is noted that the elements PDSN, AAA, AN/AAA, HLR/AuC, RNC, BSC/PCF and BTS are all standard elements in existing CDMA network, and AP, AC/BAS, WAG are the elements typically seen in carrier-grade WLAN networks. Particularly, WAG is the newly introduced converged network element, which fulfills the user authentication procedure to access to WLAN network, making use of the CDMA core network.

The signaling procedure between the terminal and WAG follows the SIP protocol. It completes the authentication procedure of user access to CDMA core networks when it is under WLAN mode. The traffic data is packaged using simple UDP tunnel. The data will pass through the Metropolitan Area Network to access the mobile packet core network and the internet.

3   The Implementation of Vertical Handover for Carrier-Grade WLAN and CDMA Networks

3.1   Signaling Procedure

The signaling procedure of handover between carrier-grade WLAN and CDMA system follows that of inter-PCF handover under the same PDSN. In the architecture of carrier-grade WLAN and CDMA interworking, the network element WAG is treated as a PCF in a manner of position and function. It signals to PDSN in the same manner of PCF.

The handover between WLAN and CDMA is hard handover, which crosses different systems. Due to the independence of CDMA and WLAN communication modules in the terminals, it can establish new communication link while at the same time sustaining the former link. After the target link is established, the terminal will relocate the PPP link route and the former communication link will be released in PDSN.

3.2   The Implementation for Android Intelligent Terminal

3.2.1   Software/Hardware Architecture

The terminal needs more modifications if it intends to handover seamlessly across the WLAN and CDMA network under the simple IP architecture for mobile core networks. The modifications assure that the PPP protocol stack is unique before and after the session handover between terminal and PDSN. The terminal will not restart the PPP negotiation when it handovers to WLAN or CDMA network. The handover control unit is installed in the application layer of terminal to sustain the PPP session connecting to PDSN. When the communication link to target system is established, the handover control unit will intercept the PPP message and handover it to the target network, and make the terminal not to restart PPP negotiation. The handover control unit communicates with the communication modules' driver by the handover control program added in adaption layer, achieves PPP datagram interception and transmission.

The CDMA and WLAN device driver are both network equipments in Android Operation System Linux core, which is controlled by standard Socket interface. The PPP data message is also monitored and intercepted using Socket interface.

3.2.2   Implementation

The mobile terminal equipment contains two processors. The operation system, user interface and applications are executed in AP (Application Processor), which is usually ARM CPU. Android, one of the open source operating system based on Linux, and WLAN communication modules are on AP. The radio communication control software of mobile terminal is operating in another separated CPU which is called Baseband Processor (BP).

This paper presents the implementation for inter-system handover based on AP. The implementation is based on networking architecture for carrier grade WLAN and CDMA interworking and the handover procedure is totally controlled by mobile terminal. No modifications are needed for existing network elements. The implementation involves the newly added handover control unit, SIP session unit, PPP protocol unit, tunneling protocol unit, WLAN communication unit, RIL interface and CDMA communication unit in BP.

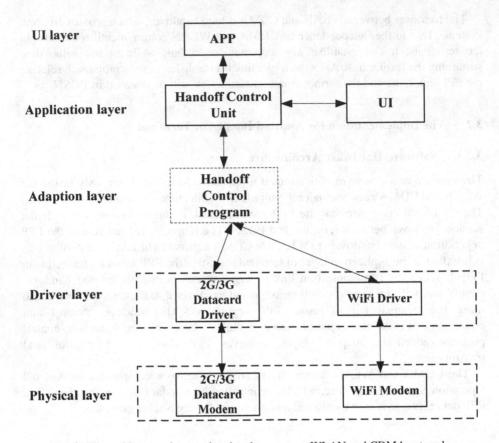

Fig. 2. The architecture for seamless handover across WLAN and CDMA network

● The handover control unit decides whether the handover condition is satisfied or not. If the handover condition is satisfied when the mobile terminal is connecting to internet using CDMA network, SIP session unit is invoked to install SIP session and trigger the handover to WLAN. After the installment of SIP session, the PPP protocol unit is invoked to start PPP dial-up process and deal with the PPP message, in order to establish the WLAN data channel. The PPP data message is intercepted and transferred to tunneling protocol unit. If the handover condition is satisfied when mobile terminal is connecting internet using WLAN, it sends Radio Link Setup Request to RIL interface to trigger the handover to CDMA network. The PPP data transferred by WLAN is intercepted and forwarded to CDMA communication unit.

● SIP session unit is called to setup SIP session by handover control unit.

● PPP protocol unit is implemented by the configuration of Linux protocol stack. (Open the Linux protocol stack management software, start the PPP protocol stack of Linux Operation System, set CONFIG_PPPOE=m and compile the PPPoE module, the PPP protocol stack is open now.) PPP protocol unit is called by the handover control unit to start the PPP dial-up and deal with the PPP message , and is

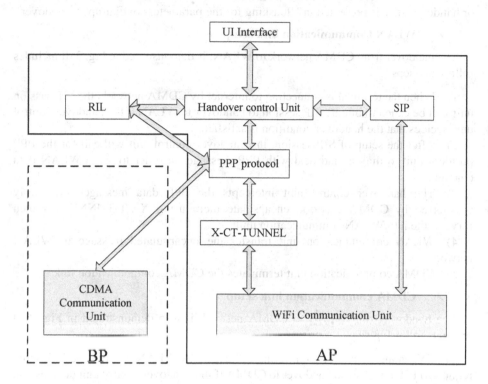

Fig. 3. The implementation based on Android terminal for seamless handover across WLAN and CDMA networks

called by the redirection request from RIL interface to use CDMA communication unit for PPP dial-up and dealing with PPP message. It means that the PPP protocol unit is used no matter the terminal is in CDMA mode or WLAN mode.

- X-CT-TUNNEL tunneling protocol unit is used for encapsulation and decapsulation of data message. The data message intercepted by handover control unit is encapsulated using specific tunneling protocol and is transferred to WLAN communication unit after encapsulation. SIP session unit, PPP protocol unit and tunneling protocol unit fulfill the communication link setup of WLAN.

- WLAN communication unit forwards the data message encapsulated by tunneling protocol unit to WLAN. It turns off the WLAN communication link when CDMA communication unit is transferring the data to CDMA network.

- RIL interface (Radio Interface Layer) redirects the communication link request from handover control unit to PPP protocol unit in AP (Application Processor). It makes use of the unique PPP protocol stack in AP both for the handover from CDMA network to WLAN and the handover from WLAN to CDMA network. RIL interface and PPP protocol unit setup the CDMA communication link.

• User Interface interacts with the handover process controller, and the dial-up or handover state is presented in UI, asking for the parameters of dial-up or handover.

➢ **WLAN Communication link setup**

The handover from CDMA network to WLAN, is demonstrated in Fig. 3. It includes following steps.

1) When the terminal is connecting to internet by CDMA network, the SIP session unit will be called to initiate SIP session to handover to WLAN if the handover control unit decides that the handover condition is satisfied.

2) After the setup of SIP session, the handover control unit will call for the PPP protocol unit to dial-up and deal with PPP message, in order to setup WLAN data channel.

3) The handover control unit intercepts the PPP data messages previously transferred by CDMA network, encapsulate them using X-CT-TUNNE and then forward them to WLAN communication unit.

4) WLAN communication unit transfer the encapsulated message to WLAN network.

5) CDMA communication unit terminates the CDMA communication link

➢ **CDMA communication link setup**

The handover from WLAN to CDMA network is also demonstrated in Fig. 3. It includes following steps.

1) When the terminal is connecting to internet by WLAN, it will send link setup request to RIL interface to handover to CDMA if the handover control unit decides that the handover condition is satisfied.

2) RIL will redirect the link setup request to PPP protocol unit in AP, and the PPP protocol unit will call for the CDMA communication unit interface to start PPP dial-up and to deal with PPP messages.

3) The handover control unit intercepts the PPP data previously transferred by WLAN and forward them to CDMA communication unit.

4) CDMA communication unit transfer the data to CDMA network

5) WLAN communication unit terminates the WLAN communication link

4   Performance Testing

The performance testing focuses on the time delay of handover between CDMA networks and WLAN of mobile phone, verification of handover result and the effect of real time service.   The statistical server records the delay of handover and the variation of data rate.

1) time delay of handover from CDMA network to WLAN

We check the time delay from CDMA to WLAN in the debug information using the debug tool DebugView. The time delay is defined as the time difference between two events that the terminal receives the 200 OK message--"sent invite message" and the message --" Switched to WiFi". It is 90ms in following example as defined :

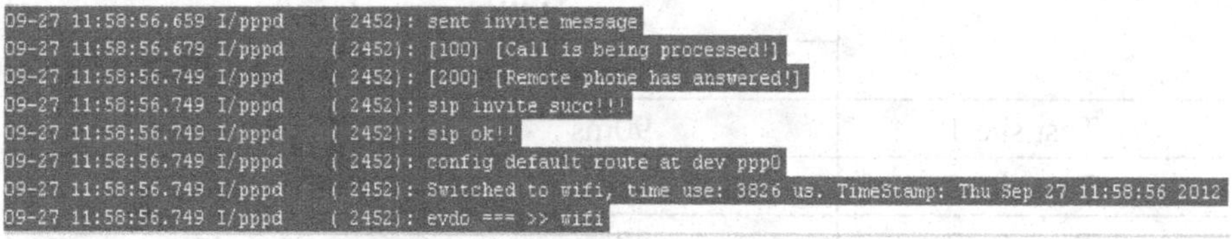

Fig. 4. One statistical example of time delay from CDMA to WLAN

2) time delay of handover from WLAN to CDMA network

We check the time delay from WLAN to CDMA network in the debug information using the debug tool DebugView. The time delay is defined as the time difference between two events that the terminal receives the message --"config default route at dev ppp0" and the message --"Switched to EVDO". It is less than 1ms in following example as defined :

Fig. 5. One statistical example of time delay from WLAN to CDMA

Conclusion of testing :

1. The handover does not affect the user experience of surfing service

1）high success rate of handover

The download service does not break off before and after the handover and during the handover. The user is not aware of the handover process, and the user experience is not disturbed. The handover success rate is 100% when the wireless signal is well. It is observed from all the test examples that the ping-pang handover will not occur. The testing shows that the performance of vertical handover between WLAN and CDMA network is overall well.

2）low time delay of handover

The time delays of handover of all the test sites are less than 90ms, which means that the service experience using wireless network card is not disturbed.

Table 1. Time delay test results of handover

Test sites	The average time delay of handover under mobility state（ms）	
	CDMA→WLAN	WLAN→CDMA
Test site 1	90ms	1ms
Test site 2	92ms	1ms
Test site 3	88ms	1ms
Test site 4	95ms	1ms
Test site 5	83ms	1ms

During the handover from CDMA network to WLAN, it will set up the tunnel with WAG via the SIP Invite message and then receives the 200 OK message. The time difference is defined as handover duration.

During the handover from WLAN to CDMA network, the radio interface of CDMA network will switch from idle to active state. Handover delay is defined between the mobile phone sends radio link establish request and receives the response of link establish. The log at mobile phone prints the time difference, which is less then 1ms.

2   It is effective to offload the data of CDMA network

The threshold of handover from CDMA network to WLAN is set to -70dBm, and the threshold of handover from WLAN to CDMA network is set to -75dBm. It makes the mobiles to reside in the WLAN for a long time, and will offload the data of CDMA network effectively.

There are three terminals in every test site, two of which are playing audio/video media file and the third is downloading file from FTP. The testing will last for more then 1 hour.

Table 2. Test results of long time keeping

Test site	Handover times		Residence duration(minute: second)			Date flow(Mbits)		
	W->C	C->W	C	W	C:W	C	W	C:W
Test site 1	79	76	27:12	74:03	36.7%	774.9	4518.45	17.15%
Test site 2	48	46	27:04	71:09	38%	790.5	3901.8	20.26%
Test site 3	36	34	48:17	97:23	49.6%	1144.04	5030.7	22.74%

Table 2. *(Continued)*

Test site 4	38	39	76:51	79:21	96.8%	1438.5	4531.95	31.74%
Test site 5	29	31	36:51	66:27	55.4%	905.48	3617.1	20.03%

5   Conclusion

Recently, China Telecom has finished the R&D work based on the scheme proposed in this paper, and the field test is also finished. It is needed to appraise the handover triggering algorithms and improve them at this moment, in order to meet the updated demand from commerce in the future. This type of implementation which does not involve protocol modification and is with minimum modifications for network and terminals, is definitely the way to future technology deployment for operators.

References

[1] 3GPP2 A.S0008-C v2.0 Interoperability Specification (IOS) for High Rate Packet Data (HRPD) Radio Access Network Interfaces with Session Control in the Access Network (2009)

[2] Technical Specification for wPDIF equipment of China Telecom (2010)

[3] Smart Wi-Fi Offload Technical Report, Draft, China Telecom (2012)

A Distributed Resource Allocation Algorithm in Multiservice Heterogeneous Wireless Networks

Juan Fan and Wuyang Zhou

Wireless Information Network Lab.,
Department of Electronic Engineering and Information Science,
University of Science and Technology of China, Hefei, Anhui, China, 230026
rosa144@mail.ustc.edu.cn, wyzhou@ustc.edu.cn

Abstract. In this paper, radio resource allocation and users to access networks assignment in heterogeneous wireless networks is studied. Mobile terminals are assumed to have the capability of using multiple radio access technologies simultaneously. A joint optimization problem is formulated, which guarantees services for terminals and maximizes the sum utility of all base stations/access points. Our model applies to arbitrary heterogeneous scenarios where the air interfaces belong to the class of interference limited systems like CDMA-based UMTS or to a class with orthogonal resource assignment such as TDMA-based GSM, WLAN or OFDMA-based LTE. Dual decomposition is employed to solve this optimization problem and a distributed iterative algorithm is developed. Simulation results demonstrate the validity of the proposed algorithm.

Keywords: heterogeneous wireless networks, resource allocation, distributed algorithm, dual decomposition.

1 Introduction

Currently there exist different wireless access networks with different capabilities in terms of bandwidth, latency, coverage area, load or cost. These networks include 2G/3G cellular, LTE, WLAN, and so on. The integration of such networks can help to support user roaming and provide various class of services with different network resource demands. However, to satisfy the required rates by the mobile terminals via different networks and make efficient utilization of the available resources from these networks, new mechanisms for resource allocation and call admission control are required.

In literature, there exist various works that study the problem of resource allocation in heterogeneous wireless networks(HWNs)[1]-[6]. The existing solutions can be classified in two categories based on whether needing a central resource manager. Most of existing solutions (such as [1]-[4]) need a central resource manager to find the optimum bandwidth allocation. While a distributed mechanism is developed in [5], only a single network is considered in obtaining the required bandwidth. In [6], although a distributed algorithm is developed to find the optimum bandwidth allocation, it neglects the heterogeneity of resource.

H. Qian and K. Kang (Eds.): WICON 2013, LNICST 121, pp. 34–43, 2013.
© Institute for Computer Sciences, Social Informatics and Telecommunications Engineering 2013

Mobile terminals(MTs) are assumed to have the capability of using multiple radio access technologies(RATs) simultaneously. This paper formulates the user assignment as a utility maximization problem which is constrained by the resource (such as power or bandwidth) of the individual base stations/access points(BSs/APs) as well as users' data rate requirements. Based on the convex formulation and by using structural properties, a decentralized algorithm is presented, which allows each network BS/AP to solve its own utility maximization problem and performs its own resource allocation to satisfy the MTs' rate requirements. The MTs play active role in the resource allocation operation by performing coordination among different BSs/APs.

The rest of this paper is organized as follows: Section 2 describes the system model. In Section 3, after the introduction of utility concept, the optimization problem formulation is developed. Algorithm that solve the problem in a decentralized way is presented in Section 4. Section 5 presents numerical simulation results and discussions. Finally, conclusions are drawn in Section 6.

2 System Model

This paper considers a geographical region where wireless access networks with different RATs is available. Any of the BSs/APs which belongs to network n, access point s can be denoted by (n, s), which $n \in \{1, 2, ..., N\}$, $s \in \{1, 2, ..., S_n\}$. The BSs/APs of each network have different coverage from those of other networks. Different networks have overlapped coverage in some areas. There are M MTs randomly distributed in the region, and MTs can be differentiated by range of rate of service request $[R_m^{min}, R_m^{max}]$, $m \in \{1, 2, ..., M\}$. An exemplary scenario with three RATs is depicted in Fig.1.

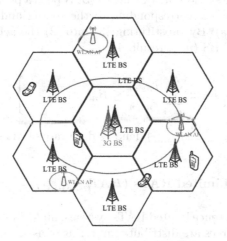

Fig. 1. An exemplary scenario with N=3

Considering the resource at the BSs/APs, the set of RATs can be divided into three subsets. $RATs = RAT_{orth,slot} \cup RAT_{inf,limit} \cup RAT_{orth,subcarriers}$.

2.1   Orthogonal Slots RATs ($RAT_{orth,slot}$)

For the class of orthogonal slots RATs systems, a fixed transmission power per BS is assumed. Bandwidth, in terms of time or frequency slots respectively, is the resource continuously distributable between MTs. The signal to interference and noise ratio (SINR) of BS (n, s) and MT m is as follows.

$$SINR_{ns,m} = \frac{g_{ns,m}\overline{P}_{ns}}{I_{ns} + N_{ns}}, \quad \forall(n, s) \in RAT_{orth,slot}, \tag{1}$$

thus depends on the channel gain $g_{ns,m}$, the BS transmission power $\overline{P}_{ns}$, the constant intercell interference I_{ns}, the noise N_{ns}. The amount of bandwidth assigned to MT m by BS (n, s) is denoted by $b_{ns,m}$. It is limited by the total, distributable bandwidth per BS $\overline{B}_{ns}$ and the constraint

$$\sum_{m=1}^{M} b_{ns,m} = B_{ns} \leq \overline{B}_{ns}, \quad \forall(n, s) \in RAT_{orth,slot}, \tag{2}$$

Due to the orthogonality of the MTs' signals and since the bandwidth is the distributable resource the relation between a MT's data rate $r_{ns,m}$ and the assigned resource is linear for this class of RATs[5]:

$$r_{ns,m} = \overline{r}_{ns,m}b_{ns,m}, \tag{3}$$

Here, $\overline{r}_{ns,m} := f(SINR_{ns,m})$ denotes the link rate per time or frequency slot between MT m and base station (n, s), where $f(SINR)$ is a positive, nondecreasing SINR-rate mapping curve corresponding to the coding and transmission technology of the BS (n, s). By substituting (3) into (2) the achievable rate region R_{ns} of each individual BS (n, s) results in:

$$\left\{ R_{ns} : \sum_{m=1}^{M} \frac{r_{ns,m}}{\overline{r}_{ns,m}} \leq \overline{B}_{ns}, r_{ns,m} \geq 0 \right\}, \tag{4}$$

which $R_{ns} = (r_{ns,1}, r_{ns,2}, ..., r_{ns,M})$ denotes data rate of MTs through BS (n, s).

2.2   Interference Limited RATs ($RAT_{inf,limit}$)

For the class of interference limited RATs systems, all MTs share the same bandwidth and that resources are distributed in terms of assigned power. The power of BS (n, s) to MT m, which denoted by $p_{ns,m}$ is limited by a sum constraint

$$\sum_{m=1}^{M} p_{ns,m} = P_{ns} \leq \overline{P}_{ns}, \quad \forall(n, s) \in RAT_{inf,limit}, \tag{5}$$

MTs are sensitive to intracell and intercell interference and the SINR between BS (n, s) and MT m is given by

$$SINR_{ns,m} = \frac{g_{ns,m}p_{ns,m}}{I_{ns} + N_{ns}},$$

$$\text{with} \quad I_{ns} = \rho g_{ns,m} \sum_{m' \neq m} p_{ns,m'} + \sum_{(n',s') \neq (n,s)} g_{n's',m}P_{n's'}, \tag{6}$$

$$\forall (n, s), (n', s') \in RAT_{inf,limit} \quad m, m' \in \mathcal{M},$$

with ρ the orthogonality factor which accounts for a reduced intercell interference. In this class of systems all links of one BS share a limited power budget and are impaired by the power assigned to other MTs in the air interface. A wellknown model for the link rate of these systems is given in [7]:

$$r_{ns,m} = C \log_2 \left(1 + DSINR_{ns,m}\right) = C \log_2 \left(1 + D\frac{g_{ns,m}p_{ns,m}}{I_{ns} + N_{ns}}\right) \tag{7}$$

There, the positive constants C, D parameterize the system characteristics such as bandwidth, modulation, and bit-error rates. However, assuming that all BS transmit with fixed transmission power and that the SINR of all links is not too low, data rate can be approximated as in [5]:

$$r_{ns,m} = C \log_2 \left(1 + D\frac{p_{ns,m}}{\beta_{ns,m} - \rho p_{ns,m}}\right) \cong \frac{CD}{I_{ns,m}}p_{ns,m} := \bar{r}_{ns,m}p_{ns,m}$$

$$\text{with} \quad \beta_{ns,m} = \frac{\rho g_{ns,m}P_{ns} + \sum_{(n',s') \neq (n,s)} g_{n's',m}P_{n's'} + N_{ns}}{g_{ns,m}}, \tag{8}$$

By solving the approximation in (8) and substitution into (5) the achievable rate region of BS $(n, s) \in RAT_{inf,limit}$ can be represented by

$$\left\{ R_{ns} : \sum_{m=1}^{M} \frac{r_{ns,m}}{\bar{r}_{ns,m}} \leq \bar{P}_{ns}, r_{ns,m} \geq 0 \right\}, \tag{9}$$

2.3 Orthogonal Subcarriers RATs ($RAT_{orth,subcarriers}$)

For the class of orthogonal subcarriers RATs systems, fixed transmission power per BS is assumed. The overall bandwidth B is divided into K subcarriers for OFDM transmission. Based on the Shannon formula, the average rate between BS (n, k) and MT m on subcarrier k in is given by

$$r_{ns,m}^k = \frac{B}{K} \log_2 \left(1 + \frac{p_{ns,m}^k l_{ns,m}|h_{ns,m}^k|^2}{\Gamma B N_0/K}\right), \tag{10}$$

where $p_{ns,m}^k$ denotes the transmission powers of BS (n, k) to MT m spent on subcarrier k. $h_{ns,m}^k$ represents the small-scale fading coefficients between BS (n, s) and MT m on subcarrier k. The path losses between BS (n, s) and MT

m is $l_{ns,m}$. Γ is the signal to noise ratio gap related to a target bit error rate (BER)[8]. N_0 denotes the power spectral density of the noise.

Assuming that BS (n, s) just allocate one subcarrier to MT m, and the SINR of all links is not too low, data rate of MT m can be approximated by

$$r_{ns,m} = r_{ns,m}^k \cong \frac{l_{ns,m}}{\Gamma N_0} p_{ns,m}^k |h_{ns,m}^k|^2 := \bar{r}_{ns,m} p_{ns,m}, \tag{11}$$

Therefore, the achievable rate region of BS (n, s) can be represented by

$$\left\{ R_{ns} : \sum_{m=1}^{M} \frac{r_{ns,m}}{\bar{r}_{ns,m}} \leq \bar{P}_{ns}, r_{ns,m} \geq 0 \right\}, \tag{12}$$

3 Problem Formulation

Let $u_{ns,m}(r_{ns,m})$ denote utility function of BS/AP (n, s) allocating resource to MT m and data rate of MT m is $r_{ns,m}$, and it is defined as in [2]:

$$u_{ns,m} = \omega \cdot log(\alpha \cdot r_{ns,m}), \tag{13}$$

where ω and α are constants indicating the scale and shape of utility function.

Having the system model and the utility concept introduced, formal problem formulation can be presented. The propose is to find the user assignment that maximizes the sum utility of all networks under the constraint that all MTs are assigned between their rate range $[R_m^{min}, R_m^{max}]$. Based on the earlier presented assumptions, the problem can be formulated as

$$\max_{R_{ns}} \sum_{n=1}^{N} \sum_{s=1}^{S_n} U_{ns}(R_{ns}),$$

$$s.t. \quad R_m^{min} \leq \sum_{n=1}^{N} \sum_{s=1}^{S_n} r_{ns,m} \leq R_m^{max}, \forall m \in \{1, 2, ...M\} \tag{14}$$

$$\sum_{m=1}^{M} \frac{r_{ns,m}}{\bar{r}_{ns,m}} \leq \Lambda_{ns}, \forall (n, s) \in RAT$$

with Λ_{ns} denoting available resources,

$$\Lambda_{ns} = \begin{cases} \bar{B}_{ns}, & \forall (n, s) \in RAT_{orth,slot} \\ \bar{P}_{ns}, & \forall (n, s) \in RAT_{inf,limit} \text{ or } RAT_{orth,subcarriers} \end{cases} \tag{15}$$

Problem (14) is convex, consequently, a variety of ready-to-use algorithms exists to solve it[9]. However, neither give these algorithms insights into the problem structure. We therefore develop a different approach based on duality[9][10]; instead of solving (14) directly we transform it into an alternative problem which is known to have the same solution as (14) but can be solved in a decentralized way by decomposition methods[11]. To obtain an expression for the dual transform the Lagrangian function of (14) is needed, which has the following form:

$$
\begin{aligned}
L(\boldsymbol{R}, \boldsymbol{\lambda}, \boldsymbol{\nu}, \boldsymbol{\mu}) = {} & \sum_{n=1}^{N} \sum_{s=1}^{S_n} U_{ns}(R_{ns}) + \sum_{n=1}^{N} \sum_{s=1}^{S_n} \lambda_{ns} \left(\Lambda_{ns} - \sum_{m=1}^{M} \frac{r_{ns,m}}{\overline{r}_{ns,m}} \right) \\
+ {} & \sum_{m=1}^{M} \nu_m \left(R_m^{max} - \sum_{n=1}^{N} \sum_{s=1}^{S_n} r_{ns,m} \right) + \sum_{m=1}^{M} \mu_m \left(\sum_{n=1}^{N} \sum_{s=1}^{S_n} r_{ns,m} - R_m^{min} \right)
\end{aligned}
\tag{16}
$$

which $\boldsymbol{\lambda}, \boldsymbol{\nu}, \boldsymbol{\mu}$ are nonnegative Lagrangian parameters. The dual function[9] of (14) is defined as

$$
g(\boldsymbol{\lambda}, \boldsymbol{\nu}, \boldsymbol{\mu}) = \max_{\boldsymbol{R}} L(\boldsymbol{R}, \boldsymbol{\lambda}, \boldsymbol{\nu}, \boldsymbol{\mu})
\tag{17}
$$

Due to nonnegativity of the Lagrangian parameters one observes that (17) is always larger than or equal to the solution of (14). Therefore, minimizing the unconstrained dual function over the Lagrangian parameters

$$
\min_{\boldsymbol{\lambda}, \boldsymbol{\nu}, \boldsymbol{\mu} \geq 0} g(\boldsymbol{\lambda}, \boldsymbol{\nu}, \boldsymbol{\mu}) = \min_{\boldsymbol{\lambda}, \boldsymbol{\nu}, \boldsymbol{\mu} \geq 0} \underbrace{\frac{\max_{\boldsymbol{R}} L(\boldsymbol{R}, \boldsymbol{\lambda}, \boldsymbol{\nu}, \boldsymbol{\mu})}{\text{Inner problem}}}
\tag{18}
$$

yields an upper bound on the original optimization problem (14) and is called the dual problem of (14). Furthermore, by convexity of (14) and since Slaters conditions[9] hold, the bound is tight and (18) and (14) have the same solution.

3.1   Inner Problem

Rearranging terms in (17) results in the following:

$$
\begin{aligned}
g(\boldsymbol{\lambda}, \boldsymbol{\nu}, \boldsymbol{\mu}) = {} & \max_{\boldsymbol{R}} L(\boldsymbol{R}, \boldsymbol{\lambda}, \boldsymbol{\nu}, \boldsymbol{\mu}) \\
= {} & \sum_{n=1}^{N} \sum_{s=1}^{S_n} \max_{R_{ns}} \left\{ U_{ns}(R_{ns}) - \lambda_{ns} \sum_{m=1}^{M} \frac{r_{ns,m}}{\overline{r}_{ns,m}} - \sum_{m=1}^{M} (\nu_m - \mu_m) r_{ns,m} \right\} \\
& + \sum_{n=1}^{N} \sum_{s=1}^{S_n} \lambda_{ns} \Lambda_{ns} + \sum_{m=1}^{M} \left(\nu_m R_m^{max} - \mu_m R_m^{min} \right)
\end{aligned}
\tag{19}
$$

Consequently, each BS/AP (n, s) can solve its own utility maximization problem, expressed as

$$
\max_{R_{ns}} \left\{ U_{ns}(R_{ns}) - \lambda_{ns} \sum_{m=1}^{M} \frac{r_{ns,m}}{\overline{r}_{ns,m}} - \sum_{m=1}^{M} (\nu_m - \mu_m) r_{ns,m} \right\}
\tag{20}
$$

The optimum allocation R_{ns} for fixed values of λ, ν, μ can be calculated by each BS/AP by applying the Karush-Kuhn-Tucker(KKT)[10] conditions on (20), and we have

$$\frac{\partial u_{ns,m}(r_{ns,m})}{\partial r_{ns,m}} - \lambda_{ns}/\overline{r}_{ns,m} - (\nu_m - \mu_m) = 0, \tag{21}$$

Using the utility function of (13), (21) results in

$$r_{ns,m} = \frac{\omega}{\lambda_{ns}/\overline{r}_{ns,m} + (\nu_m - \mu_m)}, \tag{22}$$

The optimum values of λ, ν, μ that give the optimum allocation $r_{ns,m}$ of (22) can be calculated by solving the dual problem of (18).

3.2   Outer Problem

For a fixed allocation R_{ns}, the dual problem can be expressed as

$$\sum_{n=1}^{N}\sum_{s=1}^{S_n} \min_{\lambda \geq 0}\left\{ \lambda_{ns}\left(\Lambda_{ns} - \sum_{m=1}^{M}\frac{r_{ns,m}}{\overline{r}_{ns,m}} \right) \right\} + \sum_{m=1}^{M}\min_{\nu \geq 0}\left\{ \nu_m\left(R_m^{max} - \sum_{n=1}^{N}\sum_{s=1}^{S_n} r_{ns,m} \right) \right\}$$
$$+ \sum_{m=1}^{M}\min_{\mu \geq 0}\left\{ \mu_m\left(\sum_{n=1}^{N}\sum_{s=1}^{S_n} r_{ns,m} - R_m^{min} \right) \right\} + \sum_{n=1}^{N}\sum_{s=1}^{S_n} U_{ns}(R_{ns}) \tag{23}$$

For a differentiable dual function, a gradient descent method[10] can be applied to calculate the optimum values for λ, ν, μ, given by

$$\lambda_{ns}(i+1) = \left[\lambda_{ns}(i) - \delta_\lambda\left(\Lambda_{ns} - \sum_{m=1}^{M}\frac{r_{ns,m}}{\overline{r}_{ns,m}} \right) \right]^{+} \tag{24}$$

$$\nu_m(i+1) = \left[\nu_m(i) - \delta_\nu\left(R_m^{max} - \sum_{n=1}^{N}\sum_{s=1}^{S_n} r_{ns,m} \right) \right]^{+} \tag{25}$$

$$\mu_m(i+1) = \left[\mu_m(i) - \delta_\mu\left(\sum_{n=1}^{N}\sum_{s=1}^{S_n} r_{ns,m} - R_m^{min} \right) \right]^{+} \tag{26}$$

where i is the iteration index and $\delta_\lambda, \delta_\nu$ and δ_μ are sufficiently small fixed step size. Convergence towards the optimum solution is guaranteed since the gradient of (23) satisfies the Lipchitz continuity condition[10]. As a result, the resource allocation $r_{nm,s}$ of (22) converges to the optimum solution.

4   A Distributed Resource Allocation Algorithm

Based on the optimality conditions of the inner problem and the subgradient of the outer loop in Section 3, we are able to formulate the Algorithm 1. Following the classical interpretation of λ_{ns} as the price of resources, thus, λ_{ns} serves as an indication of the capacity limitation experienced by BS/AP (n, s). ν_m and μ_m are coordination parameters used by MTs with service, and they are used to ensure that allocated resources for an MT with service lie within the specified required rate range.

Algorithm 1. Decentralized resource allocation algorithm

Initialization: Each BS/AP initializes λ_{ns} and broadcasts λ_{ns} to all MTs. Each MT initializes ν_m, μ_m and calculates $\bar{r}_{ns,m}$ for each BS/AP, then broadcasts the parameters to all BSs/APs;

while $r_{ns,m}$ *not converge* **do**

    Each BS/AP calculates $r_{ns,m}$ with (22), updates λ_{ns} with (24) and broadcasts $r_{ns,m}$ and λ_{ns} to all MTs;

    Each MT updates ν_m with (25) and μ_m with (26) , and broadcasts the parameters to all BSs/APs.

end

return $r_{ns,m}$;

---

5   Simulation Results and Analysis

In simulation, a geographical region showed in Fig.1 is considered. As a result, $N = 3$ with the LTE, 3G cellular network and WLAN indexed as $1, 2$ and 3 respectively. The MTs are randomly distributed. The simulation parameters are listed in Table 2. Numerical results are averaged over 1000 scenarios.

Table 1. Simulation parameters

Parameter	Value	Unit	Parameter	Value	Unit
video $[R^{min}, R^{max}]$	$[256, 2000]$	$Kbps$	C	1.4×10^9	-
data $[R^{min}, R^{max}]$	$[1, 10]$	$Mbps$	D	1×10^{-3}	-
LTE $\bar{P}_{BS}$	40	W	ρ	0.4	-
3G $\bar{P}_{BS}$	20	W	ω	1	-
M	$14, 16, 18, 20, 22$	-	α	0.7	-

Table 2. SINR requirements for different data rates for 802.11a[12]

Rate/Mbps	54	48	36	24	18	12	9	6
SINR/dB	24.6	24	18.8	17	10.8	9	7.8	6

An example for finding an optimal solution of the proposed algorithm is provided in Fig.2. It can be seen that MT1 which applies video service is allocated resource by LTE and 3G, and MT2 which applies data service is allocated by LTE, 3G and WLAN. Therefore, the proposed algorithm is feasible and can efficiently converge to the global optimal solution. Even though the proposed algorithm might be rather complex to implement, it could be utilized as an upper bound on the achievable gains in HWNs.

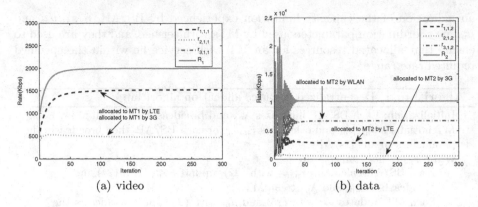

(a) video   (b) data

Fig. 2. The convergent data rate of the proposed algorithm

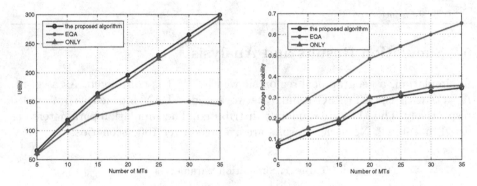

Fig. 3. Utility comparison   **Fig. 4.** Outage probability comparison

For performance comparison, we compare the proposed algorithm with EQA algorithm, which is equal resource allocation scheme, and ONLY algorithm, which is changed from the proposed algorithm and MT accesses only one RAT. Fig.3 shows the utility comparison over different number of MTs. The utility of the proposed algorithm achieves more utility than other two algorithms. In Fig.4, the outage probabilities for three algorithms are plotted. The proposed algorithm offers smaller outage probability and increases slowly over the number of MTs. The reason that our proposed algorithm outperforms EQA algorithm, is that its solution determined jointly by resource constraint and service demands. On the other hand, the proposed algorithm outperforms ONLY algorithm because of making use of multi-RAT, which is called RAT-diversity gain.

6 Conclusion

This paper develops an optimization framework for HWNs. Our model applies to arbitrary heterogeneous scenarios where the air interfaces belong to the class of interference limited systems or to a class with orthogonal resource assignment systems. A convex utility maximization problem formulation is introduced, then a distributed resource allocation algorithm is proposed. The algorithm has the following features: 1) it supports different resource (power or bandwidth); 2) Each MT can obtain its required rate from all available RAT simultaneously; 3) It is a distributed algorithm in a sense that each BS/AP solves its own utility maximization problem and performs its own resource allocation. This is very essential to be implemented in a practical environment. The performed simulations observe how the proposed algorithm would work and confirm that the proposed algorithm achieves better performance.

Acknowledgment. This work was supported by the National Major Special Projects in Science and Technology of China under grant 2010ZX03003-001, 2010ZX03005-003, 2011ZX03003-003-04.

References

1. Shen, W., Zeng, Q.: Resource management schemes for multiple traffic in integrated heterogeneous wireless and mobile networks. In: Proc. 17th Int. Conf. ICCCN, pp. 105–110 (2008)
2. Niyato, D., Hossain, E.: Noncooperative game-theoretic framework for radio resource management in 4G heterogeneous wireless access networks. IEEE Transactions on Mobile Computing 7(3) (2008)
3. Luo, C., Ji, H., Li, Y.: Utility based multi-service bandwidth allocation in the 4G heterogeneous wireless access networks. In: Proc. IEEE WCNC (2009)
4. Pei, X., Jiang, T., Qu, D., Zhu, G., Liu, J.: Radio resource management and access control mechanism based on a novel economic model in heterogeneous wireless networks. IEEE Trans. Veh. Technol. 59(6), 3047–3056 (2010)
5. Blau, I., Wunder, G., Karla, I., Sigle, R.: Decentralized utility maximization in heterogeneous multicell scenarios with interference limited and orthogonal air interfaces. EURASIP J. Wireless Communications and Networking (2009)
6. Ismail, M., Zhuang, W.: A distributed multi-service resource allocation algorithm in heterogeneous wireless access medium. IEEE Journal on Selected Areas in Communications 30(2) (2012)
7. Goldsmith, A.: Wireless Communications. Cambridge University Press, New York (2005)
8. Jang, J., Lee, K.B.: Transmit power adaptation for multiuser OFDM systems. IEEE Journal on Selected Areas in Communications 21(2), 171–178 (2003)
9. Boyd, S., Vandenberghe, L.: Convex Optimization. Cambridge University Press, New York (2004)
10. Bertsekas, D.P.: Nonlinear Programming, 2nd edn. Athena Scientific, Belmont (1999)
11. Palomar, D., Chiang, M.: A tutorial on decomposition methods for network utility maximization. IEEE Journal on Selected Areas in Communications 24(8), 1439–1451 (2006)
12. Vivek, M.: Enhanced wireless mesh networking for ns-2 simulator. ACM SIGCOMM Computer Communication Review 37(3) (2007)

Quantitative Comparison of Radio Environments for T-Ring Test System

Ming Zhao[1], Peng Dong[2], Sihai Zhang[1], and Wuyang Zhou[1]

[1] PCN&SS Lab, University of Science and Technology of China
Hefei, Anhui, China
{zhaoming,shzhang,wyzhou}@ustc.edu.cn
[2] China Mobile Research Institute
Beijing, 100053, P.R. China
Dongpeng@chinamobile.com

Abstract. T-Ring is a new integrated wireless testbed developed for scalable and reproducible evaluation and simulation of various wireless networks. Since it spans a large geographical area, the effect of signal propagation is truly real, which is a key required feature for some wireless research. For the purpose of comparing experimental results of T-Ring with similar experiments conducted on other real-world networks, quantitative comparison of the radio environments is imperative. This paper introduced a comparison method by calculating the similarity degree of the CDFs of a specific characteristic of two radio environments. Also we propose an expression of synthesized similarity degree which is a linear sum of similarity degree value of different channel characteristics. The comparison in this paper are currently made from the aspect of RSSI and RMS delay spread because of their close relation with large-scale fading and small-scale fading respectively. The contribution of each characteristic to the synthesized similarity degree is analyzed and the process of determining the weight factor of each characteristic with a pure simulation is presented. The numerical result demonstrates the feasibility of the comparison method and also shows that RMS delay spread is more effective than RSSI to show the difference of radio environments for cells with same or different sizes.

Keywords: quantitative comparison, radio environments, testbed, T-Ring.

1 Introduction

Real-world wireless network testbed has been always attracting significant attention from industry and from the research community. Most mobile wireless network research today relies on simulation. However, fidelity of simulation results has always been a concern, because simulations depend on the simplified models that do not capture real physical effects. So wireless network testbeds are necessary. However, because of the difficulty and high cost in building a full-scale testbed, most reported testbeds are simplified to some extent. For example,

H. Qian and K. Kang (Eds.): WICON 2013, LNICST 121, pp. 44–54, 2013.

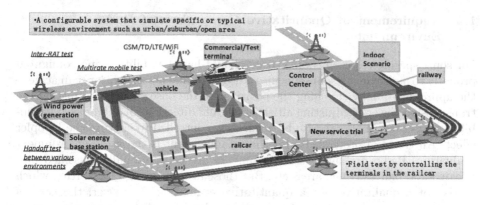

Fig. 1. General view of T-Ring system

MiNT testbed is a miniaturized one that can be deployed on a table [1]. But it inevitably encountered some problems to capture the effect of some physical effects such as node mobility and multipath fading. For this reason, there are still some full-scale testbeds reported, such as ORBIT Radio Grid Testbed [2] and APE [3]. They are all tailored toward specific applications and research areas such as Ad hoc network.

1.1 T-Ring Project Motivation and Overview

T-Ring project is a new integrated wireless testbed [4]. The key feature of the testbed is that it has a ringlike railway to carry the terminals, hence the name T-Ring. Not only will it be developed for wireless research, but it will also be used to support some industrial requirements such as field test. It is known that field test plays an important role to ensure the network quality during the construction and maintenance period. However, the performances of networks deployed in different regions sometimes differ widely because signal propagations are affected by the geographical environments etc. Therefore a testbed with real world settings is needed to evaluate the performance of wireless network protocols and to help investigate some field test problems. These considerations motivated the T-Ring project. It aims to provide a flexible and scalable experimental facility for field test and research on heterogeneous mobile networks.

T-Ring testbed spans a large geographical area and has a real-world setting. The wireless signal can be received over a large radius of the order of several hundreds or even thousands meters. T-Ring consists of several kinds of environments and can be managed to approximate some specific radio environments to help investigate field test problems. The railway in T-Ring is used to carry the terminals. It ensures the reproducibility of the experiments and makes it easy for operators to control the mobility of the terminals, which is a bottleneck for other simplified testbeds. The general view of T-Ring is illustrated in Fig. 1.

1.2 Requirement of Quantitative Comparison of Radio Environments

For some specific requirements, T-Ring should has the ability being configured properly to approximate some specific radio environments. Operators can achieve the approximation by changing the positions of the base stations, adjusting the transmission power or adjusting altitude, tilt and directions of antennas. The mobility of user terminals can also be accurately controlled to capture the Doppler effect. An essential prerequisite for that management is the radio environment evaluation. Radio propagation environments are conventionally classified into urban, suburban and open areas etc. But those are not enough for T-Ring which needs not a qualitative but a quantitative evaluation. Moreover, the cells of T-Ring are distributed over a finite area while the realistic ones may possess different sizes and some of them are very large. So comparisons between cells with different sizes are necessary.

In this paper we will introduce a comparison method of radio environments with the definition of *similarity degree*. *similarity degree* is used to describe the relations of any characteristic of two environments. Furthermore, we propose an expression of *synthesized similarity degree* which is a linear sum of similarity degree values of different channel characteristics. Consequently a method of determining the weight of each characteristic in the synthesized similarity degree is produced. The comparison in this paper are currently made from the aspect of *received signal strength indicator* (RSSI) and *root mean square* (RMS) delay spread because of their close relation with large-scale fading and small-scale fading respectively. Some large-scale propagation study can help analyzing the coverage situation of the radio signal for various carrier frequency [5][6]. Meanwhile, this paper focuses on multipath effect for its tight relationship with the small-scale fading. There are lots of illustrations about multipath measurement [7][8][9]. To describe the multipath quantitatively, RMS delay spread is selected to be involved in the analytical evaluation. It should be pointed out that the comparison method can be extended to involve more radio parameters in future work.

2 Comparison of Radio Environments

For quantitative comparison and evaluation of radio environments, we should first decide which kind of radio characteristics should be used for comparison. In this section, we present the comparison from aspects of RSSI and multipath effect which are related with large-scale fading and small-scale fading respectively. RSSI depends on path loss effect and transmission power of the base station. The small-scale fading can be quantitatively described from several aspects [10]. RMS delay spread is used here to describe the multipath effect. Another problem to be pointed out is that T-Ring is a flexible testbed and the cells in it can be configured to have different sizes. So Comparison of propagation for cells with different sizes is also a preliminary job.

2.1 Large-Scale Fading and RSSI

A terminal in T-Ring should experience a RSSI comparable with that in realistic networks. RSSI in most cases depends on path loss resulted from large-scale fading and transmission power of the base station. Large-scale fading is the result of signal attenuation due to propagation over long distance and diffraction around large objects in the propagation path. It directly affects wireless coverage. The commonly used propagation models are Cost231-Hata model for carrier frequency below 2 GHz [6] and Stanford University Interim (SUI) model for carrier frequency below 11 GHz [11]. Cost231-Hata model is represented by the following equations [6]:

$$PL[dB] = (44.9 - 6.55 \log_{10} h_{tx}) \log_{10} \frac{d}{1000} + 45.5$$
$$+(35.46 - 1.1 h_{rx}) \log_{10} f_c - 13.82 \log_{10} h_{tx} + 0.7 h_{rx} + C \qquad (1)$$

Where:
PL - Path loss, dB
h_{tx} - Transmitter height, m
d - Distance between transmitter and receiver, m
h_{rx} - Receiver height, m
f_c - Carrier frequency, MHz
C - 0 dB for suburban area and 3 dB for urban area

Equation (1) shows that path loss depends on the logarithm of distance with fixed f_c, h_{tx} and h_{rx}. Assume that a terminal moves along a route, the path loss difference between the start point and the end point is obtained as:

$$PL_{start} - PL_{end} = \alpha \log_{10}(d_{start}/d_{end}) \qquad (2)$$

Where d_{start} and d_{end} are the distances between both ends and the transmitter, α is a constant for simplicity. Let

$$d_{start}/d_{end} = \rho \qquad (3)$$

Equation (2) and (3) show that pathloss depends on the relative distance ρ. So if the length of field test route is proportional to the cell size, the path loss variations along the route will be identical to the counterpart in the realistic cell. Furthermore, by appropriately configuring the transmission power of the base station, the RSSI in the T-Ring system along a field test route will be similar to that in the corresponding commercial networks.

2.2 Small-Scale Fading and RMS Delay Spread

Small-scale fading is a characteristic describing the rapid fluctuations of received power level due to small sub wavelength changes in receiver position. It can be regarded as the joint effect of multipath and the receiver movement. There are several characteristics that can be used to quantitatively analyze the small-scale

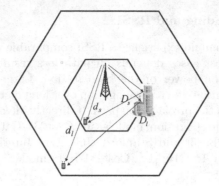

Fig. 2. Multipath for users in different-size cells

fading [10]. This paper will only focus on the multipath at present. For narrow-band wireless communication systems, multipath result in a flat fading. And for a wide-band system, multipath brings about frequency selective fading. So delay spread is a key feature for wireless channel. Here we use RMS delay spread for evaluating the similarity of multipath fading here. The RMS delay spread is defined as the standard deviation of the power delay profile [7]:

$$\tau_{RMS} = \left(\sum_{k=0}^{N} (\tau_k - \tau_e)^2 \frac{|P(\tau_k)|}{\sum_{i=0}^{N} |P(\tau_i)|} \right)^{1/2} \tag{4}$$

Where τ_e is average delay and $|P(\tau_i)|$ is the power of the ith path. Multipath results from the presence of reflection, diffraction and scattering. Since scattering is hard to model and the diffraction can be regard as reflection by virtual object, the following analysis of multipath will primarily focus on reflection. The simplification will not affect the analysis result of RMS delay spread. As shown in Fig. 2, two terminals locate in the cells with different distance from the base station. Assume there is a specific reflector with the distance D_s apart from the transmitter, the delay spread caused by the reflector is τ_1 for user at the short distance and τ_2 for users at the long distance respectively. The following relationships can be achieved

$$\tau_1 > \tau_2 \tag{5}$$

Equation (5) indicates that the multipath changes with the variation of the cell radius even for the same environment. The delay spread in a small cell will be larger than that in a larger cell. Though it is difficult to accurately control multipath effect, we still have some methods to handle some key parameters such as RMS delay spread. It is known that multipath is affected by the antenna tilt, antenna altitude and beam width. If we can make the statistical characteristic of RMS delay spread along the railway approximate that of a real-world field test, we achieve the goal of setting up a radio environment in T-Ring similar to that in a real network.

3 Quantitative Evaluation

After comparison of different-sized cells from aspects of RSSI and RMS delay spread, a quantitative evaluation expression is needed to describe the similarity of two environments. Because many parameters are conventionally investigated in statistical way, the similarity degree of two environments will also be evaluated statistically. For each radio characteristic, we analyze the measured data and calculate the probability density function (PDF) or the cumulative distribution function (CDF). Here we use CDF for evaluation. Then the similarity degree of the characteristic of two wireless environments is measured by

$$\lambda = 1 - \sqrt{\frac{\sum_i (x_i - x_i')^2}{\sum_i x_i^2}} \tag{6}$$

Where x_i and x_i' are two series of sample data of CDF which range from 0 to 1. As a result, λ also ranges from 0 to 1, with 0 denoting that the characteristic of the two environments bear no resemblance and 1 denoting the reverse. If several characteristics are taken into account, a synthesis evaluation expression is needed. Provided the similarity degree of the two wireless environments on the i th characteristic is λ_i, the synthesized similarity degree λ_{syn} of characteristics is written as

$$\lambda_{syn} - \sum_{i=1}^{K} w_i \lambda_i \tag{7}$$

Where w_i is the weight factor of each similarity degree λ_i , and K is the number of characteristics to be involved in the evaluation. To obtain a reasonable synthesized similarity degree, the weight factor should be properly determined. From information theory aspect, the more difference a characteristic shows for different environments, the heavier weight it will be given. So the weight factor is defined as

$$w_i = \frac{1 - \lambda_i}{\sum_{k=1}^{K} (1 - \lambda_k)} \tag{8}$$

Where λ_i is an calculated similarity degree of i th parameter, and K is the number of characteristics that are involved in the evaluation. For an extreme example, a characteristic with a similarity degree 1 all the time for various wireless environments will contribute zero to the synthesized evaluation. Moreover, the weight factor of each parameter is normalized in equation (8).

4 Simulation and Example

To show the feasibility of the quantitative comparison method and the process of determining the wight factors w_i in the synthesized similarity degree as (8), we set up a simulation model as shown in Fig. 3. A set of reflectors from A to

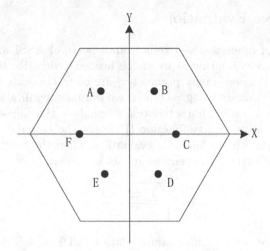

Fig. 3. Simulation Scenario

Table 1. Simulation Parameters

Parameter	Value
Height of TX antenna	30m
Height of RX antenna	1.5m
Frequency	1.9GHz
Radius of the cell	300m

F distribute in a single cell. The transmitter uses omnidirectional antennas and locates in the center of the cell. We ignore the shadowing effect to simplify the simulation. The simulation parameters are shown in TABLE 1. The coverage area is partitioned into hundreds of blocks. For each block, the power of the LOS path and the reflection path caused by the six reflectors are cumulated as RSSI. RMS delay spread can also be calculated with equation (4).

We first investigate the comparison of radio environments for cells with same sizes. We set up two simulation scenarios with the reflectors distributed in the cells uniformly or randomly. The RMS and RSSI are estimated and CDF of each characteristic is shown in Fig. 4. The result shows there is no much gap between CDFs of RSSI for the uniform distribution and random distribution, whereas the CDFs of RMS delay spread for the two kinds of distribution are quite different. With equation (6), we calculate the similarity degree and obtain $\lambda_{RSSI} = 0.9153$ and $\lambda_{RMS} = 0.6491$. The phenomenon indicates that RMS delay spread is more likely to display the difference of various environments. So RMS delay spread is expected to get a heavier weight than RSSI.

To determine the value of w_i for a specific cell size, we set up ten scenarios in which the reflectors are randomly distributed. Each scenario will be combined with another one for similarity degree evaluation. The similarity degree of RMS

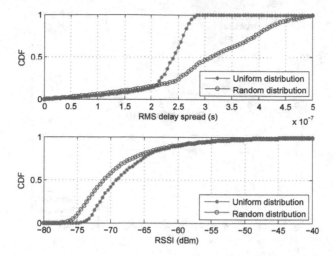

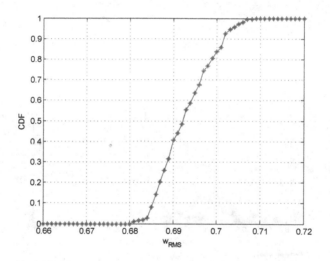

Fig. 4. CDFs of RMS delay spread and RSSI for uniform and random distributions

Fig. 5. CDF of w_{RMS} for various reflectors distribution in cells with same size

delay spread and RSSI of each possible pair is calculated as $\bar{\lambda}_{RSSI}$ and $\bar{\lambda}_{RMS}$. And corresponding w_i are acquired consequently with Equation (8). By analyzing the CDF of calculated w_{RMS} as shown in Fig. 5, w_{RMS} is obviously distributed within a narrow range of [0.680, 0.708]. That means $\bar{\lambda}_{RMS}$ is estimated with small variance. So we define the estimated as

$$\bar{w}_i = \frac{1}{N} \sum_{n}^{N} w_{i,n} \tag{9}$$

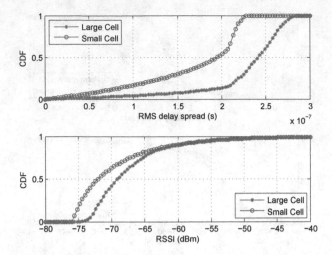

Fig. 6. CDFs of RMS delay spread and RSSI for different-sized cells

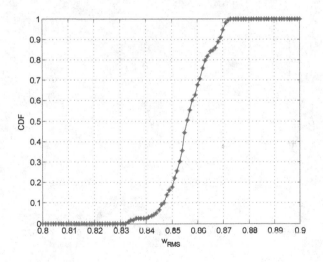

Fig. 7. CDF of w_{RMS} for different-sized cells

Where n is the index of w_i and N is the total number of the calculated w_i. Here simulation results shows $(\bar{w}_{RMS}, \bar{w}_{RSSI})$ is estimated as $(0.694, 0.306)$. Thus we obtain a comparison expression for cells with same size as

$$\lambda_{syn} = 0.694\lambda_1 + 0.306\lambda_2 \tag{10}$$

where λ_1 denotes the similarity degree of RMS delay spread and λ_2 denotes that of RSSI. The equation (10) will be used to compare the radio environments of cells with the same size.

With the same method, the comparison of cells with different size is also performed. Also we setup ten scenarios with six reflectors randomly distributed in a single cell. For each scenario, we consider two sub scenarios that the transmission power is changed so that larger coverage has a radius twice of the small one. Fig. 6 shows the CDFs of RMS and RSSI for different-sized cells, and Fig. 7 shows CDF of for different-sized cells. Consequently we estimate $\lambda_{RSSI} = 0.8778$ and $\lambda_{RMS} = 0.6879$. Thus $(\bar{w}_{RMS}, \bar{w}_{RSSI})$ is determined as $(0.85, 0.15)$. Thus we obtain a comparison expression for cells with different size as

$$\lambda_{syn} = 0.85\lambda_1 + 0.15\lambda_2 \tag{11}$$

where λ_1 denotes the similarity degree of RMS delay spread and λ_2 denotes that of RSSI. The equation (11) will be used to compare the radio environments of cells with the different size.

Through the simulation we find that the RMS delay spread differs widely for different scenarios, while RSSI are very close. That phenomenon results from the fact that the RSSI are dominated by the large-scale fading which is difficult to be demonstrated in the pure simulation scenario. But the multipath effect can be easily captured.

It should be pointed out that the above simulations and process only indicate the feasibility of the proposed method. The equation(10) and (11) only make sense for the scenario in this paper. A weight factor w_i for a special characteristic should be determined after data collection in real networks with the proposed method. So future work will concentrate on the calibration of this method and determine the comparison metric that will be used for T-Ring test system.

5   Conclusion

In this paper we introduce a new integrated wireless testbed, T-Ring. To satisfy some specific requirements, T-Ring should has the ability of being configured properly to approximate some specific radio environments. For that purpose, we present a quantitative comparison method of radio environments. We define a similarity degree to describe the relation of radio characteristics and a synthesized similarity degree to describe the relation of two radio environments. The method of determining the weight factor of each characteristic in the synthesized expression is also proposed. With the method, it is possible to describe how much a radio channel resembles another one. Simulations show that the quantitative comparison is feasible and indicate that parameters which are more likely to reveal the difference of various environments will get heavier weights. With the comparison method, we can first measure some wireless parameters in a cell and rebuild it on a computer-based simulation platform according to the evaluation metric. Then T-Ring will be adjusted to approximate the wireless environment of a real-world commercial network under the direction of the simulation platform. RSSI and RMS delay spread are currently presented to be involved in the quantitative comparison. Of course some other useful characteristics can be involved with the same method. That will be investigated in the future.

Acknowledgment. This work is supported by National programs for High Technology Research and Development (2012AA011402) and T-Ring project.

References

1. De, P., Raniwala, A., Sharma, S., Chiueh, T.: A Miniaturized Network Testbed for Mobile Wireless Research. In: IEEE INFOCOM 2005. 24th Annual Joint Conference of the IEEE Computer and Communications Societies, vol. 4, pp. 2731–2742 (2005)
2. Seskar, I., Ott, M., Ganu, S., Ramachandran, K., et al.: Overview of the ORBIT Radio Grid Testbed for Evaluation of Next-Generation Wireless Network Protocols. In: IEEE Wireless Communications and Networking Conference (WCNC), vol. 3, pp. 1664–1669 (2005)
3. Lundberg, D., Nielsen, J., Nordstrom, E., Tschudin, C.: A large-scale testbed for reproducible ad hoc protocol evaluations. In: IEEE Wireless Communications and Networking Conference (WCNC), vol. 1, pp. 412–418 (2002)
4. Ren, H., Xu, L., Zhao, M.: Equivalence Analysis of Vertical Handoff for Cells with Various Scales. In: Intelligent Computation Technology and Automation (ICICTA), vol. 2, pp. 535–539 (2011)
5. Anastasios, G., Propagation, S.S.: study and performance evaluation of a fixed access WiMAX system. In: Fourth European Conference on Antennas and Propagation (EuCAP), pp. 1–5 (2010)
6. Castro, B.S.L., Gomes, I.R., Ribeiro, F.C.J.: COST231-Hata and SUI models performance using a LMS tuning algorithm on 5.8GHz in Amazon Region Cities. In: Fourth European Conference on Antennas and Propagation (EuCAP), pp. 1–3 (2010)
7. Rappaport, T.S., Seidel, S.Y., Singh, R.: 900-MHz multipath propagation measurements for US digital cellular radiotelephone. IEEE Trans. on Vehicular Technology 39(2), 132–139 (1990)
8. Seidel, S.Y., Rappaport, T.S., Jain, S., Lord, M.L., Singh, R.: Path loss, scattering and multipath delay statistics in four European cities for digital cellular and microcellular radiotelephone. IEEE Trans. on Vehicular Technology 40(4), 721–730 (1991)
9. Sousa, E.S., Jovanovic, V.M., Daigneault, C.: Delay spread measurements for the digital cellular channel in Toronto. IEEE Trans. on Vehicular Technology 43(4), 837–847 (1994)
10. Durgin, G.D., Rappaport, T.S.: Theory of multipath shape factors for small-scale fading wireless channels. IEEE Trans. on Antennas and Propagation 48(5), 682–693 (2000)
11. Erceg, V.: Channel models for broadband fiexed wireless systems. In: IEEE 802.16 Broadband Wireless Access Working Group (2010)

Optimal Packet Length in Delay-Tolerant Networks under Mobile-to-Mobile Fading Channel

Yuan Liu[1], Sihai Zhang[1,2], Ming Zhao[1], and Wuyang Zhou[1]

[1] Wireless Information Network Laboratory,
Department of Electronic Engineering and Information Science,
University of Science and Technology of China, Hefei, Anhui, China, 230026
[2] Key Laboratory of Wireless Sensor Network & Communication,
Shanghai Institute of Microsystem and Information Technology,
Chinese Academy of Sciences, 865 Changning Road, Shanghai, China, 200050
jayliu@mail.ustc.edu.cn, {shzhang,zhaoming,wyzhou}@ustc.edu.cn

Abstract. The performance of Delay-Tolerant Networks (DTN) is deeply affected by the node mobility and time-variant wireless channel, by which the joint influence has not been investigated in depth. We analyze the optimal packet length to maximize the effective data throughput, measured by the time spent in successfully transmitting payload data with constant bit rate (CBR) during a given period, by jointly considering the impact of node mobility and wireless channel. Based on a designed simulation model which resembles the environment of mobile nodes under mobile-to-mobile fading channel, we formulate a packet length optimization mechanism to resist packet loss due to channel fading and improve the efficiency of data transmission between mobile DTN nodes, which makes significant sense in multi-hop DTN communication. Theoretically optimal packet lengths for nodes under both environment with fixed velocity and the Random Waypoint (RWP) mobility model with variable velocity are thoroughly deduced and validated by simulation results.

Keywords: mobile delay-tolerant networks, effective data transmission, optimal packet length, mobile-to-mobile fading channel model.

1 Introduction and Related Works

The application and performance of mobile Delay-Tolerant Networks (DTN) have attracted increasing attention from plenty of researchers in multiple backgrounds, like wireless communications, computer science, social science and so on. Because of DTN's huge potential for connecting wireless devices in extreme environment and delay-tolerant ability in emerging communication services or patterns. It is recognized that the performance of DTN is constrained mainly by two fundamental factors, node mobility and the time-variant wireless channel conditions, to which many research efforts have been thrown to overcome, including efficient routing algorithms, more accurate mobility models and more intelligent transmission techniques. The mobility of nodes impacts the performance

H. Qian and K. Kang (Eds.): WICON 2013, LNICST 121, pp. 55–64, 2013.

of DTN by preventing long-playing contact duration between transmission pairs and thus, bringing the unavailable end-to-end connections in the network perspective. Meanwhile, in the transmission layer, the time-variant wireless channel will influence the network performance by deep fading, path loss and interference, among which we consider the effect of channel fading in this paper.

When considering the node mobility, many research efforts have been thrown to study how to make full use of each contact duration, since locations of each communication node pair under DTN environment change real-timely therefore their mutual contact duration can be transient. [1] concentrates on improving the efficiency of data replication in DTN by establishing convex optimization problem under the premise of the awareness of contact duration. However, the accurate duration of contact is actually difficult to be obtained. [2] further considers the mutual probing delay that curtails the actual communication link time of nodes, providing a framework to compute the optimal contact-probing frequency under energy limitations and adjusting the probing frequency according to the contact rate of nodes, which can be regarded as an additional study of [1]. C. Lin et al. [3] revise the probabilistic routing scheme named $PRoPHET$ in social-based DTN by considering contact duration of nodes as an important criterion for selecting next-hop relay in multi-hop DTN communication. However, these above works are blind to the fading condition of communication channels, which makes the channel intermittent, impacts the effective transmission time between mobile DTN nodes, and moreover, causes significant packet loss, when they are within their mutual transmission range. As to the channel fading in wireless networks, several related works should be reviewed. W. Song et al. [4] study the packet loss condition under the environment of 802.11 WLANs and establish theoretical packet error model which considers both impact of channel fading and packet collision. In this work, an adaptive packetization mechanism is proposed to improve the throughput of WLANs. K. Jayaweera et al. [5] propose a sensor deployment problem in fixed wireless sensor network (WSN) under Rayleigh fading channel model, in which Bhattacharya error probability is employed as the target of optimization and the optimal length between each sensor node and the fusion center is obtained.

However, we note that the environment of mobile DTN is quite different from that of WLANs and WSN in many aspects, such as frequent node mobility and sparse node density, thus calls for a appropriate fading model to describe the mobile-to-mobile channel condition of DTN. As far as we know, there are few works considering the influence of channel fading on the performance of mobile DTN nodes, which is our main contribution in this paper. Mobile-to-mobile fading channel [6] is a commonly used model to characterize the communication channel between mobile units, under which channel condition alternates between fading duration and non-fading duration [7]. The fading characteristics in mobile-to-mobile channel model is deeply affected by the velocities of both transmitter and receiver, meaning that it is a proper channel model for mobile DTN communication. Under such fading environment, data transmission between mobile DTN nodes will encounter considerable new problems, especially in how to improve the transmission efficiency.

Our main contribution is to choose the proper or optimal packet length that could balance per packet inherent redundancy and retransmission cost, thus maximizing the effective data delivery throughput between mobile DTN nodes under mobile-to-mobile fading channel, by assuming that each packet will be lost if encountering channel fading during its transmission and then calls for a retransmission. In this paper, we present the theoretically optimal packet length, which is verified by simulation results, under given mobile DTN communication environment with mobile-to-mobile channel fading and certain mobility model, with fixed or variable node velocity.

2 Problem Formation

We assume that communication nodes move within a given square area under Random Waypoint (RWP) mobility model [8]. In RWP model each node is assigned an initial location within a given area (typically a square) and moves at a constant velocity v to a destination (named waypoint) selected uniformly in this area. v is selected uniformly from given $[V_{min}, V_{max}]$, independently of the initial location and destination. After reaching the destination, new waypoint and new velocity are reselected according to the same rule. RWP model resembles some mobility patterns in the real world.

Mobile-to-mobile fading channel is a typical channel model for communication nodes with mobility, under which the channel condition alternates between fading duration and non-fading duration. We assume that two mobile DTN nodes act as transmitter and receiver and have velocity V_T and V_R respectively, the average non-fading duration (ANFD) of nodes [7] within the transmission range of each other can be described as below:

$$ANFD = \frac{c}{\rho f_0 \sqrt{2\pi(V_T^2 + V_R^2)}} \tag{1}$$

where $\rho = \frac{R_{th}}{R_{rms}}$, R_{th} is the system-specific threshold and $R_{rms} = \sqrt{G \cdot d^{-\alpha}}$ is the root-mean-square power of the received signal, where d is the distance between nodes, G is proportional to the transmitted power and α is propagation loss coefficient. For the sake of simplicity, we assume that the R_{rms} remains constant due to the power control of transmitter, then ρ can also be thought of as a constant when node distance changes within the limit of transmission range. f_0 is the carrier frequency and c is the optical velocity. Non-fading duration represents the lifetime of a mobile-to-mobile fading channel during which data transmission can be maintained between nodes, related researches have revealed that the non-fading duration of channel is exponentially distributed [7]. When channel fading occurs and a non-fading duration is over, the transmission will be interrupted and the packet being transmitted at this moment will be lost. Similarly, a fading duration of mobile-to-mobile channel model is also exponentially distributed [7], and the average fading duration (AFD) is denoted as:

$$AFD = \frac{c(e^{\rho^2} - 1)}{\rho f_0 \sqrt{2\pi(V_T^2 + V_R^2)}} \tag{2}$$

Within a fading duration, signal envelope stays below system-specific threshold and mobile-to-mobile channel is considered as unavailable for data transmission. The inverses of $ANFD$, denoted by λ_A, is the parameter of exponential distribution which characterizes the lifetime of mobile-to-mobile channel model. Under this circumstance, data should be divided into a few packets to avoid error and packet loss due to channel fading. We assume that there is a given data service M_0, which should be divided into k packets to be transmitted through channel:

$$M_0 = k \cdot d_0 \tag{3}$$

Each packet has the effective payload data d_0 as well as the inherent overhead, including packet header, inter-frame space and link-layer ACK, represented by d_{ov}. Then the total transmitted data is:

$$M = k \cdot (d_0 + d_{ov}) = M_0 + k \cdot d_{ov} \tag{4}$$

With given constant bit rate (CBR) for transmission, we can obtain the necessary transmission time t_s for each packet:

$$t_s = \frac{d_0 + d_{ov}}{CBR} \tag{5}$$

The t_s can thus be employed to denote the packet length under the background of CBR. Now we analyze the problem of retransmission: we assume that each packet will be discarded if a deep fading occurs during its delivery duration t_s, then after the fading duration passes, the lost packet will be retransmitted. Under the background of exponentially distributed non-fading mobile-to-mobile channel lifetime, the probability for a packet to be lost during its transmission is:

$$P_f = \int_0^{t_s} \lambda_A \cdot e^{-\lambda_A \cdot t} \cdot dt = 1 - e^{-\lambda_A \cdot t_s} \tag{6}$$

where λ_A is the parameter of exponential distribution of non-fading duration which represents characteristics of communication channel and node mobility. When fading occurs, the average length that the lost packet has been transmitted at that moment is:

$$t_l = \frac{1}{P_f} \int_0^{t_s} \lambda_A \cdot t \cdot e^{-\lambda_A \cdot t} \cdot dt = \frac{1}{\lambda_A} - \frac{t_s \cdot e^{-\lambda_A \cdot t_s}}{(1 - e^{-\lambda_A \cdot t_s})} \tag{7}$$

Then the expected time spent in transmitting each packet (including retransmission cost) is:

$$EPT = \sum_{k=0}^{\infty} (1 - e^{-\lambda_A \cdot t_s})^k \cdot e^{-\lambda_A \cdot t_s} \cdot (t_s + k \cdot t_l) = \frac{1}{\lambda_A} \cdot \frac{(1 - e^{-\lambda_A \cdot t_s})}{e^{-\lambda_A \cdot t_s}} \tag{8}$$

EPT thus synthesizes the impact of both inherent packet overhead and packet retransmission overhead, then we can define the *efficiency of transmission* as the ratio of effective data per packet to EPT:

$$\epsilon = \frac{(t_s - t_{ov})}{EPT} = \frac{\lambda_A \cdot (t_s - t_{ov}) \cdot e^{-\lambda_A \cdot t_s}}{(1 - e^{-\lambda_A \cdot t_s})} \tag{9}$$

where $t_{ov} = \frac{d_{ov}}{CBR}$. If λ_A and t_{ov} are given, transmission efficiency ϵ is thus the function of packet length t_s. When ϵ obtains its maximum value, the t_s is supposed to be optimal. We can easily find that the first order derivative of ϵ equals zero when:

$$1 - e^{-\lambda_A \cdot t_s} - \lambda_A \cdot (t_s - t_{ov}) = 0 \tag{10}$$

which is a typical transcendental equation that has unique solution, the t_s value that satisfies (10) is the theoretically optimal solution of packet length under given circumstances, including velocities of transmitter and receiver, condition of mobile-to-mobile channel and carrier frequency. Here we set $CBR = 1Mbps$, then the effective throughput of wireless transmission according to equation (9) is:

$$T_\epsilon = \epsilon \cdot CBR \tag{11}$$

We assume that each packet has an inherent overhead of 1000bit which takes a $t_{ov} = 1ms$, $f_0 = 2.6GHz$ which is a typical carrier frequency that resembles TD-LTE and $\rho = 0.6$. Two communication nodes move at the velocity of $4m/s$ respectively. Fig. 1 describes the relationship of effective throughput and packet length, which shows an obvious and unique optimal packet size t_s which resembles the result in [4] under similar assumption.

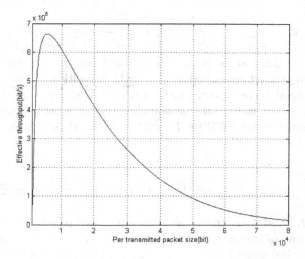

Fig. 1. The relationship between effective throughput and packet length

A theoretically optimal t_s maximizes the effective throughput under given circumstances including the velocity of nodes, fading parameter ρ and carrier frequency. However, if the environment is variable, the choice of a fixed optimal packet length which results in maximum average effective transmission throughput will be more complex. Each mobile node in RWP model will uniformly reselect its mobile velocity from given $[V_{min}, V_{max}]$ when it reaches one waypoint [8]. The change of velocity on each side of DTN communication nodes will alter the average non-fading duration of mobile-to-mobile channel according to equation (1), so the optimal packet length should maximize the mean transmission efficiency of nodes that move under RWP model.

However, the cumulative time of each velocity condition in which two communication nodes move with velocities v_1 and v_2 respectively is differently weighted, the weights are determined by the appearance probability of velocity condition (v_1, v_2), the average contact frequency (i.e., the frequency that they move into each others' transmission range) of mobile nodes under RWP model which move with v_1 and v_2 respectively and the mean duration of each contact. We notice that the velocity of RWP mobile nodes is uniformly chosen from $[V_{min}, V_{max}]$ at the waypoint and each waypoint is uniformly chosen from given area, so the appearance probability of each velocity condition (v_1, v_2) is inversely proportional to $v_1 \cdot v_2$. [9] mentions that the contact frequency of nodes under RWP model follows Poisson distribution and the mean contact frequency as the parameter of Poisson distribution is:

$$\lambda = c_0 \cdot \frac{V_r \cdot R}{A} \tag{12}$$

where A is a square area for simulation, R is the communication range of nodes, c_0 is a constant for given actual mobility model and V_r is the mean relative velocity between nodes. Obviously, only V_r is variable for different velocity condition (v_1, v_2), which is denoted as:

$$V_r(v_1, v_2) = \frac{1}{\pi} \cdot \int_0^\pi \sqrt{(v_1^2 + v_2^2) - 2v_1 v_2 cos\theta} \cdot d\theta \tag{13}$$

where θ is the included angle of v_1 and v_2. Last but not the least, the mean duration of each contact when nodes move with velocities v_1 and v_2 is also inversely proportional to their mean relative velocity. Then we obtain the weighted integral formula of the mean transmission efficiency of a pair of communication nodes, which move under RWP model with velocity chosen from $[V_{min}, V_{max}]$ respectively:

$$\overline{\epsilon(t_s)} = \frac{1}{(V_{max}-V_{min})^2} \cdot \int_{V_{min}}^{V_{max}} dv_2 \int_{V_{min}}^{V_{max}} \epsilon(v_1, v_2, t_s) \cdot \frac{c_1}{v_1 \cdot v_2} \cdot \lambda \cdot \frac{c_2}{V_r(v_1, v_2)} \cdot dv_1 \tag{14}$$

where $\epsilon(v_1, v_2, t_s)$ and λ are the same as we described in equation (9) and (12) respectively, c_1 and c_2 are constants. Then we substitute the term λ with equation (12), eliminating the term of $V_r(v_1, v_2)$. Equation (14) can thus be changed into:

$$\overline{\epsilon(t_s)} = \frac{1}{(V_{max}-V_{min})^2} \cdot \int_{V_{min}}^{V_{max}} dv_2 \int_{V_{min}}^{V_{max}} \epsilon(v_1, v_2, t_s) \cdot \frac{C}{v_1 \cdot v_2} \cdot dv_1 \qquad (15)$$

where C is a constant. We can see that $\overline{\epsilon(t_s)}$ is a typical transcendental integral function, which can be calculated by approximation algorithm, t_s is theoretically optimal when the maximum value of $\overline{\epsilon(t_s)}$ is obtained.

3 Simulation and Discussion

Our simulation background is set up as shown in TABLE I, under which the performance of data transmission between two mobile DTN nodes will be evaluated.

Table 1. Simulation settings

Simulation time	1,000,000seconds
Simulation area	1000m*1000m
Node transmission range	200m
Mobility model	Random Waypoint
Communication channel model	Mobile-to-mobile fading channel
Channel carrier frequency	2.6GHz
Inherent overhead time per packet	1ms

Where simulation time denotes the time period during which nodes move within given square simulation area, data transmission will be initiated when the distance between nodes is no more than the transmission range. Based on given CBR, the transmission performance is measured by the total time spent in successful payload data transmission during given simulation time, which excludes both inherent overhead time and retransmission time cost. Total effective data transmission time thus reflects the data throughput.

We first verify the performance of theoretically optimal packet length calculated from given environment parameters, letting two nodes select and travel towards each destination point according to the definition of RWP model. However, nodes move with fixed and equal velocity respectively, which will not be reselected at each waypoint. This setting maintains a given mobile-to-mobile fading environment. Data transmission with the optimal packet length will be performed as long as nodes move into the transmission range of each other. Control groups which have packet lengths different from the optimal one are tested under the same environment. Results of total time spent in effective payload data transmission during simulation are shown in Fig. 2. Here $\Delta t = 1ms$, we can see that the simulation group with theoretically optimal packet length calculated in each environment outperforms other control groups, the performance of control groups decreases as their packet lengths deviate further from the optimal one, which coincides with the curve in Fig .1. The effective throughput

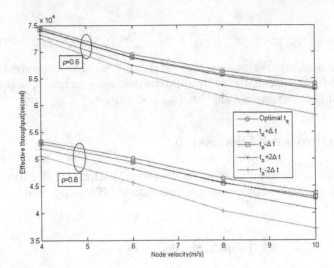

Fig. 2. Performance comparison of optimal packet length and other ones under the environment of given velocity

decreases faster in the groups that nodes move with higher velocities when their packet lengths deviate from the optimal one. Since equation (10) has the unique solution of t_s, the validity of theoretically optimal packet length is testified by the simulation.

Then we validate the fixed optimal packet length which can maximize the average effective throughput between nodes under the environment of variable velocity. We assume that communication nodes of RWP model will randomly reselect their velocity from $[V_{min}, V_{max}]$ when they arrive at each waypoint, employing the mean velocity of RWP model $\overline{V} = \frac{V_{min}+V_{max}}{2}$ as the the independent variable, where $V_{min} = 1m/s$ and $V_{max} = 2\overline{V} - V_{min}$ changes with $\overline{V}$. Simulation results of effective data transmission are shown in Fig. 3.

The simulation results validate our deduction in equation (14) and (15), proving that under the environment of RWP model with variable node velocity there still exists a theoretically optimal packet length for the transmission between DTN nodes, which results in the maximum average effective data throughput. Fig. 4 shows the comparison of theoretically optimal packet lengths deduced under the circumstances that nodes move with fixed velocity and random velocity under RWP model, respectively.

From Fig .4 we find that if ρ and f_0 are given, the optimal packet lengths of nodes under RWP model always differ from those of nodes which move with fixed velocities that equal the mean velocities of RWP model. This phenomenon emerges from the weighted mean $\overline{\epsilon(t_s)}$ as shown in equation (15), the mean cumulative contact time will be statistically longer for a pair of nodes that move with lower velocity. So the weights of different velocity conditions are differentiated, the optimal packet lengths of nodes in RWP model are determined

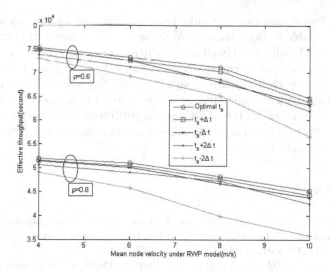

Fig. 3. Performance comparison of optimal packet length and other ones under the environment of RWP

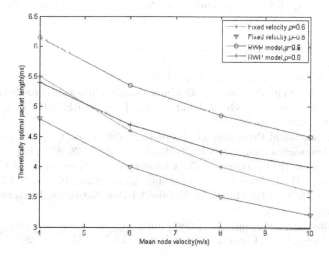

Fig. 4. Comparison of optimal packet length in nodes with fixed velocity and variable RWP velocity

more by conditions of low velocity and thus differ from the optimal packet lengths for nodes that move with the fixed mean velocity of RWP model.

4   Conclusions and Future Work

In this paper, a packet length optimization method is proposed to improve the efficiency of mobile DTN transmission, which considers the impact of mobile-to-mobile fading channel on the data transmission and formulates a thorough optimization problem. Both theoretical deductions and simulation results show that packet length will intensely affect the efficiency of data delivery in the mobile DTN under channel fading environment. A theoretically optimal packet length truly exists under both environment with fixed velocity and the RWP model with variable velocity, which can maximize the effective transmission throughput. Our future work may focus on the real-time adaptation of packet length in mobile DTN which will trace the change of environment parameters and further improve the efficiency of data transmission.

References

1. Zhuo, X., Li, Q., Gao, W., Cao, G., Dai, Y.: Contact duration aware data replication in Delay Tolerant Networks. In: Proc. IEEE International Conference on Network Protocols (ICNP), October 17-20, pp. 236–245 (2011)
2. Qin, S., Feng, G., Zhang, Y.: How the Contact-Probing Mechanism Affects the Transmission Capacity of Delay-Tolerant Networks. IEEE Transactions on Vehicular Technology 60(4), 1825–1834 (2011)
3. Lin, C.-S., Chang, W.-S., Chen, L.-J., Chou, C.-F.: Performance Study of Routing Schemes in Delay Tolerant Networks. In: Proc. 22nd International Conference on Advanced Information Networking and Applications, March 25-28, pp. 1702–1707 (2008)
4. Song, W., Krishnan, M.N., Zakhor, A.: Adaptive Packetization for Error-Prone Transmission over 802.11 WLANs with Hidden Terminals. In: Proc. IEEE MMSP 2009, Rio De Janeiro, Brazil (October 2009)
5. Jayaweera, S.K., Wimalajeewa, T.: Optimal sensor deployment for distributed detection in the presence of channel fading. In: Proc. IEEE MILCOM, November 16-19, pp. 1–7 (2008)
6. Akki, A.S.: Statistical Properties of Mobile-to-Mobile Land Communication Channel. IEEE Transactions on Vehicular Technology 43(4), 826–831 (1994)
7. Chen, X., Jones, H.M., Jayalath, D.: Channel-Aware Routing in MANETs with Route Handoff. IEEE Transactions on Mobile Computing 10(1), 108–121 (2011)
8. Groenvelt, R.: Stochastic Models in Mobile Ad Hoc Networks. University of Nice, Sophia Antipolis (2005)
9. Karaliopoulos, M.: Assessing the Vulnerability of DTN Data Relaying Schemes to Node Selfishness. IEEE Communication Letters 13(12), 923–925 (2009)

TECSS: Time-Efficient Compressive Spectrum Sensing Based on Structurally Random Matrix in Cognitive Radio Networks

Ye Tian, Quan Liu, and Xiaodong Wang

National Key Laboratory for Parallel and Distributed Processing
National University of Defense Technology
Changsha, P.R. China
{tianye172,mars-nudt}@163.com, xdwang@nudt.edu.cn

Abstract. As an advanced technology of implementing wideband spectrum sensing and enhancing the ability of secondary users to utilize multichannel diversity in cognitive radio networks, compressive sensing, without requirement of increasing ADC sampling rate, makes use of unique trait of sparse channel occupancy in cognitive radio networks to detect appearance of primary users in wide spectrum. However, current existing research works aim at highly accurate sensing based on Gaussian Random Matrix (GRM) design, but they fail to take time-efficient sensing into consideration, because GRM causes large computing volume and inefficiency, which lowers the capability of compressive sensing to quickly adapt to channel occupancy change rate of primary users and in turn decreases utility of spectrum exploitation for secondary users. In this paper, we design a Structurally Random Matrix (SRM) by combining GRM and Partial Fourier Matrix (PFM) to improve time efficiency of compressive sensing. As SRM possesses the sensing accuracy merit of GRM and the computing efficiency merit of PFM, the proposed compressive sensing scheme TECSS largely improves time efficiency at a cost of minor sensing accuracy. Simulation results reveal that the sensing accuracy of our proposed TECSS is 92.5% in average sense, slightly below that (95%) of compressive sensing schemes based on GRM, but time-efficiency is upgraded by 100%.

Keywords: spectrum sensing, compressive sensing, cognitive radio, time-efficient, structurally random matrix.

1 Introduction

The growth of wireless technology makes wireless applications flourish in past few years, which causes a large number of wireless communication systems to crowd in limited open access spectrum bands, while the other licensed spectrum bands, according to numerous experimental studies [1], is underutilized in time, frequency, or space. In order to improve spectrum efficiency, cognitive radio is regarded as the most promising technology which enables secondary users (SUs) to access to licensed spectrum bands allocated to primary users (PUs) in an opportunistic manner.

H. Qian and K. Kang (Eds.): WICON 2013, LNICST 121, pp. 65–71, 2013.

So spectrum sensing is a necessity of cognitive radio technology for SUs to monitor activities of PUs and obtain the opportunity to utilize fallow spectrum bands. So, spectrum sensing plays a key role in improving spectrum efficiency in cognitive radio networks constituted by SUs.

Wideband sensing is a kind of spectrum sensing [2], which enables SUs to get the status of multiple channels parallel. Wideband sensing is more powerful to conduct SUs to acquire the gain of multichannel diversity, because SUs can choose the best available channel from a sensing result for transmission, while it is impossible in narrow-band sensing. According to Nyquist sampling theory, wideband sensing requires high sampling rate. That is, the wider the spectrum band is sensed at a time, the higher the sampling rate is required. However, linear increase in sampling rate will cause exponential increase in technologic complexity, which limits the capability of wideband sensing [3].

Compressive sensing theory was proposed by Tao and Candès[4,5], and its principium is based on sparse matrix recoverability. According to compressive sensing theory [4], if signal has a sparse representation in some other domain by transformation from time domain, it can be sampled at sub-Nyquist rate and recovered via feasible algorithms without losing any information. The sensing performance (e.g. sensing accuracy and sensing time-efficiency) is dominated by compressive matrix [5], which must be incoherent with the sparse representation basis matrix. Consequently, compressive sensing provides a method to implement wideband sensing without stringent requirement on corresponding sampling rate, which relaxes high requirement on sampling rate of A/D Convertor. As PUs intermittently occupy licensed bands, their appearance presents sparsity in frequency domain[6], which inspires researchers with large potential of compressive sensing application in wideband spectrum sensing for cognitive radio networks[7]. However, all these existing works emphasize on performance of sensing accuracy by GRM design, but they ignore performance of sensing time-efficiency. Because GRM causes large computing volume and inefficiency, their schemes are time-inefficient in recovery. Time-efficiency of compressive spectrum sensing is of importance to cognitive radio networks. On one hand, if the sensing time can be shortened, SUs will have more time to transmit data to improve aggregate throughput. On the other hand, the status of channel occupancy may transit rapidly, which requires fast sensing of SUs to adapt to activities of PUs and protect PUs from harmful interference.

In this paper, we design SRM by combining GRM and PFM. As the SRM possesses the sensing accuracy merit of GRM and the computing efficiency merit of PFM, the proposed compressive sensing scheme not only guarantees sensing accuracy, but also improves sensing time-efficiency. Our contributions of this paper include: (1) To the best of our knowledge, we are the first to take into account the time-efficiency in compressive sensing; (2) We design a novel SRM for our compressive sensing scheme to improve the sensing efficiency at the cost of minor sensing accuracy compared to those based on GRM.

The rest of the paper is organized as follows. In section 2, we overview related work of compressive sensing in cognitive radio networks. We present our designed time-efficient compressive spectrum sensing (TECSS) in details in section 3 and evaluates the performance of TECSS by simulation in section 4. Finally, section 5 concludes our work.

2   Related Work

Most of the studies of compressive spectrum sensing in cognitive radio networks focus on the sensing accuracy, but fail to concentrate on sensing time-efficiency. Secondary users must sense the spectrum environment accuracy so as to access the spectrum without interfering primary users. Resulted from its high sensing accuracy, Gaussian random matrix is widely used for compressive spectrum sensing in [6, 7]. Its incoherence with other orthogonal matrices makes the compressive sensing accurately with minimal number of measurements [5]. But because of its randomicity it has two defects: huge memory buffering and high computational complexity. In wideband compressive sensing, the number of sub-channel will be very large, so we have to choose another matrix which can be used to deal with large scale data. Moreover, we want to get TECSS, the chosen matrix must have low computational complexity.

Partial Fourier matrix in [8] is a kind of compressive matrix that exploits the algorithm of FFT so as to speed up compressive sensing. Partial Fourier matrix can significantly reduce the complexity of the compressive sampling system. However, it is only inefficient with the signals which are sparse in time-domain, thus it can't be employed in compressive spectrum sensing because the signals are sparse in frequency domain not sparse in time domain in cognitive radio networks.

In this paper, we combine the random Gaussian matrix and partial Fourier matrix to get a kind of sensing matrix called structurally random matrix to sense the spectrum time-efficiently and accurately. So far we have not found any work on sensing time-efficiency, and this missing part is exactly what we are going to do in this paper.

3   TECSS with SRM

In this section we derive secondary users with SRM sense the state transition of primary users accurately and time-efficiently.

3.1   System Model

Consider a (ultra-)wide band that hosts both primary users and secondary users. Suppose that the spectrum of B Hz is divided into N non-overlapping sub-channels,. Signals transmitted by primary users are received by secondary users [9]. We use $r(t)$ to denote the received signal by secondary users in time-domain. r_t stands for the discrete version of $r(t)$ sampled at Nyquist rate, and r_f is the spectrum form of r_t .And T_{SRM} and T_{GRM} denote the sensing time of using SRM and GRM, respectively.

3.2   Sensing Processing of Secondary Users

Secondary users sense the spectrum using received signal, the signal given by

$$r(t) = r_p(t) + n(t) \tag{1}$$

where $r_p(t)$ denote signals from primary users, $n(t)$ is additive white Gaussian noise (AWGN).Take N-point FFT (Fast Fourier Transform) of the time discrete version of (2), then we have

$$r_f = r_{p,f} + n_f. \tag{2}$$

Secondary users estimate the spectrum $r_{p,f}$ so as to choose a better sub-channel from the unoccupied frequency band. Resulted from the low spectrum utilization of primary users, $r_{p,f}$ is sparse, compressive spectrum sensing can be used. In compressive spectrum sensing secondary users collect and compress time-domain signals using compressive matrix $C_{M \times N}$ (M<<N), the measurement signal can be calculated as

$$s_t = C \times r_t \tag{3}$$

where r_t is the sampled signal of $r(t)$ at Nyquist rate f_N .With compressive sampling, the sample rate decrease to $(M / N) f_N$,which relaxes the high requirement on ADC sampling rate. And we have

$$r_t = F_N^{-1} r_f \tag{4}$$

where F_N^{-1} is the N-Point IFFT matrix. Such that we have

$$s_t = C F_N^{-1} r_{p,f} + \tilde{n}_f \tag{5}$$

where $\tilde{n}_f = C F_N^{-1} n_f$ is still AWGN. Based on compressive sensing, secondary users reconstruct the spectrum $r_{p,f}$ with compressive matrix C and measurement s_t using the recovery algorithms [10]. According to (5), s_t is the sampled signal by C, so the choice of compressive matrix C is important in compressive spectrum sensing. Both sensing accuracy and sensing time-efficiency lie on C .

3.3   Structurally Random Matrix

The sensing accuracy depends on the incoherence of compressive sensing matrix C with IFFT matrix F_N^{-1}. The coherence is low when we choose GRM as sensing matrix, so the sensing accuracy of GRM is excellent. But when GRM is used in ultra-wideband compressive sensing, its buffering memory is huge and computation complexity is very high due to their completely unstructured nature.

Now wideband compressive sensing need to be accuracy and time-efficiency, in order to keep approximate sensing accuracy, the matrix needs to have the properties of GRM to guarantee the incoherence. To speed up the sensing, we can utilize the properties of partial Fourier matrix [8]. So SRM can be designed like this

$$C = \sqrt{\frac{N}{M}} DFP \cdot \tag{6}$$

$P \in R^{N \times N}$ is a random permutation matrix, which can permute the locations of elements of a vector randomly. With this matrix we can guarantee that SRM has approximate incoherence with F_N^{-1}, thus, the sensing accuracy is approximate to the GRM.

$F \in R^{N \times N}$ is an orthonormal matrix, like the partial Fourier matrix, we can use FFT matrix, DCT matrix, or WHT matrix to reduce the computation complexity. Resulted from their fast computation algorithms the compressive sensing is speeded up.

$D \in R^{M \times N}$ is a randomly downsampler. It can randomly abstract M rows of FP, which will generate stochastically independence among the deterministic rows [8]. With this matrix we can get sub-Nyquist rate measurements. Multiplying $\sqrt{\frac{N}{M}}$ is to guarantee the same power after down rate sample.

So with this design, SRM realizes the sensing accuracy of Gaussian matrix and sensing time-efficiency of Partial Fourier matrix. As a result, using the SRM as compressive matrix for spectrum sensing realizes approximate accuracy of GRM and higher time-efficiency than GRM.

4   Simulation Evaluation

In this section, we conduct simulations to verify the availability and efficiency of proposed TECSS with SRM compared with its counterparts with GRM.

4.1   Simulation Setup and Performance Metrics

In this section, we will compare the sensing performance of SRM and GRM. The assessed sensing performance includes sensing accuracy and sensing time-efficiency. The sensing accuracy is evaluated by the probability of detection and the sensing time-cost is evaluated by system time of the computer.

4.2   Sensing Accuracy of SRM and GRM

In Fig.1, Original signal denotes the spectrum which is occupied, Recovered signal 1 and 2 denote the sensing spectrum using GRM and SRM, respectively. Difference1 and 2 denote the differences between the original signal and recovered signals. We can find that the sensing accuracy with GRM is slightly better than SRM in accuracy. In Table 1, we list the sensing accuracies with different numbers of sub-channels, we can see the average accuracy of SRM is 92.5%, it only decreases by 2.5% compared with GRM(95%).

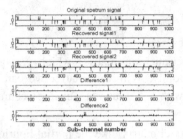

Fig. 1. the number of sub-channels is 1024, the occupied number is 40

Table 1. Sensing accuracy

Sub-channel number	GRM	SRM
500	100%	95%
1000	95%	92.5%
1500	95%	92.5%
2000	90%	90%

4.3 Sensing Time-Cost of SRM and GRM

In Fig.2, the sensing time of GRM is always longer than that of SRM. As the sub-channel numbers increase, the GRM sensing time will rapidly increases because of its high computation complexity. However, the SRM can deal with large data., the sensing time ratio is larger than 2, so the sensing speed is improved by 100% .

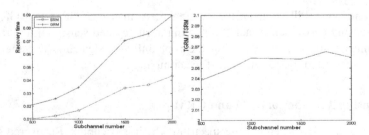

Fig. 2. Sensing time with two matrices

5   Conclusions

The former used methods of wideband compressive spectrum sensing only focused on the sensing accuracy, but failed to concentrate on the time-efficiency of sensing. Aimed at speeding up the sensing to sense fast change of spectrum and leave more time for data transmission, this paper presents TECSS based on SRM. With simulation evaluation, we verify our analysis and demonstrate the significant performance gain of TECSS with SRM. To deal with situations where primary users appear and disappear even faster, the real-time compressive spectrum sensing is our future work.

Acknowledgments. This work has been supported by Natural Science Foundation of China with grants No. as 61070203, 61202484.

References

1. Akyildiz, I.F., Lee, W., Vuran, M.C., Mohanty, S.: NeXt generation dynamic spectrum access cognitive radio wireless networks: A survey. Computer Networks 50(13), 2127–2159 (2006)
2. Xie, S., Liu, Y., Zhang, Y., Yu, R.: A parallel cooperative spectrum sensing in cognitive radio networks. IEEE Transactions on Vehicular Technology 59(8), 4079–4092 (2010)
3. Akyildiz, I., Lo, B., Balakrishnan, R.: Cooperative spectrum sensing in cognitive radio networks: A survey. Physical Communication (2010)
4. Candes, E., Romberg, J., Tao, T.: Robust uncertainty principles: Exact signal reconstruction from highly incomplete frequency information. IEEE Transactions on Information Theory 52(2), 489–509 (2006)
5. Baraniuk, R.: A lecture on compressive sensing. IEEE Signal Processing Magazine (2007)
6. Tian, Z., Giannakis, G.: Compressed sensing for wideband cognitive radios. In: IEEE International Conference on Acoustics, Speech and Signal Processing, ICASSP 2007, vol. 4 (2007)
7. Wang, Y., Tian, Z., Feng, C.: Sparsity order estimation and its application in compressive spectrum sensing for cognitive radios. IEEE Transactions on Wireless Communications 11(6), 2116–2125 (2012)
8. Do, T., Gan, L., Nguyen, N., Tran, T.: Fast and efficient compressive sensing using structurally random matrices. IEEE Transactions on Signal Processing (99), 1–11 (2011)
9. Csurgai-Horvath, L., Bito, J.: Primary and secondary user activity models for cognitive wireless network. In: Proceedings of the 2011 11th International Conference on Telecommunications (Con-TEL), pp. 301–306 (2011)
10. Havary-Nassab, V., Hassan, S., Valaee, S.: Compressive detection for wide-band spectrum sensing. In: 2010 IEEE International Conference on Acoustics Speech and Signal Processing (ICASSP), pp. 3094–3097 (2011)

An Overlay Architecture for MISO Cognitive Radio Systems

Monirosharieh Vameghestahbanati, Hasan S. Mir, and Mohamed El-Tarhuni

Department of Electrical Engineering
American University of Sharjah
United Arab Emirates
{g00041221,hmir,mtarhuni}@aus.edu

Abstract. A multiple-input-single-output (MISO) wireless overlay system is developed in the context of cognitive radio (CR) applications. Whereas conventional CR architectures require spectrum sensing and only allow the overlay system to operate when the legacy system is idle, the proposed architecture enables simultaneous operation of the overlay and legacy systems. The overlay system exploits transmit-path diversity in order to optimize its own self performance while mitigating interference into the legacy system. Simulation results using the proposed architecture demonstrate significant performance gains vis-a-vis single-input-single-output (SISO) schemes.

Keywords: Mean square error (MSE), multiple-input-single-output (MISO), crosstalk, overlay system, cognitive radio (CR).

1 Introduction

The problem of frequency spectrum congestion has been increasing due to the demand for higher date-rate services combined with the need to accommodate diverse types of users and applications [1]. Novel paradigms are thus needed in order to meet such demands. The recently developed technology of cognitive radio (CR) [2] provides an intelligent wireless communication system that is able to adapt itself to the environment via dynamically and autonomously adjusting its operating parameters [3],[4].

The operating paradigm of a CR system consists of *legacy* users that hold the primary spectrum license and have usage priority, and *overlay* that users have lower usage priority and are only allowed to operate in the legacy band if doing so does not cause unacceptable interference to legacy users. It is thus important that the overlay system be capable of spectrum sensing, which involves determining the existence of active legacy users within a geographical area of interest. Relevant algorithms for doing so, however, suffer from degraded performance in the presence of channel shadowing and fading [5]. As such, we propose in this paper a multiple-input-single-output (MISO) CR paradigm wherein overlay users can operate *simultaneously* with legacy users without the need of spectrum sensing. The simultaneous operation paradigm, combined with the spatial

H. Qian and K. Kang (Eds.): WICON 2013, LNICST 121, pp. 72–77, 2013.
© Institute for Computer Sciences, Social Informatics and Telecommunications Engineering 2013

diversity afforded by the multiple transmit antennas, may potentially unveil an even more efficient utilization of the shared spectrum. Furthermore, the design of the optimal transmitter and receiver of the overlay system must be done in such a manner that mitigates the mutual interference between the overlay and legacy users.

This contribution is broadly related to previous work on joint transmitter/ receiver optimization under the MSE criterion. The design of an overlay system in the context of non-coordinated digital subscriber lines is considered in [6], wherein the performance metric consists of the overlay system MSE and the excess MSE to the legacy system caused by the introduction of the overlay system. Joint transmitter/receiver optimization for multiple uncoordinated users is investigated in [7] under the assumption that the direct and cross talk channel responses seen by each user are symmetric. A narrowband spatial multiplexing system with a jointly optimal transmitter and receiver is addressed in [8] by decoupling the MIMO channels into parallel sub-channels via the transmit and receive filters. [9] studied the problem of joint precoder and receiver design using the MSE between the transmitted signal of the new system and its estimate in the receiver for the system downlink. It should be noted, however, it does not consider the optimal overlay system pulse shape or the effect of interference from the legacy system on the performance of the overlay system.

In this paper, we study the problem of jointly optimizing the transmitter/ receiver pulse shape for a MISO system overlaid onto an existing legacy system using a composite MSE criterion. The criterion consists of the overlay system MSE and the excess MSE introduced into the legacy system.

This paper is organized as follows. Section 2 introduces the proposed MISO system and its design. Section 3 provides simulation results. We conclude the paper in Section 4.

2   Multiple-Transmit-Antenna System

Figure 1 shows a block diagram of the proposed system architecture. The legacy system is assumed to be single-input-single-output (SISO), whereas the overlay system is assumed to be MISO. Thus, the single legacy transmitter has impulse response $h_t^{(l)}(t)$, whereas the M overlay transmitters have impulse responses $h_t^{(o_m)}(t)$, $m = 1 \ldots M$. Since both the legacy and overlay system have only a single output, they consist of only one receiver with respective impulse responses $h_r^{(l)}(t)$ and $h_r^{(o)}(t)$.

The direct channel with impulse response $h_c^{(ll)}(t)$ is used for communication by the legacy system, but is contaminated by the AWGN signal $w_2(t)$ and the interference path with impulse response $h_c^{(o_m l)}(t)$, $m = 1 \ldots M$, that originates at the mth overlay transmitter and terminates at the legacy receiver. Similarly, the direct channel with impulse response $h_c^{(o_m o)}(t)$, $m = 1 \ldots M$, is used for communication by the overlay system, but is also contaminated by the AWGN signal $w_1(t)$ and the interference path with impulse response $h_c^{(lo)}(t)$ that originates at the legacy

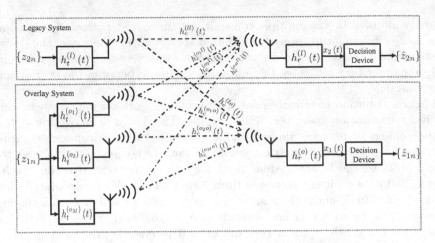

Fig. 1. Multiple-transmit-antenna system model

transmitter and terminates at the overlay receiver. It is assumed that knowledge of these channels is available through appropriate feedback mechanisms.

The independent and identically distributed (i.i.d) input sequences z_{1n} and z_{2n} form the input to the overlay and legacy systems. The legacy and overlay receivers process these respective sequences and produce the respective output signals $x_1(t)$ and $x_2(t)$. Decision devices are used to produce the final outputs denoted as $\hat{z}_{1n}$ and $\hat{z}_{2n}$.

The objective is to design the jointly optimal overlay transmitters $h_t^{(o_m)}(t)$, $m = 1 \ldots M$, and overlay receiver $h_r^{(o)}(t)$, so that mutual interference between the overlay and legacy systems can be mitigated and thus permit simultaneous operation of the two systems. The design is posed as an optimization whose cost function consists of the performance of the overlay system and the performance degradation of the legacy system due to the introduction of the overlay system. Furthermore, the design is subject to two constraints - the legacy transmitter and receiver $h_t^{(l)}(t)$ and $h_r^{(l)}(t)$ *cannot* be modified (and are thus not design variables), and the average transmitter power on the overlay user is constrained to some level P_t, where

$$P_t = \sum_{m=1}^{M} P_{tm} \tag{1}$$

and P_{tm} represents the average transmitter power from the mth antenna of the overlay system. As such, an appropriate cost function is the composite MSE:

$$MSE = MSE_1 + MSE_2^e + \sum_{m=1}^{M} \lambda_m P_{tm} \tag{2}$$

where MSE_1 represents the overlay system MSE, MSE_2^e represents the excess MSE into the legacy system due to the interference from the overlay system, and λ_m, $m = 1 \ldots M$, represents the Lagrange multipliers. By transforming (2) into the frequency domain, the following conditions for the jointly optimal overlay transmitter and receiver are obtained:

$$\mathbf{H_t^{(o)}}^{\mathsf{T}}\mathbf{M_1}\mathbf{H_t^{(o)}} = \left|H_r^{(o)}(f)\right|^2 M_2 \tag{3}$$

$$\left[\mathbf{H_t^{(o)}}^{\mathsf{T}}\mathbf{M_3}\mathbf{H_t^{(o)}} + M_2\right] H_r^{(o)}(f) = T\mathbf{H_t^{(o)}}^{\mathsf{T}}\mathbf{H_c^{(oo)}} \tag{4}$$

$$\left[\left|H_r^{(o)}(f)\right|^2 \mathbf{M_3} + \mathbf{M_1}\right] \mathbf{H_t^{(o)}} = T H_r^{(o)}(f)\mathbf{H_c^{(oo)}} \tag{5}$$

where $\mathbf{M_1} = \left|H_r^{(l)}(f)\right|^2 \mathbf{H_c^{(ol)}}\mathbf{H_c^{(ol)}}^{\mathsf{T}} + \lambda$, $M_2 = \left|H_t^{(l)}(f)\right|^2\left|H_c^{(lo)}(f)\right|^2 + \eta^{-1}$, $\mathbf{M_3} = \mathbf{H_c^{(oo)}}\mathbf{H_c^{(oo)}}^{\mathsf{T}}$, and

$$\mathbf{H_t^o} = \left[\, H_t^{o_1}(f)\; H_t^{o_2}(f)\ldots H_t^{o_M}(f)\,\right]^{\mathsf{T}} \tag{6}$$

$$\mathbf{H_c^{(oo)}} = \left[\, H_c^{o_1 o}(f)\; H_c^{o_2 o}(f)\ldots H_c^{o_M o}(f)\,\right]^{\mathsf{T}} \tag{7}$$

$$\mathbf{H_c^{(ol)}} = \left[\, H_c^{o_1 l}(f)\; H_c^{o_2 l}(f)\ldots H_c^{o_M l}(f)\,\right]^{\mathsf{T}} \tag{8}$$

In equations (3)–(8), $H_t^{(l)}(f)$, $H_r^{(l)}(f)$, $H_r^{(o)}(f)$, $H_c^{(ll)}(f)$, $H_c^{(lo)}(f)$, $H_t^{(o_m)}(f)$, $H_c^{(o_m o)}(f)$, and $H_c^{(o_m l)}(f)$ represents the Fourier transform of $h_t^{(l)}(t)$, $h_r^{(l)}(t)$, $h_r^{(o)}(t)$, $h_c^{(ll)}(t)$, $h_c^{(lo)}(t)$, $h_t^{(o_m)}(t)$, $h_c^{(o_m o)}(t)$, and $h_c^{(o_m l)}(t)$, respectively. Because (3), (4), and (5) do not have a closed-form solution, an efficient sequential optimization algorithm is used to find the optimum overlay receiver ($H_r^{(o)}$) which is then applied to (5) in order to find the optimum overlay transmitter ($\mathbf{H_t^{(o)}}$). Moreover, the approximate values for the Lagrange multipliers λ_1 through λ_M that satisfy the desired power constraint are determined using non-joint optimization which does not necessarily yield the optimum solution. While the optimum solution (which can be computed using e.g. trust-region-reflective optimization techniques) will yield better performance (i.e. lower composite MSE), it is computationally more complex.

3 Simulation Results

Performance comparisons are provided in this section for which the overlay transmitter has a single antenna ($M = 1$) and dual antennas ($M = 2$). The case $M = 1$ serves as a baseline against which we can compare the improvement in performance afforded through the use of spatial diversity, as is the case when $M = 2$. It is assumed that the system operates over a flat Rayleigh fading channel in the presence of AWGN. Also, without loss of generality, we assume that both the legacy and the overlay systems occupy a common bandwidth of 15 MHz and the legacy transmitter power is 0 dB.

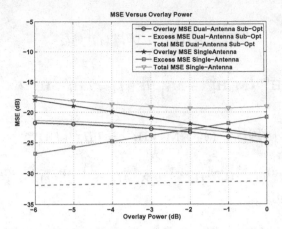

Fig. 2. Effect of varying overlay power in a system with sub-optimum dual transmit antenna overlay, and a system with single antenna overlay

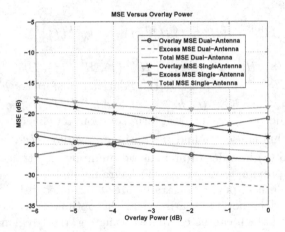

Fig. 3. Effect of varying overlay power in a system with optimum dual transmit antenna overlay, and a system with single antenna overlay

Figure 2 shows the variation of the MSE with the overlay transmitter power for the dual-transmit-antenna and single-transmit-antenna overlay systems for the case in which the sub-optimum (but computationally efficient) method (non-joint optimization) is used to compute the overlay transmitter and receiver. For the dual-transmit-antenna system, the overlay transmitter power is the total available power at the overlay transmitter, which is allocated to each overlay transmitter by sequentially optimizing the Lagrange multipliers, λ_1 and λ_2, in (2). It can be seen that the overall performance of the dual-transmit-antenna system is better compared to the single-transmit-antenna system.

Figure 3 shows the variation of the MSE with the overlay transmitter power for the dual-transmit-antenna and single-transmit-antenna overlay systems for the case in which the optimum (but computationally complex) method is used to compute the overlay transmitter and receiver. Like Figure 2, it can be seen that the overall performance of the dual-transmit-antenna system is better compared to the single-transmit-antenna system. Moreover, the improvement in performance has increased relative to the sub-optimum solution. Nonetheless, this margin of increased performance comes at the cost of increased computational burden.

4   Conclusion

A cognitive radio paradigm was proposed wherein an overlay system can simultaneously operate with the legacy user over the same spectrum without the need of spectrum sensing. The overlay system employs a MISO architecture that enables it to exploit transmit path diversity. Based on a composite MSE that consists of the sum of the MSE of the overlay system and the excess MSE introduced to the legacy system, necessary conditions that jointly optimize the overlay transmitter/receiver filters were derived. Simulation results show that the proposed overlay system architecture yields significant performance gains over the conventional SISO implementation and thus more efficiently exploits the shared spectrum.

References

1. Chen, J., Zhang, X., Kuo, Y.: Adaptive Cooperative Spectrum Sharing Based on Fairness and Total Profit in Cognitive Radio Networks. ETRI Journal, 512–519 (2010)
2. Mitola, J.: Cognitive Radio: Making Software Radio More Personal. IEEE Personal Communications 06(04), 48–52 (1999)
3. Haykin, S.: Cognitive Radio: Brain-empowered Wireless Communications. IEEE Journal on Selected Areas in Communications 23(2), 201–220 (2005)
4. Federal Communications Commission: Notice of Proposed Rule Making and Order: Facilitating Opportunities for Flexible, Efficient, and Reliable Spectrum Use Employing Cognitive Radio Technologies. ET Docket No. 03-108 (2005)
5. Yucek, T., Arslan, H.: A Survey of Spectrum Sensing Algorithms for Cognitive Radio Application. IEEE Communications Surveys Tutorials 11(1) (2009)
6. Mir, H., Roy, S.: Optimum Transmitter/Receiver Design for a Narrowband Overlay in Noncoordinated Subscriber Lines. IEEE Transactions on Communications 52(6), 992–998 (2004)
7. Kumar, P., Roy, S.: Optimization for Crosstalk Suppression with Noncoordinating Users. IEEE Transactions on Communications 44, 894–905 (1996)
8. Sampath, H., Paulraj, A.: Joint Transmit and Receive Optimization for High Data Rate Wireless Communication Using Multiple Antennas. In: Conference Record of the Thirty-Third Asilomar Conference on Signals, Systems, and Computers, vol. 1, pp. 215–219 (1999)
9. Seo, B.: Joint Design of Precoder and Receiver in Cognitive Radio Networks Using an MSE Criterion. Signal Processing 91(11), 2623–2629 (2011)

A Scalable Feedback-Based Approach to Distributed Nullforming

Muhammad M. Rahman, Soura Dasgupta, and Raghuraman Mudumbai*

Department of Electrical & Computer Engineering, University of Iowa,
Iowa City IA 52242
{mrahmn,dasgupta,rmudumbai}@engineering.uiowa.edu

Abstract. We present a novel approach to the problem of distributed nullforming where a set of transmitters cooperatively transmit a common message signal in such a way that their individual transmissions precisely cancel each other at a designated receiver. Under our approach, each transmitter iteratively makes an adjustment to the phase of its transmitted RF signal, by effectively implementing a gradient descent algorithm to reduce the amplitude of the overall received signal to zero. We show that this gradient search can be implemented in a purely distributed fashion at each transmitter assuming only that each transmitter has an estimate of its own channel gain to the receiver. This is an important advantage of our approach and assures its scalability; in contrast any non-iterative approach to the nullforming problem requires centralized knowledge of the channel gain of every transmitter. We prove analytically that the gradient search algorithm converges to a null at the designated receiver. We also present numerical simulations to illustrate the robustness of this approach.

Keywords: distributed nullforming, cooperative transmission, virtual antenna arrays.

1   Introduction

We consider the problem of distributed nullforming where a set of transmitters in a wireless network cooperatively transmit a common message signal in such a way that their individual transmissions cancel each other at a designated receiver. In effect the transmitters form a *virtual antenna array* and shape the array's antenna pattern to create a null at the desired location. The technique of distributed nullforming has many potential applications including interference avoidance for increased spatial spectrum reuse [1], cognitive radio [2], physical-layer security [3] and so on.

Distributed nullforming requires precise control of the amplitude and phase of the radio-frequency signal transmitted by each cooperating transmitter to ensure

---

* This work was partly supported by US NSF grants CPS-1239509, CCF-0830747, CNS-1239509, CAREER award ECCS-1150801 and EPS-1101284, and a grant from the Roy J. Carver Charitable Trust.

H. Qian and K. Kang (Eds.): WICON 2013, LNICST 121, pp. 78–84, 2013.

that they cancel each other. This is an extremely challenging problem because each transmitter usually obtains its RF signal from a separate local oscillator (LO), and signals obtained from different LOs invariably have Brownian motion driven phase drifts due to manufacturing tolerances and temperature variations. The nullforming algorithm must estimate, track and compensate for the effect of these drifts.

While the idea of cooperative communication has been studied for decades [4], the early work in this area neglected the RF synchronization issues that are crucial for the practical implementation of these ideas. Recently, however, there has been a significant amount of research activity on distributed transmit beamforming [5], [6], [7], including implementation on commodity hardware [8, 9].

While the synchronization techniques developed for distributed beamforming can be adapted for nullforming, there are two important differences that make nullforming significantly more challenging: (a) While beamforming gains are highly robust and insensitive to small phase errors (upto about 30 degrees [5]), nullforming is substantially more sensitive [13] to even modest errors. (b) One implication of this sensitivity to small phase errors is that the simple 1-bit feedback algorithm [10] that has proved to be effective for beamforming does not work for nullforming. However, we show in this paper that a gradient descent algorithm using multi-bit feedback similar to [11] works very well for nullforming. (c) For beamforming, each transmitter only needs the knowledge of the phase of its own transmitted signal at the receiver. In contrast for nullforming, the amplitude and phase of the transmitted signal at each node cannot be chosen independently of the amplitudes and phases of other nodes [13]. Nullforming essentially depends on a node's transmitted signal cancelling the signals from all other transmitters. Therefore state-of-the-art distributed nullforming algorithms, [12] and [13] assume that each transmitter knows *every transmitter's* complex channel gain to the receiver. This requirement poses a severe challenge for scalability.

In contrast to previous work on distributed nullforming [12, 13], in this paper we assume that each transmitter knows *only its own channel gain* to the null location. Using this in Section 2 we formulate our gradient descent based algorithm, in which each node adjusts its transmitted phase knowing only its channel gain, and a common feedback signal from the receiver at which the null is desired. This feedback signal is simply the complex baseband signal received by the receiver. Section 3 presents an analysis of the stability and convergence properties of the algorithm under simplifying assumptions. Section 4 provides simulations, that include the effect of channel phase offsets and oscillator drift. Section 5 concludes.

2   Scalable Algorithm for Nullforming

We now describe a scalable gradient descent algorithm for distributed nullforming in a node. As noted in the introduction, we assume that at the beginning of a nullforming epoch, each transmitter has access to its own complex channel gain to the receiver, using which it equalizes its channel to the receiver. This is in sharp contrast to [12] and [13] where each transmitter knows the Channel State Information (CSI) for every transmitter. We assume there are N transmitter nodes that have been synchronized in frequency, using the techniques of [12], [13] and [11].

Assume at time slot k, the i-th node transmits the baseband signal $e^{j\theta_i[k]}$. The total baseband signal at the receiver is thus:

$$s[k] = R[k] + jI[k], \tag{1}$$

where

$$R[k] = \sum_{i=1}^{N} r_i \cos\left(\theta_i[k] + \phi_i[k]\right), \tag{2}$$

$$I[k] = \sum_{i=1}^{N} r_i \sin\left(\theta_i[k] + \phi_i[k]\right), \tag{3}$$

r_i is the equalized channel gain from the i-th transmitter and $\phi_i[k]$ is a small uncompensated channel phase from the i-th transmitter. The receiver feeds back at each time slot the signal $s[k]$. Consequently, at each time slot the i-th transmitter has access to $R[k]$, $I[k]$, r_i and $\theta_i[k]$; $\phi_i[k]$ is not available to any one. Define, $\theta[k] = [\theta_1[k], \cdots, \theta_N[k]]^\top$. The total received power in the k-th time slot is:

$$J(\theta[k]) = I^2[k] + R^2[k]. \tag{4}$$

Throughout we make the following standing assumption:

Assumption 2.1. *The r_i are such that there is a choice of θ_i for which $J(\theta) = 0$.*

Since the r_i are equalized gains, each receiver can always choose its r_i to equal 1, ensuring the existence of a choice of θ_i that achieve the null mandated by Assumption 2.1. For a suitably small $\mu > 0$, in our algorithm the i-th transmitter updates its phase according to:

$$\theta_i[k+1] = \theta_i[k] + \mu r_i \left(\sin\left(\theta_i[k]\right) R[k] - \cos\left(\theta_i[k]\right) I[k]\right). \tag{5}$$

Few features are of note. The algorithm is totally distributed, as each node only needs the common feedback signal $s[k]$ and r_i and $\theta_i[k]$, to implement it. This contrasts with [12], [13] where much more information is needed. Second, suppose in vector form the algorithm were expressed as:

$$\theta[k+1] = \theta[k] - f[k]. \tag{6}$$

Then, when the phase offsets $\phi_i[k]$ are all zero, the $f[k]$ corresponding to (5) is simply:

$$f[k] = \mu \left.\frac{\partial J(\theta)}{\partial \theta}\right|_{\theta=\theta[k]}. \tag{7}$$

In other words the algorithm attempts the gradient descent minimization of the received power. Finally, the fact that the algorithm works from a common feedback signal supplied by the receiver, makes it *totally scalable* as the feedback overhead does not grow with the size of the transmitter array.

3 Stability

Our stability analysis will be conducted under the idealized assumption of no noise and zero $\phi_i[k]$. The underlying philosophy is driven by total stability theory, [14], that states in essence that should the algorithm uniformly converge to desired stationary points in the idealized (zero noise, zero ϕ_i) case, uniformity being with respect to the initial time, then it will exhibit robustness to noise and small ϕ_i. Indeed we will demonstrate the *practical* uniform convergence of (5) under the following assumption:

Assumption 3.1. *In (2) and (3) for all $i \in \{1, \cdots, N\}$ and all k, $\phi_i[k] = 0$.*

Let us clarify what we mean by *practical* uniform convergence. As will be evident from the sequel, under Assumption 3.1 the algorithm in (5) has entire manifolds of stationary points at least to one of which the algorithm converges uniformly. Some stationary correspond to nulls. The rest, which we dub as being *spurious*, do not. We will show that the latter are locally unstable. Thus they are rarely attained, and even if attained not practically maintained as the slightest noise would drive the phase trajectories away from them. Thus, by showing the local stability of the stationary points corresponding to nulls, we would have demonstrated the practical uniform converence of the algorithm to a null.

We relax Assumption 3.1 to permit non-zero but constant ϕ_i. Under these conditions from (5) we obtain that the stationary points fall into the following categories. (A) $R[k] = I[k] = 0$. (B) If $R[k] \neq 0$, then for all i, $\tan \theta_i[k] = \frac{I[k]}{R[k]}$. (C) If $I[k] \neq 0$, then for all i, $\cot \theta_i[k] = \frac{R[k]}{I[k]}$. Clearly [A] corresponds to stationary points reflecting nulls. Both [B] and [C] reflect the condition that for all i, l, $\tan \theta_i = \tan \theta_l$. Some of these may still correspond to nulls. The rest are spurious.

We will now invoke Assumption 3.1. We have the following Theorem.

Theorem 3.1. *Under Assumption 3.1, (2), (3), (5) and (4), there exists a $\mu^* > 0$, such that for all $0 < \mu < \mu^*$, $\theta[k]$ converges uniformly to one of the stationary points in (A-C) above.*

Standard theory shows that the local instability of the algorithm in (5) is assured if the algorithm linearized around that stationary point has poles outside the unit circle. Under 3.1 this in turn is assured if the Hessian of $J(\cdot)$ evaluated at such a stationary point has a negative eigenvalue. As under (B,C) all off diagonal elents of Hessian are ± 1, this is in turn assured by the Hessian evaluated at such a stationary point having a nonpositive diagonal element. The (i, l)-th element of such an Hessian obeys:

$$[H(\theta)]_{il} = \begin{cases} -2 \sum_{m \neq i}^{N} \cos(\theta_i - \theta_m) & i = l \\ 2 \cos(\theta_i - \theta_l) & i \neq l \end{cases}$$

It is readily seen that for arbitrary $N \geq 2$ at least one diagonal element is negative or zero.

Thus practical uniform convergence is guaranteed by showing that all stationary points corresponding to a true null are locally stable. To this end we must examine the Hessian at these points corresponding nulls. Assumption 2.1 guarantees the existing of stationary points. Under Assumption 3.1 at a stationary point corresponding to a null, i.e. when $R = I = 0$, there holds:

$$[H(\theta)]_{il} = \begin{cases} 2 & i = l \\ 2\cos(\theta_i - \theta_l) & i \neq l \end{cases}$$

It is readily seen that at such a stationary point, with $c = \begin{bmatrix} \cos\theta_1 \cdots \cos\theta_N \end{bmatrix}^T$ and $s = \begin{bmatrix} \sin\theta_1 \cdots \sin\theta_N \end{bmatrix}^T$ the Hessian is $2cc^T + 2ss^T$. Thus the Hessian evaluated at a null is positve semidefinite, but with rank at most 2. There are several zero eigenvalues of the Hessian. Using as we did in [15], center manifold theory, one can nonetheless show that these stationary points are indeed locally stable. The proof being complicated is omitted. This thus proves the practical uniform convergence of (5) to a null is guaranteed under Assumptions 2.1 and 3.1.

4   Simulations

We now provide simulations that attest to the efficacy of the algorithm. All simulations involve 10 transmitters. In the following discussion, SNR is defined as the ratio of the per-node received power to the noise power.

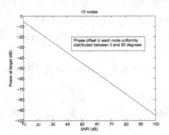

Fig. 1. Power at null target vs. SNR

Fig.1 shows a simulation plot of time-averaged total power at null target as a function of SNR when there are no phase drifts at the oscillators, but each of the ten transmitters sees a phase offset ϕ_i, that is uniformly distributed between 0 and $\pi/2$. The SNR limits the accuracy of the individual phase estimate and this in turn leads to fluctuations in the estimated gradient and therefore the overall received signal strength at the null target. As expected the power at the null target decreases monotonically with increase in SNR.

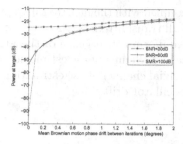

Fig. 2. Power at null target vs. phase drift for equal channel gains

Fig. 2 shows the variation of time-averaged total power at null target as a function of the Brownian motion phase drift for different SNRs. It can be seen that for very small Brownian motion drifts, the null power is determined by the SNR. However once drift increases to about a tenth of a degree between two iterations of the gradient descent, the null is largely limited by the drift and is more or less independent of the SNR. Observe that the highest phase drift of two degrees between phase updates corresponds to the very low feedback rate of 5 Hz, for even the cheapest of oscillators.

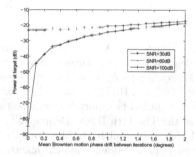

Fig. 3. Power at null target vs. phase drift for unequal channel gains

Fig. 3 is very similar to Fig. 2, except that unlike Fig. 2, that involves a setting where all gains are 1, in Fig. 3 the actual gains are obtained from a Rayleigh distribution and then equalized to one. As can be seen Fig. 3, the resulting potential noise amplification, has virtually no effect on the performance of the gradient descent nullforming algorithm.

5   Conclusion

We have provided a new gradient descent based distributed nullforming algorithm that requires far less feedback than all its predecessors, in that each transmitter is required by this algorithm to only know its channel state information to the receiver. In constrast, previous algorithms required that channel state information to the receiver from each transmitter be known to each other transmitter in the virtual array. This coupled with the fact that it requires an additional *common* signal fed back by to all transmitters by the receiver, ensures its scalability. We have proved practical uniform convergence of the algorithm to a null. This ensures robustness to noise and channel phase estimation errors., verified by simulations, that involve nontrivial channel phase estimation errors compounded by Brownian motion driven oscillator drift.

References

[1] Ozgur, A., Lévêque, O., Tse, D.N.C.: Hierarchical cooperation achieves optimal capacity scaling in ad hoc networks. IEEE Transactions on Information Theory, 3549–3572 (2007)

[2] Yucek, T., Arslan, H.: A survey of spectrum sensing algorithms for cognitive radio applications. IEEE Communications Surveys & Tutorials, 116–130 (2009)

[3] Dong, L., Han, Z., Petropulu, A.P., Poor, H.V.: Cooperative jamming for wireless physical layer security. In: Proceedings of SSP (2009)

[4] Cover, T., Gamal, A.E.L.: Capacity theorems for the relay channel. IEEE Transactions on Information Theory 25(5), 572–584 (1979)

[5] Mudumbai, R., Barriac, G., Madhow, U.: On the feasibility of distributed beamforming in wireless networks. IEEE Trans. on Wireless Communication 6(5), 1754–1763 (2007)

[6] Mudumbai, R., Brown III, D.R., Madhow, U., Poor, H.V.: Distributed transmit beamforming: Challenges and recent progress. IEEE Communications Magazine 47(2), 102–110 (2009)

[7] Seo, M., Rodwell, M., Madhow, U.: A feedback-based distributed phased array technique and its application to 60-ghz wireless sensor network. In: 2008 IEEE MTT-S International Microwave Symposium Digest (June 2008)

[8] Rahman, M.M., Baidoo-Williams, H.E., Mudumbai, R., Dasgupta, S.: Fully wireless implementation of distributed beamforming on a software-defined radio platform. In: Proceedings of the The 11th IPSN, Beijing, China (2012)

[9] Quitin, F., Rahman, M.M.U., Mudumbai, R., Madhow, U.: Distributed beamforming with software-defined radios: frequency synchronization and digital feedback. In: IEEE Globecom 2012 (December 2012)

[10] Mudumbai, R., Hespanha, J., Madhow, U., Barriac, G.: Scalable feedback control for distributed beamforming in sensor networks. In: ISIT, Adelaide, Australia (September 2005)

[11] Mudumbai, R., Bidigare, P., Pruessing, S., Dasgupta, S., Oyarzun, M., Raeman, D.: Scalable feedback algorithms for distributed transmit beamforming in wireless networks. In: Proceedings of ICASSP (March 2012)

[12] Brown, D.R., Madhow, U., Bidigare, P., Dasgupta, S.: Receiver-coordinated distributed transmit nullforming with channel state uncertainty. In: Proceedings of 46th CISS (March 2012)

[13] Brown, D.R., Bidigare, P., Dasgupta, S., Madhow, U.: Receiver-coordinated zero-forcing distributed transmit nullforming. In: Proceedings of SSP (August 2012)

[14] Hahn, W.: Stability of motion. Springer (1967)

[15] Summers, T.H., Yu, C., Dasgupta, S., Anderson, B.: Control of minimally persistent leader-remotefollower and coleader formations in the plane. IEEE Transactions on Automatic Control 56(12), 2778–2792 (2011)

System on a Programmable Chip Design of a Wireless Transceiver Prototype for Smart Grid Applications

Dan Shan[1], Weidong Xiang[1], Paul Richardson[1], and Hua Qian[2]

[1] ECE Department, University of Michigan, Dearborn, MI 48128, USA
[2] Shanghai Institute of Microsystem and Information Technology, Shanghai, China
{danshan,xwd,richarpc}@umich.edu,hua.qian@shrcwc.org

Abstract. When compared to digital signal processors (DSPs), filed programmable gate arrays (FPGAs) have more computation power where functions are realized by hardware modules operating in parallel, instead of by instructions executing in sequence in DSPs. In this contribution, a large scale low duty smart utility network (SUN) radio upon the IEEE 802.15.4g standard (draft) for smart grid applications is implemented. Unlike the current wireless sensor network (WSN) using Zigbee radios, which is mainly used in a local scale, say less than tens of meters, SUN focuses on large scale WSN, which is able to access to the infrastructure at a distance up to kilometers. At the moment of composing this article, the IEEE 802.15.4g standard is still under developed. However, the narrow band, less than 1MHz, orthogonal frequency multiplexing division (OFDM) technology is identified to be adopted to realize robust link in large scale outdoor environments. Funded by Argonne National Laboratory (ANL), Department of Energy (DoE) in 2011 and then collaborated with Shanghai Research Center for Wireless Communications, a SUN radio prototype based on an Altera FPGA chip is firstly implemented and evaluated. The system design, baseband signal processing, medium access control (MAC) protocols and interfaces to computers are detailed in the article. An embedded processor within the FPGA chip is used to realize MAC protocol simplifying the system design. Moreover, such a FPGA based prototype serves as a universal *system on programmable chip* for a board range wireless communications. Experiments results demonstrate satisfied processing latency and bit error rate (BER) for smart grid applications.

Keywords: SUN, IEEE 802.15.4g, FPGA, Smart Grid.

1 Introduction

By the aid of an intelligent sensing and control system, smart grid possesses enhanced resolutions of energy accessibility, flexibility, manageability, and reliability than traditional power grid current in use. However, smart grid requires intensive effort including research, design and development of smart equipment, communications sbusystems, data management center, security and applications

H. Qian and K. Kang (Eds.): WICON 2013, LNICST 121, pp. 85–95, 2013.

softwares [1]. Like the Internet, smart gird is a network of networks, subsystems and subnets of which have different configuration and ownership and need to interconnect each other. Such a realization highly relies on the effective network and media access control (MAC) protocols. Moreover, as an important nation wide infrastructure, smart gird is expected to accommodate with diverse applications, which will be added on or defined in the decades to come. The applications have distinguished requirements on network topology, transmission range, data rate, delay, bit error rate (BER) and package error rates (PER) under various channel environments. Unfortunately, the current wireless sensor network (WSN) based on local Zigbee radios cannot offer the claimed feature [2]. Instead, a geographically diverse and large scale low duty WSN should be presented to provide seamless connectivity among the equipments in smart gird.

In 2008, IEEE 802.15 smart utility networks (SUN) Task Group 4g was founded to focus on the amendment to Zigbee and provide a global standard named IEEE 802.15.4g, one of the main applications of which is smart grid [3]. The new standard upgrades data rate from 250kb/s to 800kb/s through adopting orthogonal frequency multiplexing division (OFDM), an advanced modulation scheme that has been widely applied. OFDM outperforms traditional modulation schemes over deep fading channels. It is believed that the IEEE 802.15.4g standard adopting a mature and market success technology will take over smart grid communications networks. Since the standard is still under development, few effort has been reported on the the hardware prototyping and evaluation of SUN radio, which motivates our work.

Wireless systems are normally prototyped upon digital signal processor (DSP) or/and field programmable gate array (FPGA). In this effort, we select FPGA due to its more powerful computation and versatile processing ability. A *programmable system on chip* design strategy is adopted to realize the SUN radio including baseband processing, MAC protocol and data interface to computers, all upon the IEEE 802.15.4g standard (draft). The prototype can serve as a hardware platform to evaluate the performance of SUN as well as the benchmark for next step application specific integrated circuit (ASIC) design.

An overview on the hardware solutions to the prototyping on wireless communications systems are discussed in Section 2. Section 3 details the design of SUN radio including both the hardware and software while Section 4 presents corresponding experimental results. Finally conclusions are withdrawn.

2   Hardware Solutions to Prototyping on Wireless Transceivers

Due to the high computation load of the digital signal processing algorithms including fast Fourier transformation (FFT), viterbi decoding, timing synchronization and channel estimation, wireless communications systems are normally built upon ASIC. However, ASIC is more suitable for radios that have massive product. At its early development and prototyping stage, a general wireless prototype is a more feasible solution.

2.1   Computers Based Wireless Prototyping Solution

Matlab is a convenient tool to realize baseband signal processing. The built-in functions such as fast Fourier transformation (FFT) and matrix operations make easy the implementation. We normally start with Matlab simulation of a wireless communications system and then implement it upon a prototype. A typical computer based prototyping solution to wireless systems is shown in Fig. 1. Through the peripheral component interconnect (PCI) interfaces, data can be exchanged between the analog-to-digital (ADC) and digital-to-analog (DAC) boards and computers. For example, the digitizer board from the *Signatec* Company [4] and the arbitrary waveform generator (AWG) from the *Strategic-test* Company [5] both have drivers and application programming interface (API) to Matlab. The transmitter and receiver locates within computers resulting in a compact solution. Normally, PCI supports high-speed data transfer between wireless systems and hard disks of computers.

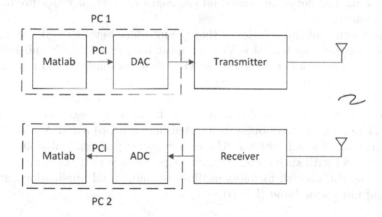

Fig. 1. The computer based wireless prototyping solution

There exists several disadvantages in this solution. The foremost is the limited computation power and comparably slow operation speed. It may take up to tens or hundreds ms for Matlab functions to complete the processing for one package. Such solution normally is not suitable for high-speed transceiver running in a real-time mode. Another issue is its lump size consisting of at least two desktop computers with PCI interfaces, inappropriate for portable applications.

2.2   DSP Based Solution

The architecture for DSP solution is shown in Fig. 2. The advantage of the solution lies on that there are a lot of open source codes and free libraries for typical baseband processing on various DSPs, including FFT and synchronization. *GNU Radio* is one of such toolkits [6]. Since the processing is completed by software,

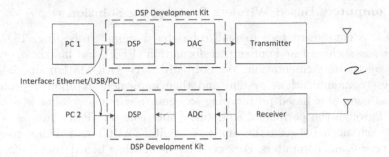

Fig. 2. The DSP based wireless prototyping solution

this solution is also called *software defined radio*. The implementation complexity for this solution is similar to the computer based solution. The data interfaces need to be further developed based on the *board support packages* provided by DSP manufactures.

A disadvantage of this solution is that the interface between DSPs and ADCs and DACs requires additional work since most high-speed ADCs and DACs do not contain on-chip buffers. Taking the ADC as an example, the output data at the I/O pins last only one clock cycle (for example, 100ns at a sampling rate of 10MSPS). A DSP running an operating systems or enabling interrupts may miss of one or more samples of data resulting in seriously degradation in performance. Therefore, an extra buffer is inserted between DSPs and ADCs. A lot of DSP development kits insert a FPGA or a complex programmable logic device (CPLD) to deal with such an issue. Another problem is that the computation is still not powerful enough for most medium or high-speed applications, such as Wi-Fi and ultra-wide band (UWB).

2.3 FPGA Solution

Baseband processing in wireless communications systems normally requires intensive computation to complete up to hundreds of multiplications, additions and others during one sampling cycle. DSP and FPGA are the two most commonly used programmable devices that meet the requirements of computation. Furthermore, the computation capability can be estimated by the number of 16-bit multiplications that can be executed within one second. A high-speed DSP is TMS320C6474 from TI has a computation power of 28,800 MIPS (million instructions per second) at a unit price of \$170. At the comparable price, a FPGA chip of EP3C55 from Altera can be bought, which contains 156 multipliers when operating at a clock of 250MHz, or 55k logic elements (LEs) at a clock of 437.5MHz. Every 266 LEs can also be synthesized to form a 16-bit multiplier. The total number of multiplications that this FPGA chip can accommodate with within a second is therefore $156 * 250M + (55000/266) * 437.5M = 129,460M$, which has several times of computation power than DSP. With higher prices,

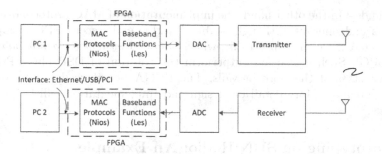

Fig. 3. The FPGA based wireless prototyping solution

FPGA chips with a triple number of LEs operating at a double clock can be purchased, while there seems no faster DSP can be found on the market.

The FPGA based architecture of wireless communications prototype is shown in Fig. 3. An obvious drawback of FPGA based solution lies on that the high requirements on the programmers's skills and training as well as the long development period when compared to that upon DSP. However, in recent years the advance of the development software and tools largely assuages such an issue. Another drawback is that the coding and programming of signal processing algorithms on FPGA using VHDL is more difficult than that over DSP using C language. This is the price that we have to pay for the benefit gained from the FPGA based solution. Meanwhile, it normally takes more synthesis time for FPGA than compilation time when DSP is adopted to implement similar modules.

In addition, the high-speed user data interface, such as USB, PCI and Ethernet, are non-trivia for FPGA when they are implemented through using VHDL codes upon LEs than C codes over DSP. Solutions to such issue will be further discussed in the followings.

2.4   DSP+FPGA Solution

As we mentioned above, DSP is good at data interfacing while FPGA at parallel computing and interfacing to ADC and DAC modules, the combination of DSP and FPGA seems to be a *good* approach, such as the development kits from Sundance [7] and Lyrtech [8]. However, the foremost factor that prevent such a solution from being widely employed lies in the complexity of hardware, across development environment and soaring high price more than $10K. Moreover, both platforms use third party *Diamond* operating system, even worsening the situation.

2.5   FPGA + Embedded Processer Solution

We can conclude that FPGA is the feasible solution and dominate the wireless communications prototyping but require significant experience and sufficient backgrounds. On the other hand, the implementation of MAC protocol over LEs is tedious and onerous, although doable. To this end, recent FPGA chip fortunately embeds a micro-processor, which is called *system on a programmable chip* (SoPC). Such a solution outperform the solution of DSP plus FPGA in many aspects and therefore prevails. The FPGA board used in this project costs $1,200/unit. More detail on design and implementation will be given in followings.

3   Prototyping on SUN Radio: An Example

A SUN radio prototype upon the IEEE 802.15.4 standard is built up according to the FPGA based solution. The Cyclone III development kits and data conversion HSMC boards containing dual channel ADC and DAC, both from the *Terasic* company are selected. The FPGA kit integrates a EP3C120F780C FPGA chip, 256MB dual-channel DDR2 SDRAM, 8MB SRAM, 64MB flash memory, an Ethernet transceiver chip, and a USB port for debugging. The data conversion board has a dual channel DAC (DAC5672) and two ADC chips (AD9254), both having a 14-bit resolution and an operation clock of 100MSPS. For quadrature modulation, the I and Q channels require dual channel ADC and DAC. The data conversion boards connect to the FPGA kit through the HSMC interface, which is defined by the *Altera* company.

Fig. 4. The snapshot of the prototyping based on the Cyclone III FPGA FPGA development kit

Fig. 3 and Fig. 4 show the diagram and snapshot of the prototype. The programs consist of the C codes running over the embedded Nois II processor within the FPGA chip and VHDL codes on LEs.

1) **C programs upon Nios II processor:** The C codes realize the MAC protocol as well as Ethernet interface. Two tasks named as *Package Receiving*

and *MAC Processing* running on μCOS operating system are established to realize the above two functions. Inter-task communications and synchronization are realized by a message queue. The data flow chart of the program at the transmitter is shown in Fig. 5 and Fig. 6. The codes at the receiver is similar but with reverse processing. At transmitter, the task "Package Receiving" keep polling the Ethernet interface using Socket API. Once a user datagram protocol (UDP) package is received, its address will be copied to the message queue. The task "MAC processing" watches on the message queue in a non-blocking manor. After picking up an arrival packet from the queue, it starts the process of the MAC protocol. The flowchart of the processing at transmitter is demonstrated in Fig. 5. The two tasks are synchronized by the message queue.

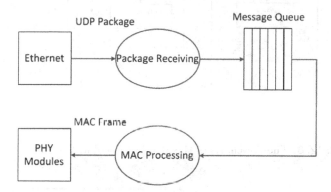

Fig. 5. Data interface and MAC protocol running over the Nios II processor at transmitter

2) **VHDL programs on LEs:** The baseband processing is realized upon LEs using VHDL codes. Fig. 7 and Fig. 8 show the diagrams of the baseband processing at transmitter and receiver, respectively. In addition to the FIFOs and drivers for ADCs and DACs, other function blocks are well defined by the IEEE802.15.4g standard (draf). Nios II processor works in an asynchronous mode while LEs in a synchronous mode. The FIFO needs to be carefully designed to seamlessly pass data between physical layer and MAC layer. Fig 9 shows the interface between them and Fig. 10 the ping-pong mode of the FIFO where a dual buffer is adopted. In the meantime, Quartus provides IP cores for typical function modules including FFT, IFFT and Viterbi decoding. Fig. 11 shows the realization of the time synchronization, consisting of 18 processing in parallel. The flexible trading off between complexity and speed validates our comments on FPGA based solution to wireless system prototyping.

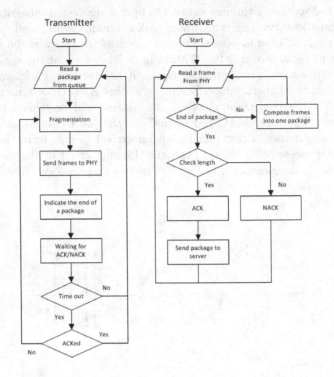

Fig. 6. The flowcharts of the MAC protocol at transmitter

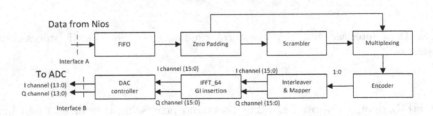

Fig. 7. The baseband processing at transmitter

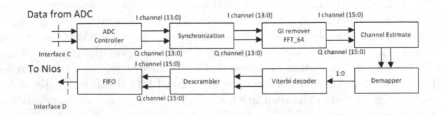

Fig. 8. The baseband processing at receiver

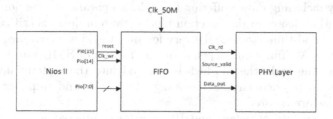

Fig. 9. The interface between PHY and MAC modules

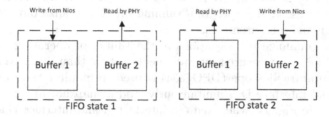

Fig. 10. The ping-pong mode of the FIFO

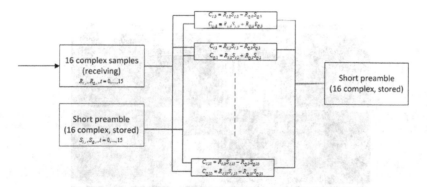

Fig. 11. The realization of time synchronization

4   Results of the SUN Radio Prototype

The performance of the SUN radio is tested in the terms of data rate, processing latency, bit error rate (BER) versus signal-to-noise ratio (SNR). A trial on the application is conducted by transferring a MP3 file from the transmitter to the receiver. Through the time used and the size of the file, the estimate throughout is 110 kbits/s.

The processing latency between the interface A and interface B in Fig. 7, and the latency between the interface C and interface D in Fig. 8, represent the transmission delay and receiving delay. The summation of two delays is system delay including data buffering for serial-to-parallel conversion as well as the computation delays of the function blocks. System delay is critical for SUN which require real-time message delivery for smart grid applications. The delay generated by MAC functions depends on the factors of SNR, interferences, re-transmission time and others, which is counted into the systems delay. Other delays caused by physical circuits including ADC, DAC and amplifiers are much small and thus are ignored.

The measurements of delays and BERs were conducted within a loopback where the interface B and interface C are connected and the delay between the interface A and interface D is measured. Test data from the Nios processor are input to interface A and finally recovered at interface D and thereafter read back to the processor. A C program running on Nios realize data generation, data collection and measurements.

In order to minimize the variations of the timing of operating system, the transmission delay is measured by equipments rather than using Nios itself. A Tektronix digital oscilloscope (DPO7354) is used to monitor the waveforms at interface A and interface D, simultaneously, and a snapshot of captured wave-forms is shown in Fig. 12, where data at interface A and interface D are colored in yellow and blue, respectively. The delay is estimated as 1.89ms, meeting the requirement of real-time delivery for smart grid applications.

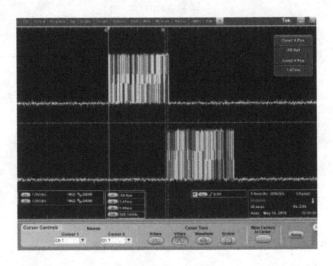

Fig. 12. The captured waveforms at interface A and interface D

For BER testing, a set of digitalized additive white Gaussian noises (AWGNs), of which the powers are adjusted according to the required SNR, are added at the interface C by LEs. BERs under each SNR were calculated by Nios processor through comparing the bit streams at interface A and interface D. Fig. 13 shows the BER-SNR curve. Finally, the delay of the Ethernet interface is tested by using the *ping* command at the server. Result shows that the round delay of the Ethernet interfaces at the transmitter and receiver including SUN radios is less than 1ms.

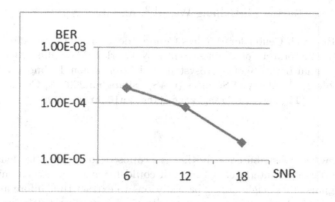

Fig. 13. The measured BER-SNR curve of the SUN radio

5   Conclusions

A SUN radio prototype for smart grid applications upon the new IEEE 802.15.4g standard (draft) is implemented based on the FPGA based solution. Experiments verifies the designed specifications including delay and BER. The prototype features in a single chip solution integrating both baseband modules and MAC protocols that operate upon the embedded Nios processor. RF front ends are adding on and outdoor field testing will be conducted to further evaluate the performance of SUN radios adopting narrow OFDM for large scale low duty WSN applications, such as smart grid, vehicular networks, eHealth and the internet of things.

References

1. Electric Power Research Institute: Report to NIST on the Smart Grid Interoperability Standards Roadmap, http://www.nist.gov/smartgrid/
2. "ZigBee" IEEE Std 802.15.4
3. Preliminary draft P802.15.4g-d0.2
4. Signatec Company, http://www.signatec.com/products/daq/high-speed-fpga-pcix-digitizer-board-pda16.html
5. Arbitrary waveforms generator,http://www.strategic-test.com/eng/Instruments/Arbitrary-Waveform-Generators2
6. GNU Radio, http://gnuradio.org/redmine/wiki/gnuradio
7. Sundance, http://www.sundance.com/
8. Lyrtech, http://www.lyrtech.com/

A Distributed Synchronization Algorithm for Femtocells Network

Ligang Liu[1], Jiang Wang[1,2], and Jing Xu[1,2]

[1] Shanghai Research Center for Wireless Communication, Shanghai, 200335, China
[2] Key Laboratory of Wireless Sensor Network & Communication,
Shanghai Institute of Microsystem and Information Technology,
Chinese Academy of Sciences (CAS), Shanghai 200335, China
{ligang.liu,jiang.wang,jing.xu}@shrcwc.org

Abstract. A distributed algorithm is proposed to synchronize femtocells through air interface. A femtocell could listen to the synchronization signals of its neighbouring base stations to extract time information of these neighbours. Then it updates its time according to the neighbours' time, directed by a global optimization criterion in a distributed manner. Finally all femtocells will have same time information. A common framework is summarized to deal with many scenarios with different configuration of weight coefficients.

Keywords: Wireless communication, femtocell, synchronization, gossip algorithm, distributed communication.

1 Introduction

Synchronization among femtocells is very important [1, 2]. Just like a typical macrocell, femtocells require a certain level of synchronization (frequency or phase/time). On the one hand, frequency synchronization is required to ensure a tolerable carrier offset. On the other hand, time synchronization is of great importance especially for time division duplex (TDD) systems. It is necessary to align received signals, otherwise inter-slot interference will occur. Furthermore, synchronization is also required for macrocell users to handover to a femtocell, or vice versa [3–5].

Many solutions have been developed to synchronize base stations in wireless communication systems. GPS is the most popular synchronization method for current wireless networks because of its maturity and convenience. For a femtocell deployed inside buildings, a stable satellite signal indoor will be very weak so that it will take long time to obtain synchronization information, even lead to receivers out of work. Alternatively, femtocells could achieve synchronization through the backbone connection using IEEE 1588 PTP (Precision Time Protocol). However, PTP could suffer delay jitter because the delays on the Internet has a relative large dynamic range depending on the traffic, which is unpredictable. Another challenge for PTP is that it requires new investment to deploy

H. Qian and K. Kang (Eds.): WICON 2013, LNICST 121, pp. 96–103, 2013.

PTP-enabled routers throughout the path between the servers and the clients. In a word, it is difficult for PTP to be directly applied in femtocell.

An approach is proposed to employs the clock drift ratio information to achieve synchronization between non-interacting femtocells and macrocells [6]. But it requires information of user-equipments.

Another approach is to listen to the synchronization signals of neighbouring macrocells to synchronize the clock. This method is normally called *network listening* [7, 8]. For a femtocell, an efficient solution would be to listen to the nearest macrocell. Unfortunately, in a scenario where the macrocell coverage is poor, this method will be out of work. In the case of dense femtocells deployment, it is possible that the coverage of many cells will overlap each other. An acceptable solution for the synchronization could be to use the neighbouring femtocells, not only listening to the macrocells.

Alternatively, femtocells could achieve synchronization in a distributed manner. By listening to neighbouring femtocells, a femtocell calculates its synchronization time using a well-defined algorithm on certain criterion. This method is efficient especially when there are a large amount of nodes. These kinds of algorithms, so called gossip algorithms, have been studied in sensor networks to distribute the information among the different nodes [9].

In this paper we propose a synchronization scheme of femtocells in a distributed way in the case of dense femtocell deployment. The remainder of this article is organized as follows. In Section 2 we present a distributed synchronization algorithm for femtocells network along with analysis and discussion of some simple extensions. Section 3 presents computer simulations to evaluate performance of the proposed algorithm, and finally Section 4 concludes the paper.

2   Distributed Synchronization Algorithms for Femtocells

2.1   System Model

Let the femtocell network is composed of J femtocells, and we get a set of J nodes $V = \{v_1, v_2, \cdots, v_J\}$. There is a set of edges $E = \{e_{ij}\}$, where $e_{ij} \in E$ if and only if node v_i can listen to synchronization signal from node v_j. It leads to a graph $G = \{V, E\}$. Note that G is a directed graph because $e_{ij} \in E$ does not imply $e_{ji} \in E$. This would happen in the case where different nodes have different transmission power, or different link has different path loss. Every node v_i carries information t_i, which represents synchronization time of node v_i. It is assumed that the initial value of $t_i(0)$ is uniformly distributed in a limited range $[-c, c]$, where c is a positive number. The goal of the problem is to update t_i iteratively so that all nodes achieve same value as soon as possible, $t_1(n) = t_2(n) = \cdots = t_J(n)$ when n is greater than a certain number. Here n is the iteration number.

2.2   Distributed Synchronization Algorithm

At any iteration n, node v_i senses its neighbour node v_j and estimates time of v_j as t_{ij} where $1 \leq j \leq J(j \neq i)$. In order to determine new time, node v_i tries to optimize a cost function. An efficient cost function $u(t_i)$ could be the weighted sum of squared time difference between v_i and v_j,

$$u(t_i) = \sum_{j=1}^{J} \alpha_{ij} \left(t_i - t_{ij} \right)^2. \tag{1}$$

Here α_{ij} is a weighting coefficient and note that for a node v_j that v_i cannot sense, $\alpha_{ij} = 0$. The existing of α_{ij} is because time information measured over different link should be assigned different weight. For example, time sensed from a strong synchronization signals should be assigned more weight than that from a weak neighbour, thus rendering the algorithm robust against measurement errors. It is necessary to pose a constraint, $\sum_{j=1}^{J} \alpha_{ij} = 1$.

A reasonable α_{ij} could be defined as ratio of total received synchronization signal power to that from node v_j,

$$\alpha_{ij} = \frac{P_{ij}}{\sum_{k=1}^{J} P_{ik}} \quad (i \neq j) \tag{2}$$

where P_{ij} is the synchronization signal power that node v_i has received from node v_j, and it is assumed here $\alpha_{ii} = 0$.

The distributed synchronization problem is to find an optimal t_i so that it can minimize $u(t_i)$ defined in equation (1) at every iteration for every node. It can be written as

$$t_{i,opt} = \underset{t_i}{\arg\min}\, u(t_i) \tag{3}$$

It is a simple problem and its solution is $t_{i,opt} = \sum_{j=1}^{J} \alpha_{ij} t_{ij}$.

Ideally, t_{ij}, i.e. time of node v_j that node v_i has sensed, is exactly equal to t_j. However, estimation error z_{ij} is inevitable and $t_{ij} = t_j + z_{ij}$. Here we assume that z_{ij} is a zero-mean Gaussian variable with variance of σ_{ij}^2 and we assume that z_{ij} is independent to t_j. As a result, the time updating equation for node v_i from iteration $n-1$ to n is written as in a iterative way:

$$t_i(n) = \sum_{j=1}^{J} \alpha_{ij}[t_j(n-1) + z_{ij}]. \tag{4}$$

Note that here we have removed the effect of time component that has proceeded during an iteration, for the sake of concise. A femtocell could update its synchronization time in two ways, i.e. in synchronous way and asynchronous way.

2.3   Convergence Analysis of Synchronous Updating

In synchronous way, at every iteration, all of the femtocells update its time at same time. Here we temporarily assume that for all nodes, their weight coefficients are invariant.

For the sake of concise, we consider estimation error free algorithm first, i.e. $z_{ij} = 0$. Let $\mathbf{T}(n) = \{t_1(n), \ldots, t_J(n)\}^T$ and $\boldsymbol{\alpha}$ is a $J \times J$ matrix, $\boldsymbol{\alpha} = \{\alpha_{ij}\}$, the above equation is rewritten as

$$\mathbf{T}(n) = \boldsymbol{\alpha}\mathbf{T}(n-1) \tag{5}$$

Extend this series, it becomes $\mathbf{T}(n) = \boldsymbol{\alpha}^n\mathbf{T}(0)$. The convergence behavior of the algorithm is determined by properties of weight coefficient matrix $\boldsymbol{\alpha}$. It is obvious that $\boldsymbol{\alpha}$ is a row stochastic matrix, whose each row sum is unity. For a row stochastic matrix $\boldsymbol{\alpha}$, its largest eigenvalue is 1 and the others are absolutely smaller than 1. It is obvious that $\boldsymbol{\alpha}^n$ is convergent when $n \to \infty$ and $\boldsymbol{\alpha}^\infty$ is a $J \times J$ constant matrix $\mathbf{1}\mathbf{b}^T$, whose all rows are same to $\mathbf{b}^T$. Here $\mathbf{1}$ is a $J \times 1$ column vector that all elements are 1 and $\mathbf{b}$ is a $K \times 1$ column vector that is determined by eigenvector of α. Consequently, $\mathbf{T}(\infty) = \mathbf{b}^T\mathbf{T}(0)\mathbf{1}$. It means that the proposed algorithm is convergent and the final time value of all nodes is determined by $\boldsymbol{\alpha}$ and $\mathbf{T}(0)$.

The second order convergence of the proposed algorithm can be analyzed through $\xi = E\{\|\mathbf{T}(n) - \mathbf{T}(\infty)\|_2^2\}$. After some trivial mathematics manipulations, it can be drawn that $\xi = 0$.

Consider the case of non-zeroes estimation error, $z_{ij} > 0$, the same conclusion can be drawn after some trivial mathematics manipulations, remembering the independence assumption of z_{ij} and t_j. However, in this case, the second order convergence is different. It has $\xi = \sum_{i=1}^{J}\sum_{j=1}^{J}\alpha_{ij}^2\sigma_{ij}^2$. Because $0 \le \alpha_{ij} \le 1$, it can be derived that the synchronization error in distributed manner will be less than that of synchronization from only one neighbour. For example, if synchronization error of node v_1 from node v_2 or v_3 is $\sigma_{12}^2 = \sigma_{13}^2 = \sigma^2$, now let node v_1 gets synchronization time from both node v_1 and v_2 using above distributed algorithm, with same weight coefficients $\alpha_{12} = \alpha_{13} = 1/2$. Then the new synchronization error will be reduced to $\sigma^2/2$.

2.4   Convergence Analysis of Asynchronous Updating

In asynchronous way, at every iteration, only one femtocell updates its time and the others do nothing. It is assumed that at iteration n, node v_i synchronizes from node v_j. Let us construct a time-varying weight coefficients matrix $\alpha(n)$, which is a identity, except the i-th row is replaced by weight coefficients $\boldsymbol{\alpha}_i = \{\alpha_{i1}, \cdots, \alpha_{iJ}\}$. Note that $\boldsymbol{\alpha}(n)$ still is a row stochastic matrix. Hence the time updating equation is written as

$$\mathbf{T}(n) = \boldsymbol{\alpha}(n)\mathbf{T}(n-1) \tag{6}$$

Extend this series, it becomes $\mathbf{T}(n) = \prod_{m=n}^{1} \boldsymbol{\alpha}(m)\mathbf{T}(0)$.

Because $\boldsymbol{\alpha}(m)$ is row stochastic, it has been proved that the limit existed [9],

$$\lim_{n\to\infty} \prod_{m=n}^{1} \boldsymbol{\alpha}(m) = \mathbf{1}\mathbf{b}^T \tag{7}$$

It means that after certain n iterations $\prod_{m=n}^{1} \boldsymbol{\alpha}(m)$ has all its rows are identical. Hence $\mathbf{T}(n)$ has all its elements same as $\mathbf{b}^T \mathbf{T}(0)$. It should be noted that in asynchronous updating, the final value of $\mathbf{b}$ is determined by not only the value of $\boldsymbol{\alpha}(m)$ but also the order of $\boldsymbol{\alpha}(m)$.

Compared to the synchronous updating, the asynchronous updating will converge in a lower rate because it only synchronizes one node in one iteration while the synchronous method will update all nodes in one single iteration.

The proposed approaches are different from the gossip algorithms used in wireless sensor networks. In a gossip algorithm, in one iteration, a selected *pair* of neighboring nodes (v_i, v_j) exchange their current estimates and then update the estimates of both nodes as same value, $t_i(n) = t_j(n) = f(t_i(n-1), t_j(n-1))$, where f is a predefined function. The weight matrix in gossip algorithm usually is doubly stochastic. Although the doubly stochastic matrix has better characteristics than a row stochastic matrix, this condition is too strong for the synchronization problem. The the proposed algorithm in this paper is a kind of extension of the gossip algorithm and it is expected to be applied in more wide area.

2.5   Variant

The updating in equation (4) does not consider the current time of v_i itself. It would cause the time of v_i change dramatically. The time updating could use a moderate manner. For node v_i, another approach is to update its time based on its current time by adding a weighted item of time obtained from the neighbours. It can be written as

$$t_i(n) = \beta t_i(n-1) + (1 - \beta) \Delta t_i(n-1) \tag{8}$$

$$\Delta t_i(n-1) = \sum_{j=1, j \neq i}^{J} \alpha_{ij}[t_j(n-1) + z_{ij}] \tag{9}$$

This modification can be represented accordingly by a new definition of $\boldsymbol{\alpha}$, where $\alpha_{ii} = \beta$ and

$$\alpha_{ij} = (1 - \beta) \frac{P_{ij}}{\sum_{k=1}^{J} P_{ik}}, (j \neq i) \tag{10}$$

With this definition, it holds that $\sum_{j=1}^{J} \alpha_{ij} = 1$ for any $1 \leq i \leq J$, i.e. $\boldsymbol{\alpha}$ is still row stochastic. Consequently, this variant has similar convergence performance compared to the ones discussed in the previous subsections. The different is it will converge in a relatively lower rate, but in a smoother manner.

There should be a scenario where one node, v_i for example, obtain its synchronization from an external source, such as GPS. It is not necessary for it to synchronize from any neighbour, although it could provide synchronization to the other nodes. In this case, its weight coefficients should be defined as a zero vector except the i-th element is 1. The resultant $\boldsymbol{\alpha}$ is still row stochastic. It can be expected that in this case, when the algorithm has converged, all nodes has identical synchronization time same to that of v_i.

Summarily, the proposed algorithm can be represented by equation (6). Different definition of $\alpha(m)$ will lead to different implementation of the proposed algorithm, which is suitable in the designed scenario.

3   Computer Simulations

In this section, performance of the proposed algorithm is verified by computer simulations. There are 20 femtocells randomly deployed in two building stripes. The transmission power of all femtocells are 20dBm.

$$PL(\text{dB}) = 38.46 + 20\log_{10} D + 0.7d_{\text{in}} + q_{\text{i}}L_{\text{iw}} + q_{\text{o}}L_{\text{ow}} \tag{11}$$

Here, D presents distance between two femtocells and d_{in} is indoor part (all distance is in meters). The item $0.7d_{\text{in}}$ is energy loss caused by indoor materials. q_{i} is the number of inner walls between two femtocells and L_{iw} is energy loss through inner walls (5dB). q_{o} is the number of outdoor walls between two femtocells (0 for femtocells in same stripe and 2 for femtocells in different stripe) and L_{ow} is energy loss through outdoor walls (20dB).

3.1   Convergence and Influence of β

Fig. 1 illustrates convergence in the first 30 iterations of the proposed synchronous updating algorithm with different parameter β. Each line represents the time of one femtocell during the convergence period. It can be seen that the algorithm can converge in very fast rate. The asynchronous updating method has similar performance, except it has much slower convergence rate, so the result is not presented here.

The parameter β is used to adjust behavior of the algorithm. Smaller the β is, less weight the current time poses to its new time. It can be seen from the two subfigures that when $\beta = 0.0$ the new time of each femtocell changes dramatically, while the convergence rate is faster than that of $\beta = 0.5$. Contrarily, the convergence of $\beta = 0.5$ looks smoother than that of $\beta = 0.0$.

In order to compare their convergence rate, the convergence performance is quantified using the definition as *deviation* $\chi(n) = \sum_{i=1}^{J}[t_i(n) - \bar{t}(n)]^2$, where $\bar{t}(n) = \sum_{i=1}^{J} t_i(n)/J$, i.e. the squared sum of difference between $t_i(n)$ and their average $\bar{t}(n)$.

Fig. 2 compares three $\chi(n)$ with $\beta = 0.0$, $\beta = 0.5$ and $\beta = 0.9$ respectively. It is obviously seen that smaller β has faster convergence rate.

3.2   Case of One Femtocell is Fixed

It has been discussed that when a femtocell has an external synchronization source, it is not necessary to update its time at any iteration but it can provide synchronization to the others. As a result, all the other femtocells can achieve synchronization of this special femtocell. Fig. 3 illustrates the convergence in this

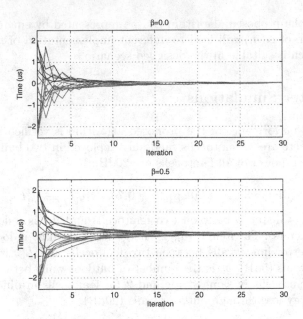

Fig. 1. Convergence of the proposed synchronous updating algorithm

case, where femtocell 1 located in the left bottom apartment has a fixed time 0. When the algorithm has converged, all femtocells have the same synchronization time of 0.

4   Conclusion

We have proposed a kind of distributed synchronization algorithms for femto-cells network. Through minimizing the time difference between femtocells, the proposed algorithms can achieve all related femtocells be time synchronized. It is distinguished from the existing approaches that maintain synchronization only

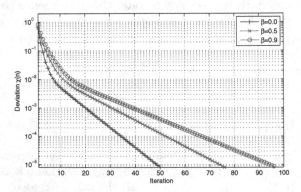

Fig. 2. Comparison of $\chi(n)$ with different β

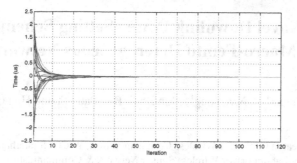

Fig. 3. Convergence in the case of one femtocell is fixed

with a single neighbour. The proposed algorithms get synchronization from multiple neighbours. This method can lead a cluster of femtocells synchronized in a faster rate than the method of single source. At the same time, this method has better synchronization accuracy than its single source counterpart. It does not require a central control node and it is self-organized and self-optimized.

Acknowledgments. This work was supported by National Science and Technology Major Project (NO. 2012ZX03003009-003), and project of Constructions of Innovative Service Platform for Wireless Mobile Communication Technology (No. 11DZ2290100), and project of New Generation Wireless Communication Network Architecture (No. 12JC1404202).

References

1. Zhang, J., Roche, G.: Femtocells: technologies and deployment. John Wiley & Sons, Ltd. (2010)
2. Chandrasekhar, V., Andrews, J.G.: Femtocell networks: a survey. IEEE Communications Magazine 46(9), 59–67 (2008)
3. 3GPP, Synchronization in UTRAN Stage 2 (Release 10), TS 25.402 (June 2011)
4. 3GPP, TDD Home eNode B Radio Frequency requirement analysis (Release 10), TR 36.922 (April 2011)
5. Jungnickel, V., Wirth, T., Schellmann, M., Haustein, T.: Synchronization of cooperative base stations. In: ISWCS (2008)
6. Mehrpouyan, H., Blostein, S.D., Svensson, T.: A New Distributed Approach for Achieving Clock Synchronization in Heterogeneous Networks. In: GLOBECOM, pp. 1–5 (2011)
7. Amin, P., Tirkkonen, O.: Network Listening based Synchronization techniques for Femtocell Systems. In: PIMRC, pp. 1–5 (2011)
8. Lien, S., Lee, H., Shih, S., Chen, S., Chen, K.: Network synchronization among femtocells. In: GLOBECOM, pp. 248–252 (2011)
9. Dimakis, A.G., Kar, S., Moura, J.M.F., Rabbat, M.G., Scaglione, A.: Gossip Algorithms for Distributed Signal Processing. Proceedings of the IEEE 98(11), 1847–1864 (2010)

A Novel Downlink Power Setting Scheme
For Macro-Femto Heterogeneous Networks

Haitao Cheng[1,2,3], Xin Yang[1,2], Jun Zhu[3], Ben Pan[1,2,3], and Hua Qian[1,2]

[1] Shanghai Research Center for Wireless Communications, WiCO, Shanghai, P.R. China
Key Laboratory of Wireless Sensor Network & Communication,
[2] Shanghai Institute of Microsystems and Information Technology (SIMIT),
Chinese Academy of Sciences (CAS), Shanghai, P.R. China
[3] Key Laboratory of Intelligent Computing & Signal Processing of Ministry of Education,
Anhui University, Hefei, P.R. China
6/F International Business Park, 280 Linhong Road Changning District, Shanghai, China
{haitao.cheng,xin.yang}@shrcwc.org, junzhu@ahu.edu.cn

Abstract. In heterogeneous networks containing macro cells and femto cells, power setting is one of the effective techniques to reduce downlink inter-cell interference. In order to diminish inter-cell interference level of the systems and improve system spectrum efficiency, a novel adaptive power setting scheme is proposed and evaluated with other conventional power setting schemes by simulation. Simulation results show that the proposed scheme can improve the edge and average spectrum efficiency of femto cell significantly when there are few indoor macro UEs and reduce system inter-cell interference when there exist macro users close to the femto cell.

Keywords: power setting, heterogeneous network, power control, inter-cell interference, femto.

1   Introduction

Femto cell i.e. Home eNB (HeNB) comes into the spotlight due to its commercial potential [1-2]. It uses an access point (AP) regarded as a small base station (BS) which is connected to service provider's internet network. HeNB is the home base station with low cost and ordinary subscribers can buy and set it by them easily.

Although femto cell solves the coverage problem involving indoor users, there are still lots of problems to be solved in wireless network, which the most important is the interference problems. Since many service providers do not have enough frequency resource to provide services, macro cells and HeNB cells might use the same frequency resources. Consequently, when a macro user exists nearby a HeNB, the receiving signal of macro users will be interfered from the HeNB transmission signals. Similarly in downlink transmission, because of the interference, the SINR will be becomes lower and the data rate of macro user also reduces. [3-5].

In order to maintain the performance of macro users, the interference problem is a critical problem from the view point of service providers. Moreover, the notified users

H. Qian and K. Kang (Eds.): WICON 2013, LNICST 121, pp. 104–112, 2013.
© Institute for Computer Sciences, Social Informatics and Telecommunications Engineering 2013

of the HeNB will be connected HeNB access point, so that only the owner of the HeNB could get benefits from the HeNB. Thus, non-authorized macro users nearby the HeNB access point can't access to the HeNB and suffer from significant interference from the HeNB even if the received signal power of the HeNB is larger than that of their current serving macro eNB [6-7]. In previous research on reduction of inter-cell interference for heterogeneous networks, a technique of setting eNB's transmit power receives considerable attention [8]. However, all the existing power setting schemes are setting HeNB's transmit power statically and not considering whether there are victim macro users close to the HeNB or not.

In this paper, a novel adaptive power setting scheme for a HeNB is proposed and verified by simulation. The adaptive scheme tries to reduce the inter-cell interference to the nearby victim macro users if they exist. On the other hand, the proposed scheme tends to improve the edge and average spectrum efficiency of the femto cell when there are few macro users close to the HeNB. Because of coverage problem, the macro eNB can't consider to control the power.

The rest of the paper is organized as follows. System model is presented in section 2. Conventional power setting schemes are introduced in section 3. And a new power setting scheme is proposed in section 4. Simulation results and analysis is presented in section 5. And a conclusion is drawn in Section 6.

2   System Model

We consider a simple Macro-Femto heterogeneous network scenario, where several HeNBs are deployed in a Macro cell. The scenario is illustrated in Fig.1, in which 2 HeNBs are shown for simplicity. HeNBs use the same frequency band as the Macro eNB. Therefore, for user equipment (UE), there are two kinds of downlink interference. One kind of downlink interference is from neighboring non-serving MeNB. The other kind is from neighboring non-serving HeNBs.

As in a 3GPP Long Term Evolution (LTE) system, transmission of downlink control channel signal employs the whole frequency bandwidth. In this paper, we consider UE's receive performance based on the whole frequency bandwidth.

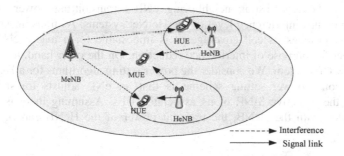

Fig. 1. Macro-Femto HetNet scenario

For a UE, we can obtain it's receive power as following:

$$R_{UE} = P_{SeNB} - PL_{SeNB\_UE} \tag{1}$$

Where R_{UE} is receive power of a UE in dB; P_{SeNB} is transmit power of its serving eNB in dB; PL_{SeNB_UE} is pathloss between the serving eNB to the UE in dB.

Similarly, we can obtain its suffering interference power as following:

$$I_{UE} = \sum_i P_{NSeNB,i} - PL_{NSeNB,i\_UE} \tag{2}$$

Where I_{UE} denotes interference power suffered by a UE in dB; $P_{NSeNB,i}$ is transmit power of the ith non-serving eNB in dB; PL_{NSeNB,i_UE} is pathloss between the ith non-serving eNB to the UE in dB.

Then the signal-to-interference plus noise-ratio (SINR) of a UE can be given as following:

$$SINR_{UE} = 10^{R_{UE}/10} / (10^{I_{UE}/10} + 10^{\sigma_n^2/10}) \tag{3}$$

Where σ_n^2 is the noise power at UE receiver in dB.

From above deviation, it is can be shown that there are several factors affect the SINR performance of a UE. These factors are transmitting power of neighboring non-serving eNBs, pathloss between the neighboring non-serving eNBs and the UE, and its receiver power from its serving eNB. In order to reduce interference and improve the receive performance of the UE, we need to either improve receiver power of the UE, or decrease the transmit power of its neighboring eNBs. However, decreasing transmit power of the neighboring eNBs may lead into problems, such as low system throughput, poor UE experience and shrunk cell coverage.

3   A Conventional Power Setting Scheme

As mentioned above, adjusting neighboring eNB's transmitting power is one of techniques to reduce interference level of the HetNet systems. As transmit power of a macro eNB determines its cell coverage, it is impossible for a macro eNB adjusts transmit power for purpose of interference reduction. On the other hand, a home eNB may serve few UEs indoor. We consider the power setting algorithms for a HeNB.

A conventional power setting scheme is that an eNB adjusts transmit power according to the objective SINR of its associated UEs. Assuming there is only one HUE associated with the HeNB, the transmit power of the HeNB can be given as follows.

$$P_{HeNB} = \max\left(P_{min}, \min\left(PL_{HeNB\_HUE} + R_{HUE}, P_{max}\right)\right) \tag{4}$$

Where P_{HeNB} denotes the transmit power of HeNB in dB; PL_{HeNB_HUE} is the pathloss between HeNB and the home UE (HUE) in dB; P_{max} and P_{min} are the maximum and the minimum transmit power limit of a HeNB in dB; respectively, R_{HUE} denotes the receive power of HUE in dB and can be obtained as following.

$$R_{HUE} = 10\log_{10}\left(10^{I_{HUE}/10} + 10^{\sigma_n^2/10}\right) + T \tag{5}$$

Where I_{HUE} denotes the interference power suffered by HUE; T is target SINR of the HUE.

As can be seen from the equation (4) and (5), a HeNB can adjust transmit power by setting the target SINR of its associated HUE. If the target SINR is set as a large value, the close-by non-associated UEs will suffer much heavy interference and may even experience radio link failure. On the contrary, if the target SINR is set as a low value, the nearby non-associated UEs will suffer the least interference from the HeNB. However, with a low target SINR, the HUE has to receive signal with a much low data rate.

4   New Power Setting Scheme

In order to diminish system interference level and improve cell throughput when there is no nearby victim non-associated UEs, we propose a new power setting scheme. In our proposed scheme, a HeNB may detect if there is a MUE close to it and estimate its pathloss to the closest MUE. There are some papers researches the calculation of pathloss between a HeNB and its close-by non-associated MUE [9-10].

Then the HeNB can set transmit power by adjusting the target SINR of its associated HUE according to its pathloss to the closest MUE.

Thus, the target SINR of an associated HUE can be given as equation (6).

$$T = T_{\min} + \Delta \tag{6}$$

Where $T_{\min}$ denotes the minimum limit of the target SINR of a HUE; Δ denotes an adaptive factor and can be given as follows.

$$\Delta = \max\left(\alpha(PL_{HeNB\_MUE} - PL_{HeNB\_MUE,\min}), 0\right) \tag{7}$$

Where PL_{HeNB_MUE} is the estimated pathloss between the HeNB to its closest MUE; $PL_{HeNB\_MUE,\min}$ is a predetermined minimum threshold of the pathloss from the HeNB to MUE; α denotes coefficient for mapping rang of pathloss to the range of target SINR of the HUE.

Then, the receive signal power at HUE can be obtained by substituting equation (6) into equation (5). And the transmit power of the HeNB can be obtained by substituting equation (5) to equation (4).

From equation (6) and equation (7), we can see that the proposed new power setting scheme can adjust the target SINR of the associated HUE dynamically according to the pathloss difference of actual value to a minimum threshold. If the closest MUE is far from the HeNB, the adaptive factor Δ will be large as PL_{HeNB_MUE} is much greater than the minimum threshold $PL_{HeNB\_MUE,\min}$. In this case, the target SINR of the HUE is accordingly set as a large value and the transmit power of the HeNB will be high. It is reasonable the HeNB can transmit with a large power to increase its cell throughput when there is no close MUE. If the closest MUE is near the HeNB, the adaptive factor Δ will be small or even zero because PL_{HeNB_MUE} is approaching to the minimum threshold $PL_{HeNB\_MUE,\min}$. Then the target SINR of the HUE is accordingly set as a low value approaching to the minimum limit $T_{\min}$ to enable the associated HUE not to suffer a radio link failure. And the transmit power of the HeNB will be low to protect the closest MUE to keep a radio link connect to its serving MeNB.

5   Simulation and Analysis

In order to verify performance of our proposed power setting scheme, computer simulation is conducted. Furthermore, the conventional power setting scheme, i.e. PS1, and scheme of HeNB's transmit power being the maximum limit, i.e. no power setting, are simulated. In PS1, the target SINR is set as a lower value of -4 dB to protect nearby non-associated MUEs. In the simulation, we consider a cellular system containing 7 macro cells with 3 sectors in a macro cell [11]. Simulation scenario is illustrated in Fig.2. HeNBs are modeled as a Dual-stripe and deployed in a sector of the center macro cell.

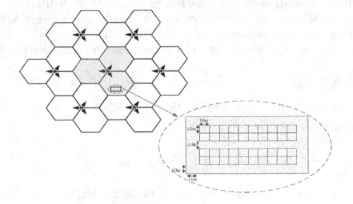

Fig. 2. simulation scenario

In the following figures, P_{in} represents the probability of MUEs being indoors. PS1 is the conventional power setting scheme with fixed -4dB target SINR and PS2 denotes our proposed power setting scheme. NO PS is the scheme that HeNB transmit downlink control signal with the maximum power.

Fig.3 and Fig.4 are curves of UEs' SINR of the proposed power setting scheme when 35% of macro UEs being indoors.

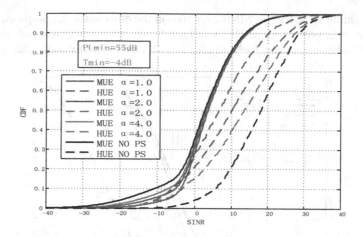

Fig. 3. CDF curve of SINR with different coefficient α

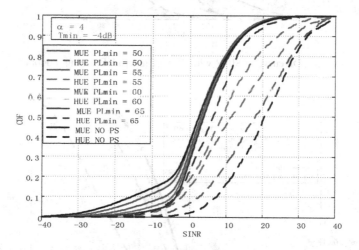

Fig. 4. CDF curve of SINR with different $PL_{HeNB\_MUE,\min}$

In Fig.3 with the minimum pathloss threshold $PL_{HeNB\_MUE,\min}$ invariant, the probability of HUEs with high SINRs increases when coefficient α increases. In the meantime, the probability of MUEs with low SINR also increases. In Fig.4 with α fixed invariant, the probability of HUEs with high SINRs decreases with the increase of $PL_{HeNB\_MUE,\min}$. Meanwhile, the probability of MUEs with low SINR also decreases. As can be seen from Fig.3 and Fig.4, $PL_{HeNB\_MUE,\min}$ and α have different effects on the system performance, $PL_{HeNB\_MUE,\min}$ is supposed to protect MUEs close to the HeNB and α is supposed to improve the throughput of HUEs when there is no nearby MUEs.

Fig.5 and Fig.6 illustrate SINR performance of different power setting schemes with different probability of MUEs being indoors. It is shown form the both figures that the proposed scheme has the similar probability of MUEs in low SINR range with the scheme of setting HUE's target SINR as -4dB. On the other hand, the proposed scheme has a much great probability of HUEs in high SINR range compared with the fixing target SINR scheme, especially when 11% of MUEs are randomly distributed indoors.

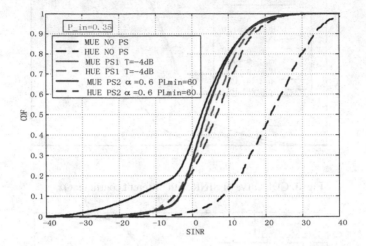

Fig. 5. CDF curve of SINR with 35% of macro UEs being indoors

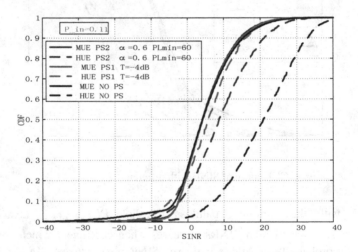

Fig. 6. CDF curve of SINR with 11% of macro UEs being indoors

Performance of different power setting schemes in terms of spectrum efficiency (SE) and the outage probability is listed in Table 1 and Table 2.

As can be seen from the tables, the proposed scheme has similar outage performance with the fixed target SINR scheme while has much higher edge and average throughput for the femto cell. Simulation parameters are in table 3.

Table 1. Performance of different power setting scheme with 35% MUE indoors

Throughput	NO PS	PS1	PS2
Outage for MUE (assuming -6dB)	18.25%	5.01%	5.37%
Outage for HUE (assuming -6dB)	0.58%	8.17%	8.21%
Edge HUE SE [bps/Hz]	1.10 (100%)	0.10 (-90.90%)	0.13 (-88.18%)
Ave HUE SE [bps/Hz]	3.57 (100%)	1.52 (-57.42%)	1.69 (-59.17%)

Table 2. Performance of different power setting scheme with 11% MUE indoors

Throughput	NO PS	PS1	PS2
Outage for MUE (assuming -6dB)	5.83%	1.84%	2.18%
Outage for HUE (assuming -6dB)	0.58%	8.12%	4.04%
Edge HUE SE [bps/Hz]	1.0 (100%)	0.12 (88%)	0.22 (-78%)
Ave HUE SE [bps/Hz]	3.49 (100%)	1.57 (-55.01%)	2.06 (-40.97%)

Table 3. Simulation parameters for HeNB deployment

Parameter	Assumption
Carrier bandwidth	10 MHz
Femto Frequency Channel	same frequency and same bandwidth as macro layer
Cell Radius	10 m
Min separation UE to femto	3m
Number of Tx antennas at femto	1
Femto antenna pattern	Omni antenna elements
Femto antenna gain	5 dBi
Min/Max Tx power femto	-10/20 dBm
Maximum number of femto UE per femto	1

6   Conclusions

In a heterogeneous system deployed with macro eNBs and home eNBs, a macro UE may move to a position close to a home eNB. However, the macro UE can't access to the home eNB as the home eNB serves for a closed subscribe group. In this case, the macro UE will suffer heavy interference from the home eNB and may loss radio link connect to the serving macro eNB. An adaptive power setting scheme is proposed in this paper to diminish inter-cell interference to macro UEs and improve the edge and average spectrum efficiency of the femto cell when there is no macro UE surrounding the home eNB. Simulation results show that the proposed scheme can reduce inter-cell interference to the macro users close to the femto cell and improve the throughput of femto cell significantly especially when few MUEs being indoors.

Acknowledgments. The authors would like to thank the anonymous reviewers for their careful reviews and insightful comments. This work was supported by National Science and Technology Major Project (NO.2010ZX03003-002); Tri-networks Integration Oriented Novel Wireless Telecommunication Equipment Research and Development (No.11QA1406300); the Key Technology Demonstration Test Platform for Fusion Terminals of TD-LTE and Satellite Mobile Communication (No.11511502702); Constructions of Innovative Service Platform for Wireless Mobile Communication Technology (No. 11DZ2290100).

References

1. Claussen, H.: Performance of Macro- and Co-channel Femtocells in a Hierarchical Cell Structure. In: IEEE International Symposium on Personal, Indoor and Mobile Radio Communications (PIMRC 2007), pp. 1–5 (September 2007)
2. Bharucha, Z., Hass, H., Cosovic, I., Auer, G.: Throughput Enhancement through Femto Cell Deployment. LNEE, pp. 311–319 (April 2009)
3. Chandrasekhar, V., Andrews, J.G., Gatherer, A.: Femtocell Networks: A Survey. IEEE Communications Magazine 46(9), 59–67 (2008)
4. 3GPP, 3GPP TR 25.820. Tech. Rep. (2008), http://www.3gpp.org
5. Claussen, H., Ho, L.T.W., Sanuel, L.G.: An overview of the femtocell concept. Bell Labs Technical Journal 13(1), 221–245 (2008)
6. R1-105081, Summary of the description of candidate eICIC solutions, CMCC, 3GPP TSG-RAN, WG1, #62
7. TR 36.921, Home eNode B (HeNB) Radio Frequency (RF) requirements analysis. V9.0.0
8. Chandrasekhar, V., Andrews, J.G., Shen, Z., Muharemovic, T., Gatherer, A.: Distributed Power Control in Femtocell-Underlay Cellular Networks. In: IEEE Global Telecommunication Conference (GLOBECOM 2009), pp. 1–6 (November-December 2009)
9. R1-104537, HeNB power setting scheme with penetration loss consideration, NEC Group, 3GPP TSG-RAN, WG1, #62
10. R1-104539, DL power control for HeNB with victim UE detection, Pico Chip, Kyocera, 3GPP TSG-RAN, WG1, #62
11. 3GPP TR 36.942 V10.1.0 (2010-09) p100

A Cluster Head Assisted UE Switching Solution
for Device-to-Device Communications

Jinling Du[1], Bin Zhou[1,2], Jing Xu[1,2], Zhenhong Li[3], Haifeng Wang[3], and Ligang Liu[1]

[1] Shanghai Research Center for Wireless Communications, WiCO, Shanghai, P.R. China
[2] Key Laboratory of Wireless Sensor Network & Communication,
Shanghai Institute of Microsystem and Information Technology (SIMIT),
Chinese Academy of Sciences (CAS), Shanghai, P.R. China
[3] Wireless modem R&D Renesas Mobile Corp, Shanghai, P.R. China
{jinling.du,bin.zhou,jing.xu,ligang.liu}@shrcwc.org,
{zhenhong.li,haifeng.wang}@renesasmobile.com

Abstract. Device-to-Device (D2D) cluster communication underlaying cellular networks has been proposed as a means of increasing the resource utilization, and improving the spectral efficiency. However, when D2D links cannot satisfy the connection requirements, in order to keep the connection, D2D communication has to switch back to cellular communication. Consider that the previous switching methods mainly concentrated on the network centralized controlled D2D communications, so we propose a novel switching solution aided by a cluster head for (semi-) distributed controlled D2D communications. We propose the switched D2D user itself search and access the target base station. The cluster head determines transmission mode based on the channel state information after switching. The numerical simulation demonstrates the hybrid mode outperforms the D2D mode in some conditions.

Keywords: Device-to-Device/D2D, cluster head, switching, hybrid mode, semi-distributed controlled.

1   Introduction

With the development of broadband networks, wireless data traffic is expected to continue strong growth in the near future. Mobile devices are dramatic increasing in the access to the limited frequency bands in the recent years while the limited available bands are more and more strained. It requires more efficient new solutions for use of existing spectrum resources. Device-to-Device (D2D) [1-7] communication technology is expected to become a promising resolution, which has been introduced to the conventional cellular communications. As an underlay of an LTE Advanced network, D2D enables new service opportunities, reduces the overhead for short range time intensive services and increase power and spectrum efficiency, which is becoming a beneficial complement of the IMT-Advanced system.

D2D communication [3], as the name implies, denotes a group of devices (e.g., UEs (User Equipments)) that are close and communicate with each other. As an

H. Qian and K. Kang (Eds.): WICON 2013, LNICST 121, pp. 113–122, 2013.
© Institute for Computer Sciences, Social Informatics and Telecommunications Engineering 2013

underlay cellular networks, D2D has two distinct links: D2D links and cellular links. D2D users exchange information with each other via D2D links directly, rather than via cellular wireless networks relaying within a D2D cluster (including D2D pair). When a D2D UE connects to the base station (evolved NodeB, eNB), it uses cellular links. D2D communication has two operating types. One is a network (e.g., eNB) centralized controlled D2D communications [1-2], i.e. eNB controls and manages D2D cluster communications, every D2D UE interacts control signalling with eNB respectively. Another is a cluster head (CH) semi-distributed controlled D2D cluster communications, i.e. the CH is responsible for managing and maintaining intra-cluster control signalling and data transmission, besides, it also interacts necessary control signaling such as synchronization, access, resource allocation and (re-)allocation with eNB via cellular links. eNB only has context information of the CH while it possibly has no information of other cluster members. These cluster UEs connect with the CH via D2D links and they are possibly without connection to the eNB. CH managed the cluster UEs.

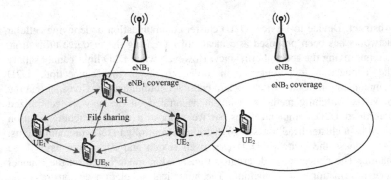

Fig. 1. D2D cluster communication and UE movement scenario

D2D cluster dynamically changes as user mobility within varying and unstable channel conditions, which might lead to the D2D link quality sharply deteriorate, even it could not meet connection requirements. As a result, D2D cluster might need to update, re-establishment. Under such condition, if D2D UEs were communicating with each other directly, in order to guarantee service continuity, D2D UEs might try to switch to the cellular networks to continue the communication. Since the introduction of D2D communication mode, there exist two communication modes for UEs: D2D mode and cellular mode. Therefore, the selection of communication mode should not only consider the link quality between UEs but also the link quality between eNB and UEs. To obtain the more efficient communications at any time, switching between D2D and cellular is inevitable.

For eNB centralized controlled D2D communications, eNB receive measurement reports from UEs periodically, eNB handles D2D link and cellular link conditions. Once D2D link quality is less than some limit value, the eNB determines D2D UEs switch back to cellular communications, vice verse. But for a CH semi-distributed controlled D2D communication, if eNB is lack of UE context, switching aided by eNB is not applicable. In this paper, we propose a D2D cluster UE switching to cellular wireless communications solution for CH semi-distributed controlled D2D cluster communications, and it can reduce routing latency and save radio resources.

This paper is organized as follows. Section 2 reviews related works and problem description. Section 3 presents the switching solution and implementation. The Section 4 presents numerical simulation and results.

2   Related Works and Solved Problem

In the existing literature, most research focuses on eNB centralized controlled D2D communications. [1-2] presented the concept of D2D communication as an underlay to a cellular network. In this system, eNB controls and manages D2D cluster (pair) UEs. If D2D links cannot provide good service quality, eNB is responsible for UEs switching to cellular communication mode from D2D mode. But in a CH semi-distributed controlled D2D cluster communication, for a certain amount of the cluster members, since those common cluster UEs have no dedicated channels to connect with eNB, taking Fig. 1 as an example, intra-eNB (CH and UE_2 is in the same eNB coverage) switching between D2D mode and cellular mode is hard to implement. It becomes much harder to implement inter-eNB switching when UE_2 moves to the other eNB. Even if communication mode switching can be processed, it would cost significant signalling overhead and time delay, and further degrade systems capacity and throughput.

Conventional cellular networks support UEs mobility and roaming. When users move from one cell to another one, in order to achieve call continuation during boundary crossings, handover is a key step. [8] discussed the handover initiation techniques and the handoff decision protocols, which decrease forced termination probability while not increasing call blocking probability significantly, when users transferring an active call from one cell to another. In cellular networks, the source eNB determines the target eNB for a UE who intends to make handover in cellular wireless networks [9]. Due to the limited range, D2D radio should be designed for rather stationary links. Nevertheless, it should also offer limited mobility support. In a cellular centralized controlled D2D communications, a handover from a D2D connection to a cellular connection is initiated when the cellular connection achieves higher throughput than the D2D or if one of the policies for D2D connections is violated. Obviously, eNB-based handover decision can be also applicable to a network centralized controlled D2D communications. In eNB centralized controlled D2D pair communications, once D2D link quality no longer satisfies communication requirements, eNB can make decision require D2D UEs in D2D mode switch to cellular mode. Assuming a pair of D2D UEs are located in the same eNB coverage area, and control signalling can be interacted between every D2D UE and eNB. The straightforward phases are as follows: Once D2D link quality is below some pre-ordered threshold value, D2D UEs can send request to eNB for switching to cellular mode respectively; After receiving the switching request, eNB allocates radio resources for cellular communication to UEs; if the cellular link quality is above some pre-ordered radio link threshold value in cellular mode, both UEs can switch back to cellular mode. This solution will be applicable for a group of UEs formed a D2D cluster communication as well, but it would be no doubt cost significantly radio resource and signalling. Worse still, the solution is hard to implement a cluster UE switches seamlessly to cellular mode. For the CH semi-distributed controlled D2D communications, due to lack of a centralized controller node, we have to search a new switching solution to mitigate data loss.

Within a D2D cluster as illustrated in Fig. 1, a group of UEs directly exchange information (e.g., file sharing) with each other via D2D links, without eNB relaying. All D2D UEs are in the coverage of eNB_1. The data source is elected as the CH of the cluster, which is responsible for managing and maintaining the operation within the cluster and keeping connection with eNB_1. Actually, any of UEs within the cluster can serve as a CH. Here just for convenient expression. In this case, if a D2D user UE_2 leaves from the cluster and UE_2 wishes to keep the existing service, even in an extreme case, UE_2 maybe leave from eNB_1 to eNB_2, how to keep communication connection? A straight-forward solution is the UE switches to cellular communication. It is also useful for a CH semi-distributed controlled D2D cluster communications. However, due to eNB is lack of UE context, D2D UE(s) switching to cellular communication mode has a bigger challenge to reduce resources consumption and time delay as much as possible and still provide existing service QoS to the communicating UEs. In this paper, our contribution has two points: on the one hand, if a D2D UE has to switch back to conventional cellular mode for communication, the D2D UE selects the identifier (ID) of the target eNB by itself for switching to the conventional cellular mode from D2D mode; on the other hand, the CH will use a new hybrid mode to transmit the data in case the leaving UE and current D2D users want to receive the same data information. The hybrid mode includes two cases based on the MCS (Modulation Coding Scheme) information: one is CH broadcasts data packets to D2D cluster and the target eNB (or CH itself eNB, then forward to the target eNB); the other is CH multicasts packets within the cluster in a dedicated resource while CH unicasts to the target eNB (or CH itself eNB, then forward to the target eNB) in another dedicated resource.

3   Protocol Implementation

We assume that D2D communication utilizes the eNB uplink resource orthogonally. As illustrated in Fig. 2, at the beginning, a data source CH multicasts files to a D2D cluster, CH can listen all of the cluster members. Afterwards, UE_2 gradually moves far away from CH. Once the D2D link quality between UE_2 and CH cannot satisfy the connection conditions, in this case, UE_2 still want to receive the present file, UE_2 will have to switch to the conventional cellular communication mode. The switching procedure includes the switching preparation phase, the switching execution phase, the data transfer phase.

In the switching preparation phase, UE_2 first initiates a cell search and a random access procedure. If eNB ID of the D2D UE_2 who intends to access is the same as eNB ID of the D2D CH as illustrated in Fig. 2(a), then UE_2 will access to eNB_1 and establish RRC connection with eNB_1. Otherwise, if UE_2 transfers to eNB_2 (Fig. 2(b)), in this case, the D2D UE_2 will intend to access to eNB_2 and establish RRC connection with eNB_2, which is different from eNB (eNB_1) of the D2D CH.

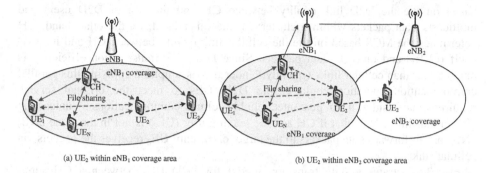

(a) UE_2 within eNB_1 coverage area   (b) UE_2 within eNB_2 coverage area

Fig. 2. Implementation process

In the switching execution phase, UE_2 sends a switching request to the CH via D2D link for keeping the existing service. The request includes the UE_2 accessed eNB ID. Note that it's different from handover procedure of the conventional cellular wireless network. In the cellular network, the source eNB finds and determines the target eNB for its UE, and the source eNB assists the UE to access the target eNB. Here the UE itself searches and accesses to the target eNB and informs the target eNB ID to the CH. Then the CH (not the source eNB) sends the switching request of UE_2 together with UE_2 accessed eNB ID to eNB_1 (the eNB ID of the CH) via the cellular links. Once eNB_1 receives the request message from CH, eNB_1 will know to which eNB UE_2 has accessed. If UE_2 accessed eNB ID is the same as eNB_1, the procedure will turn to the data transfer phase. Otherwise, if UE_2 accessed eNB ID is the eNB_2, the two cellular eNBs will have to exchange the switching request and confirmed message for UE_2. After CH receives the switching command via the cellular links, CH sends a switching confirmation message to UE_2 via D2D links, as a result, UE_2 receives the rest of packets via cellular links. UE_2 disconnects D2D links.

In the data transfer phase, CH adopts a hybrid communication mode. In hybrid mode of communication, D2D mode and cellular mode communicate simultaneously. That is, CH transmits packets to UE_2 via cellular links, while CH transmits packets to the rest of the D2D members via D2D links. In detailed implementations, CH compares the MCS between CH and eNB_1 with MCS between D2D links to determine the resource assignment. It has two cases.

(1) $MCS_{CH-eNB1}$ is (approximately) equal to MCS_{D2D}: In this case, CH uses a dedicated resource to broadcast the data packets to both the D2D cluster (the rest of D2D member UEs) and eNB_1, which saves the radio resources. It notes that if CH and UE_2 is not in the same eNB, eNB_1 would have to forward the packets to the target eNB (e.g., it is eNB_2 in Fig. 2(b)), until the data packets are sent to UE_2 via cellular links at last.

(2) Great difference to compare $MCS_{CH-eNB1}$ with MCS_{D2D}: In this case, CH selects a parallel communication operation using two dedicated resources, i.e., multicasting data packets via D2D links and unicasting via cellular links. The two communication modes are independently exist at the CH. On the one hand, CH determines the MCS based on the the D2D link quality between CH and the rest of D2D users and multicasts data packets within a cluster; on the other hand; on the other hand, CH determines the MCS based on the the cellular link quality between CH and its eNB itself (eNB$_1$) and unicasts data packets. Since D2D link transmission efficiency is much better than cellular links typically. Under this assumption, applying this parallel communication operation could enable D2D UEs to meet the original service requirements; besides, it can guarantee reliable cellular communications by unicasting via cellular links. Note that if CH and the leaving user (UE$_2$) is not in the same eNB, eNB$_1$ has to forward data packets to the target eNB, until UE$_2$ receives the packets via cellular links.

Fig. 3 illustrates a state transition model for D2D UEs between a CH semi-distributed controlled D2D communication mode and conventional eNB centralized controlled cellular communication mode. At the beginning, all UEs stay in D2D mode (The CH still connects with eNB). When D2D links of a cluster member UE within a cluster can't satisfy direct communication requirement as the position of the D2D UE and communication environment changes, in order to accomplish some communication service, the D2D UE will have to switch to cellular mode from D2D mode. In this case, the UE keeps the previous D2D link to maintain D2D communication, while the UE establishes a cellular link. If the UE can satisfy the cellular communication requirement, the UE will leave the D2D connection state and enter cellular connection state. At this time, the CH communicates with the UE via cellular links, while CH communicates with the rest of cluster members via D2D links. That is, for the original cluster, it enters hybrid state.

On the contrary, if at the beginning, UEs are in cellular communication mode. When a cellular UE multicasts data through eNB relaying, if the data source UE and one of receiver UEs satisfy the requirement for D2D communication and UEs have D2D communication capability, eNB shall instruct the UEs to switch from cellular mode to D2D mode. In this case, eNB designates the source UE to serve as a cluster head which still keeps connection with eNB, meanwhile, the source UE and the receiver UE try to establish D2D links. When a D2D link is already established between the two UEs successfully, both UEs respectively enter D2D communication state. However, if the D2D link quality between the source UE and the rest of receiver UEs cannot satisfy the requirement, they would continue to communicate through cellular links, that is, the network enters hybrid communication mode. But when all the rest of receiver UEs can enter D2D communication state, this network enters D2D mode.

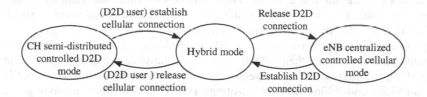

Fig. 3. Cluster member state transition and mode switching

4   Numerical Simulation and Results

In this section, we analyze the cost of time-frequency resource in D2D mode and hybrid mode respectively. As shown in Fig. 1, for simplified calculation, only one user UE_2 moves far away from D2D, other users are static. In D2D mode, we assume the communication radius of the D2D is large enough, even if the user moves far away from D2D, the communication is still via D2D links. In hybrid mode, we assume the moving user UE_2 is still in the coverage of eNB_1, besides, only UE_2 communicates with CH via cellular links, other D2D members communicate with CH via D2D links. D2D and cellular communication use orthogonal resource, assuming frequency resource is the same in D2D multicast and cellular uplink/downlink unicast. The channel model considers only path loss. We do not consider shadowing or fast fading. In this case, we compare D2D mode and hybrid mode in the single-cell. Shannon's capacity formula is used to calculate the sum cost of time-frequency resources of unit-bit. In D2D mode,

$$Sum_{D2D} = \frac{1}{B_{D2D} \cdot R_{D2D}} = \frac{1}{B \log_2 (1 + SNR_{D2D})} \tag{1}$$

Wherein, B_{D2D} denotes the transmission bandwidth of D2D mode, e.g, one physical resource block (PRB). For convenience, we assume that the bandwidth of both D2D mode and cellular mode are B. R_{D2D} is the D2D multicast transmission rate on each PRB (including the leaving UE_2), and SNR_{D2D} is the signal to noise radio of the D2D links.

In the hybrid mode, in order to make the updated D2D keep transmitting data, the networks still allocate the same frequency resource (B). In this case, the sum cost of time-frequency resources of unit-bit is

$$Sum_{hybrid} = \frac{1}{B_{rD2D} \cdot R_{rD2D}} + \frac{1}{B_{UL} \cdot R_{UL}} + \frac{1}{B_{DL} \cdot R_{DL}}$$
$$= \frac{1}{B \log_2 (1 + SNR_{rD2D})} + \frac{1}{B \log_2 (1 + SNR_{UL})} + \frac{1}{B \log_2 (1 + SNR_{DL})} \tag{2}$$

Wherein, R_{rD2D} is the transmission rate of the rest D2D members (excluding UE_2), which forms a updated D2D, compared to the original D2D. RUL and R_{DL} are the cellular uplink/downlink transmission rate on each PRB respectively. SNR_{rD2D} denotes the SNR among the rest D2D links, and SNR_{UL} and SNR_{DL} are cellular uplink and downlink SNR.If we do not consider interference, assuming the channel model considers only path loss, when the transmission power and thermal noise is fixed, larger distance, lower SNR, and larger resource cost.

From (1) and (2), we perform the numerical simulations. Table I summarizes a list of simulation parameters and their default values. The simulation tool is developed in MatlabTM. In the first scenario, we keep fixed the distance between CH and eNB (e.g., 23m, 73m and 140m) and the positions of the cluster users excluding the moving UE_2. As shown in Fig. 4, when UE_2 moves far away from the CH, the distance attenuation increases, the sum resource cost of the time-frequency of D2D mode increases as well. For hybrid mode, if the distance between CH and eNB was fixed, UE_2 mobility has a tiny influence for the cost of the cellular uplink/downlink and the rest of D2D members, the resource cost increases slowly. Obviously, at the beginning, the performance of the D2D mode is better, however, as the distance between CH and UE_2 increases, the performance of the hybrid mode will outperform the D2D mode. So the crossing point can be as 'switching point', it represents the best switching location found in each case, considering D2D modes and hybrid modes. We can conclude that if the hybrid mode is chosen in some occasions, it will be a gain in the system capacity.

Table 1. Simulation parameters and values

Parameters	Values
Carrier frequency	2 GHz
Max eNB Tx power	46 dBm
UE Tx Power	10 dBm
Tx bandwidth	1 PRB
Distance attenuation	128.1+37.6lg(d), with d in km
UE noise figure	9 dB
UE thermal noise density	-174 dBm/Hz

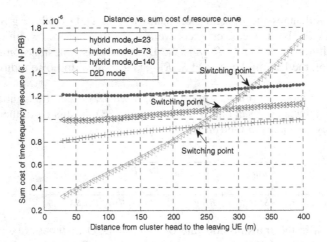

Fig. 4. Sum cost of time-frequency resource in the first scenario

In the second scenario, we keep fixed the communication radius of D2D and eNB varies its position. Fig. 5 illustrates the resource cost of the hybrid mode increases with the distance and the cost of D2D mode in some special D2D coverage distances. Due to in hybrid mode, some packets are transmitted via eNB relaying, so when the distance between CH and eNB increases, the gain of the hybrid mode degrades. But as expected, the hybrid mode has better performance than D2D mode when we consider the short distance between CH and eNB. Actually, when the D2D coverage is 250m, and the cellular communication distance is below 60m, the resource cost of the hybrid mode is lower than those required in the D2D mode. Once the distance between CH and eNB is beyond 60m, the sum resource cost of the hybrid mode will be larger. In this case, the crossing point can become a switching threshold value. If the coverage distance of D2D mode and cellular mode increase, the switching threshold value will increase as well.

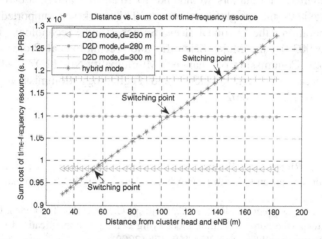

Fig. 5. Sum cost of time-frequency resource in the second scenario

In short, the simulations illustrate that the D2D communication and cellular communication should not be applied all the time, but only in some favorable conditions. Therefore, switching between D2D communication and cellular communication is inevitable. It notes that D2D is a short-range communication technology. Only when UE is close to each other, D2D communication may allow for extreme high bit rates, low delays and low power consumption. So when a part of D2D users have to switch to cellular communication from D2D communication, the proposed hybrid communication mode adopts the hybrid communication mode, that is, the integration of D2D communication and cellular communication to improve the system efficiency significantly.

5   Conclusion

In this paper, we investigated a switching solution between cellular communications and D2D communications. It can speed up routing lookup process and reduce time delay, especially for inter-eNB switching to cellular links from D2D links, compared with cellular handover. As in the cellular handover, in order to lookup the target eNB, the source eNB has to resort to Mobility Management Entity (MME), and its latency is much longer. While in the proposal, the D2D CH reports the target eNB ID to the source eNB, then the source eNB knows who is the target eNB in advance. This process is without need to relocation procedure signalling and MME routing lookup, and it reduces latency.

The proposal also improves spectrum efficiency. From the simulations, the hybrid communication mode can save radio resources and improve spectrum efficiency while without degrading D2D transmission rate.

In this paper, either centralized or semi-distributed D2D communication utilizes licensed spectrum resources. Consider the unlicensed bands are used inefficiently and D2D communications technology can increase power and spectrum efficiency, in the near future, we would study D2D utilization on unlicensed bands.

Acknowledgments. The authors would like to thank the anonymous reviewers for their careful reviews and insightful comments. This work was supported by Renesas Mobile Corporation, the National Key Science and Technology Project No. 2011ZX03003-003-04, the Major Scientific and Technological Projects of Science and Technology Commission of Shanghai Municipality No. 11DZ2290100 and the Key Basic Research Project of Science and Technology Commission of Shanghai Municipality No. 12JC1404202.

References

1. Doppler, K., Rinne, M., Wijting, C., Ribeiro, C.B., Hugl, K.: Device-to-Device communication as an underlay to LTE-Advanced networks. IEEE Commun. Mag. 47(12), 42–49 (2009)
2. Jänis, P., Yu, C., Doppler, K., Ribeiro, C., Wijting, C., Hugl, K., Tirkkonen, O., Koivunen, V.: Device-to-device communication underlaying cellular communications systems. Int. J. Commun., Network and Sys. Sci. 2(3), 169–178 (2009)
3. Timo, K., Sami, H., Tao, C., Janne, L.: Clustering concept using device-to-device communication in cellular system. In: IEEE WCNC, pp. 1–6 (2010)
4. Seppala, J., Koskela, T., Chen, T., Hakola, S.: Network controlled device-to-device (D2D) and. cluster multicast concept for LTE and LTE-A Networks. In: IEEE WCNC, pp. 986–991 (2011)
5. Yang, W., Sun, W., Li, L.: Reliable multicasting for device-to-device underlaying radio cellular networks, http://arxiv.org/pdf/1008.3741
6. Rêgo, M., Lucena, E., Maciel, T., Cavalcanti, R.: On the performance of the device-to-device communication with uplink power control, http://www.dee.ufma.br/~fsouza/Anais_SBrT_2011/papers/completos/85605.pdf
7. Yu, C.H., Tirkkonen, O., Doppler, K., Ribeiro, C.: On the performance of device-to-device underlay communication with simple power control. In: Proc. IEEE Vehicular Technology Conference, pp. 1–5 (Spring 2009)
8. Ekiz, N., Salih, T., Küçüköner, S., Fidanboylu, K.: An overview of handoff techniques in cellular networks. Int. J. Inf. Technol. 2(3), 132–136 (2005)
9. 3GPP TS 36. 300 V9.0.0. Evolved universal terrestrial radio access (E-UTRA) and evolved universal terrestrial radio access network (E-UTRAN) overall description (2009)

An Algorithm for Finding Energy Efficient Relay Positions in Cellular Network

Ming Zhao, Saifeng Ni, Sihai Zhang, and Wuyang Zhou

PCN&SS Lab, University of Science and Technology of China
Hefei, Anhui, China
{zhaoming,shzhang,wyzhou}@ustc.edu.cn,
saifeng@mail.ustc.edu.cn

Abstract. In this paper, we propose an iterative algorithm for finding near-optimal Energy Efficient Relay Positions(EERP) in Amplify-and-Forward (AF) and Decode-and-Forward (DF) relay-assisted cellular networks. Each iteration of EERP algorithm contains two steps, i.e. energy efficient cell division and energy efficient center searching. Close-form expressions of energy efficient cell division boundaries are provided. And two-dimensional Fast Fourier Transform (FFT) is adopted to reduce the complexity of energy efficient center searching. Simulation results show near-optimal relay positions of different pathloss factors, relay scenarios and relay numbers, and demonstrates the effectiveness of EERP.

Keywords: relay position, energy efficiency, green communication.

1 Introduction

Statistics about energy consumption of cellular system show that a lot of energy is wasted owing to low utilization of cellular systems, especially base station (BS), resulting from low traffic. In order to save energy consumption of cellular networks, traffic-aware energy efficient network planning becomes essential and attracts a lot of attention recently[1][2][3]. Based on traffic fluctuation, many switching on/off schemes are proposed in both academia and industry to avoid wasting BS operation energy. Cell zooming, which adaptively adjusts cell size according to traffic load, has the potential to balance traffic load and reduce energy consumption [3]. However, it may easily cause coverage hole, and additional modules are needed to support cell zooming. Moreover, more powerful hardware is needed to get more information such as real-time traffic load and neighbor cell information for cell zooming.

Relaying is one of the features proposed for the 4G LTE-Advanced system. Therefore relay position in cellular network is a hot topic. Relay can enlarge coverage and increase network capacity, and it can also improve energy efficiency. Traffic-aware relay placement can effectively improve energy efficiency. Currently, most research on relay placement in wireless network focuses on improving relay-assisted network radius [4] and throughput [5][6], or minimize outage probability [7]. On the other hand, energy-efficient design of sensor and ad

H. Qian and K. Kang (Eds.): WICON 2013, LNICST 121, pp. 123–136, 2013.

hoc networks has received significant attention for decades with emphasis on prolonging battery life-time for sensor nodes and mobile terminals [8], but the networking planning problem in cellular network is different with those in sensor or ad hoc networks. As energy efficiency becomes one of the major goals in designing cellular system, the work [9] is among very few that optimizes relay station (RS) positions to reduce energy consumption, but it focuses on one-dimensional cellular network scenario.

Real-time traffic distribution in a cellular cell changes randomly. However, from a macro point of view, traffic distribution in a cell has statistical pattern, e.g. some subareas in the cell is hot-spot while some are sparsely populated. on the other hand, some mobile stations can be dynamically assigned as relay nodes according to the optimal relay position searching in future cellular networks. In this paper, we focus on traffic-aware energy-efficient relay position searching problem in a hexagon cell. By optimizing RS locations base on statistical traffic distribution, energy consumption will decline. To find the optimal RS locations, a near-optimal heuristic iterative algorithm named Energy Efficient Relay Position (EERP) is proposed in both AF and DF relay scenarios, which is based on the idea of *Lloyd algorithm*. Each iteration of EERP executes two steps: First, the cell is divided into small regions covered by RSs and BS. The division is based on the result of the most energy efficient power allocation. Close-form expressions of cell separation boundary and shapes of cell separation boundary in some specific pathloss factors are provided. Based on cell separation diagram, energy efficient RS locations are calculated according to traffic distributions. After several iterations, we can get the near-optimal positions for N RSs. Two-dimensional FFT is used to largely reduce the complexity.

2   System Model and Problem Description

2.1   System Model

Consider a hexagon cell with radius R_{cell} and N RSs in it. BS is located in cell center as shown in Fig. 1 and transmits signal to mobile station(MS) directly or through a RS for downlink. h_{BR}, h_{RM}, h_{BM} denote BS-RS channel, RS-MS channel and BS-MS channel respectively. Channel gain between position i and j is formulated as $h_{ij} = ad_{ij}^{-b}$, where d_{ij} is the distance between i and j; a,b are constants, where b denotes pathloss factor. Here, the channel model we adopted is Urban Macro Model in ITU-R M.2135, and the details can be found in Section 4. With orthogonal resource allocation technology, intra-cell interference can be avoided.

For DF relays, downlink data rate R_{DF} is formulated as [10]

$$R_{DF} = \min\left(\frac{1}{2}\log_2\left(1 + P_s|h_{BR}|^2\right), \frac{1}{2}\log_2\left(1 + P_r|h_{RM}|^2\right)\right) \tag{1}$$

where P_s, P_r is transmission power of BS and RS, and Gaussian noise power N_0 is normalized. Channel gains are modeled as $|h_{RM}|^2 = a_1 d_{RM}^{-b_1}$, $|h_{BR}|^2 = a_2 d_{BR}^{-b_2}$,

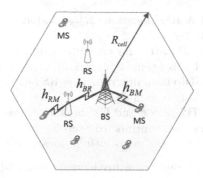

Fig. 1. System Model

$b_2 \leq b_1$.For AF relays, downlink data rate R_{AF} is

$$R_{AF} = \frac{1}{2} \log_2 \left(1 + \frac{P_s |h_{BR}|^2 P_r |h_{RM}|^2}{1 + P_s |h_{BR}|^2 + P_r |h_{RM}|^2} \right) \tag{2}$$

If BS directly communicates with MS, downlink data rate will be expressed as

$$R_{DT} = \log_2 \left(1 + P_s |h_{BM}|^2 \right) \tag{3}$$

2.2 Problem Description

The objective is to find optimal positions for N RSs based on statistical traffic distribution to maximize cell energy efficiency i.e. minimize cell power consumption $h(\mathbf{H})$. We suppose cell traffic distribution follows function $f(\mathbf{X})$, where $\mathbf{X}$ denotes user's position (x, y) and $f(\mathbf{X})$ is the corresponding traffic requirement in bits. The problem can be formulated as

$$\min_{\mathbf{H}} h(\mathbf{H}) = \iint_S \frac{P_s(\mathbf{X}, \mathbf{H}) + P_r(\mathbf{X}, \mathbf{H})}{R} f(\mathbf{X}) d\mathbf{X} \tag{4}$$

where R is data rate, $\mathbf{H}$ denotes RS location (η_i, ζ_i), $i = 1, \ldots, N$ and S denotes the cell area over wich the double integral is computed. BS is located at $(0, 0)$. Transmission power of BS and RS is expressed as $P_s(\mathbf{X}, \mathbf{H})$ and $P_r(\mathbf{X}, \mathbf{H})$. So our goal is to find $\mathbf{H}^*$ which can minimize $h(\mathbf{H})$. Energy efficiency is defined as $EE = (P_r + P_s)/R$ in Joule/bit. The minimum $h(\mathbf{H}^*)$ is obtained when RSs' position and power allocation among all downlinks are most energy efficient.

3   Algorithm for Finding Energy Efficient Relay Position

To get the optimal solution $\mathbf{H}_i^*$ for MS i, BS will choose the optimal RS to forward its data, and RSs must be at the optimal position. According to the two principles, we proposed a heuristic algorithm for finding Energy Efficient Relay Position, namely EERP, based on the idea of *Lloyd algorithm*[11]. EERP is executed in following steps.

- **Step 1:** Initiate the N RSs' locations H^k_{RS} randomly with BS in cell center, where $k = 1$ is a counter.
- **Step 2:** After power allocation for each link with minimum energy cost, cell is divided into $N + 1$ subregions $S^k_i, i = 1, 2, \ldots, N + 1$.
- **Step 3:** Based on cell division diagram, new RS locations $\mathbf{H}^{k+1}_{RS}$ are obtained according to traffic distribution $f(\mathbf{X})$.
- **Step 4:** If $\|\mathbf{H}^{k+1}_{RS} - \mathbf{H}^k_{RS}\| > \varepsilon$ and $k < max\_iter$, then set $k = k + 1$ and go back to Step 2; otherwise, continue to Step 5.
- **Step 5:** Return $\mathbf{H}^{k+1}_{RS}$ as the near-optimal locations for N RSs.

In the above algorithm, ε denotes a predefined threshold and max_iter is the maximal iteration times.

Suppose that RS locations are $\mathbf{H_{RS}}$. Cell separation generates two kinds of subregion boundaries. One is between subregions of two RSs; the other is between subregions of the BS and one RS, which is determined by whether directly communication between BS and MS is better than BS transmitting its message through any RS to MS. AF and DF RS are illustrated as follows respectively.

3.1   Cell Division for DF Relays Assisted Networks

First, power allocation of P_s and P_r is to maximize energy efficiency of every downlink under the premise of guaranteeing data rate requirements R_{th}. The power allocation problem can be formulated as

$$\min_{P_s, P_r} \frac{P_s + P_r}{R_{DF}}$$
$$s.t.\ \ 0 < P_s, P_r < P_{max}$$
$$R_{DF} > R_{th} \tag{5}$$

where R_{DF} is defined as (1). Under the condition $P_{max} > (2^{2R_{th}} - 1)/|h_{SR}|^2, P_{max} > (2^{2R_{th}} - 1)/|h_{RD}|^2$[8], the optimal solution of (5) is

$$P^*_s = (2^{2R_{th}} - 1)/|h_{SR}|^2$$
$$P^*_r = (2^{2R_{th}} - 1)/|h_{RD}|^2 \tag{6}$$

3.1.1 Boundary Between Subregions of Two RSs

According to (6), energy cost of choosing RS_i is defined as

$$EE_{RS_i}(\mathbf{X}, \mathbf{H_i}) = \frac{(2^{2R_{th}} - 1)(a_2^{-1}d^{b_2}_{BR_i} + a_1^{-1}d^{b_1}_{R_iM})}{R_{th}} \tag{7}$$

The optimal subregion boundary between two RSs satisfies $EE_{RS_i}(\mathbf{X}, \mathbf{H_i}) = EE_{RS_j}(\mathbf{X}, \mathbf{H_j})$. By substituting (7), we can get

$$d^{b_1}_{R_iM} - d^{b_1}_{R_jM} = a_1 a_2^{-1}(d^{b_2}_{BR_j} - d^{b_2}_{BR_i})$$
$$\|\mathbf{X} - \mathbf{H_i}\|^{b_1} - \|\mathbf{X} - \mathbf{H_j}\|^{b_1} = a_1 a_2^{-1}(d^{b_2}_{BR_j} - d^{b_2}_{BR_i}) \tag{8}$$

where $\|\mathbf{X} - \mathbf{H}_i\|$ is the distance between MS and RS_i; the right parts of the two equalities in (8) are a constant since the distance between RS and BS is already known.

Theorem 1: Cell division among DF RSs satisfies (8).

Corollary 1: When $b_1 = 1$, the cell separation boundary is a hyperbola; when b1=2, cell separation boundary is a straight line. And when LOS exists between BS and RS, cell separation boundary tends to be a straight line.

Proof: When $b_1 = 1$, (8) turns to be $d_{R_i M} - d_{R_j M}$=const, which is a hyperbola; when $b_1 = 2$, (8) will be transformed to $\|X - \eta_i\|^2 - \|X - \eta_j\|^2$ =const, which is a straight line; when LOS exists between BS and RS, which means $b_2 < b_1$, then $d_{BR_i}^{b_2}$ is smaller than $d_{R_i M}^{b_1}$, and can be ignored, so (8) turns into $\|X - \mathbf{H}_i\| = \|X - \mathbf{H}_j\|$, which is a straight line.

3.1.2 Boundary Between Subregions of BS and RSs

When BS directly communicate with MS, P_s satisfy $P_s = (2^{R_{th}} - 1)a_1^{-1}d_{BM}^{b_1}$, so $EE_{BS}(\mathbf{X})$ can be expressed as

$$EE_{BS}(\mathbf{X}) = P_s/R = \frac{(2^{R_{th}} - 1)a_1^{-1}d_{BM}^{b_1}}{R_{th}} \qquad (9)$$

Boundary between subregions of the BS and a RS satisfies,

$$d_{BM}^{b_1} - (2^{R_{th}} + 1)d_{RM}^{b_1} = a_1 a_2^{-1}(2^{R_{th}} + 1)d_{BR}^{b_2}$$
$$\|\mathbf{X}\|^{b_1} - (2^{R_{th}} + 1)\|\mathbf{X} - \mathbf{H}_j\|^{b_1} = a_1 a_2^{-1}(2^{R_{th}} + 1)d_{BR}^{b_2} \qquad (10)$$

Theorem 2: When RS adopts DF strategy, cell separation between BS and RS satisfies(10).

Corollary 2: When $b_1 = b_2 = 2$, cell separation boundary must be behind the line which passes RS point and is vertical to the connection of BS and RS. When LOS exists between BS and RS, cell separation boundary is a parabola.

Proof: When $b_1 = b_2 = 2$, from (7) and (9), we can get

$$EE_{RS}(\mathbf{X}, \mathbf{H})/EE_{bs}(\mathbf{X}) > (2^{R_{th}} + 1)((d_{RM}^2 + d_{BR}^2)/d_{BM}^2)^2 \qquad (11)$$

Law of cosines tells us that cell separation boundary between BS and RS must be behind the line which is vertical to the connection between BS and RS and passes RS. When LOS exists between BS and RS, cell separation boundary can be approximated to $(2^{R_{th}} + 1)^{1/b_1}d_{RM} = d_{BM}$, which is a parabola.

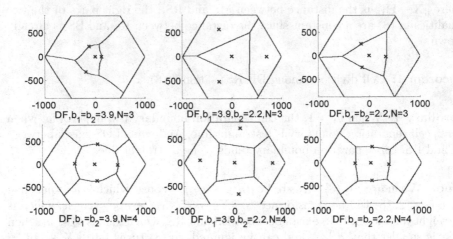

Fig. 2. Cell separation diagram (DF)

When DF strategy is adopted, cell separation boundary is shown in Fig. 2. The 'x' mark denotes RS locations. Based on RS locations, cell separation is done. Cell separation boundary is changing with fading factor b. As the growing of b_1, b_2, the curvature of cell separation boundary becomes larger, which matches with the theoretic results.

3.2   Cell Division for AF Relays Assisted Networks

With data rate expression (2) energy efficient power allocation problem can be modeled as

$$\min_{P_s, P_r} \frac{P_s + P_r}{R_{AF}}$$
$$s.t. \quad 0 < P_s, P_r < P_{max}$$
$$R_{AF} \geq R_{th} \tag{12}$$

With high SNR assumption, data rate expression (2) is approximated to

$$R_{AF} = \frac{1}{2} \log_2 \left(\frac{P_s |h_{SR}|^2 P_r |h_{RD}|^2}{1 + P_s |h_{SR}|^2 + P_r |h_{RD}|^2} \right) \tag{13}$$

Then the optimal result of (11) is

$$P_s = \frac{\left(2^{2R_{th}} - 1\right) |h_{RD}|^2 + \sqrt{2^{2R_{th}} \left(2^{2R_{th}} - 1\right) |h_{SR}|^2 |h_{RD}|^2}}{|h_{SR}|^2 |h_{RD}|^2}$$

$$P_r = \frac{\left(2^{2R_{th}} - 1\right) |h_{SD}|^2 + \sqrt{2^{2R_{th}} \left(2^{2R_{th}} - 1\right) |h_{SR}|^2 |h_{RD}|^2}}{|h_{SR}|^2 |h_{RD}|^2} \tag{14}$$

We omit the proof of the result due to space limitation.

3.2.1 Boundary between Subregions of Two RSs

The energy cost of RS_i is expressed as

$$EE_{RS_i}(\mathbf{X}, \mathbf{H_i}) = \frac{1}{R_{th}} \left((2^{2R_{th}} - 1)\left(a_1^{-1}d_{R_iM}^{b_1} + a_2^{-1}d_{BR_i}^{b_2}\right) \right.$$

$$\left. +2\sqrt{2^{2R_{th}}(2^{2R_{th}} - 1)a_1^{-1}a_2^{-1}d_{R_iM}^{b_1}d_{BR_i}^{b_2}} \right) \qquad (15)$$

When $EE_{RS_i}(\mathbf{X}, \mathbf{H_i}) \approx (2^{2R_{th}} - 1)/R_{th} \left(\sqrt{a_1^{-1}d_{R_iM}^{b_1}} + \sqrt{a_2^{-1}d_{BR_i}^{b_2}} \right)^2$, cell separation boundary can be expressed as

$$\sqrt{a_1^{-1}d_{R_iM}^{b_1}} - \sqrt{a_1^{-1}d_{R_jM}^{b_1}} = \sqrt{a_2^{-1}d_{BR_j}^{b_2}} - \sqrt{a_2^{-1}d_{BR_i}^{b_2}}$$

$$\|\mathbf{X} - \mathbf{H_i}\|^{b_1/2} - \|\mathbf{X} - \mathbf{H_j}\|^{b_1/2} = \sqrt{a_1a_2^{-1}d_{BR_j}^{b_2}} - \sqrt{a_1a_2^{-1}d_{BR_i}^{b_2}} \qquad (16)$$

Theorem 3: When RS adopts AF strategy, cell separation boundary between RSs similarly satisfies(14).

Corollary 3: When $b_1 = 2$, cell separation boundary between RSs is a hyperbola; when $b_1 = 4$, cell separation boundary is a straight line. When LOS exists between BS and RS, cell separation boundary becomes a straight line.

Proof: When $b_1 = 2$, cell separation boundary (14) can be translated into $d_{R_iM} - d_{R_jM} =$ const, which is a hyperbola. When $b_1 = 4$, cell separation boundary (14) turns to be$\|\mathbf{X} - \mathbf{H_i}\|^2 - \|\mathbf{X} - \mathbf{H_j}\|^2$, which is a straight line. When LOS exists between BS and RS, cell separation boundary (14) is approximated to $\|\mathbf{X} - \mathbf{H_i}\| - \|\mathbf{X} - \mathbf{H_j}\|$, which is a straight line.

3.2.2 Boundary between Subregions of BS and RSs

Cell separation boundary satisfies $EE_{RS_i}(\mathbf{X}, \mathbf{H_i}) = EE_{BS}(\mathbf{X})$,then from (9) and (15), we can get

$$\sqrt{d_{BM}^{b_1}/(2^R + 1)} - \sqrt{d_{RM}^{b_1}} = \sqrt{a_1a_2^{-1}d_{BR}^{b_2}}$$

$$(2^{R_{th}} + 1)^{-1/2}\|\mathbf{X}\|^{b_1/2} - \|\mathbf{X} - \mathbf{H_j}\|^{b_1/2} = \sqrt{a_1a_2^{-1}d_{BR}^{b_2}} \qquad (17)$$

Theorem 4: When RS adopts AF strategy, cell separation between RS and BS approximately satisfies(17).

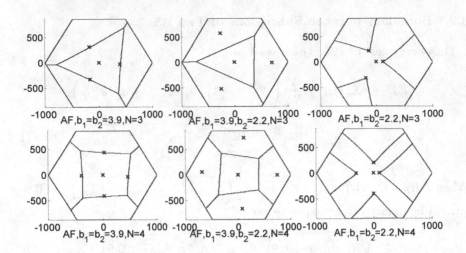

Fig. 3. Cell separation diagram (AF)

Corollary 4: When $b_1 = b_2 = 2$, no RS is needed. When $b_1 = b_2 = 4$, cell separation boundary between BS and RS is behind the line which is perpendicular to the connection of BS and RS and pass RS. When LOS exists BS and RS, cell separation boundary is a parabola.

Proof: If $b_1 = b_2 = 2$,then

$$EE_{RS}(\mathbf{X}, \mathbf{H}) > \frac{2^{2R_{th}} - 1}{R_{th}} \left(\sqrt{a_1^{-1} d_R^{b_1} M} + \sqrt{a_2^{-1} d_{BR}^{b_2} / d_{BR}} \right)^2 \qquad (18)$$

So,

$$EE_{RS}(\mathbf{X}, \mathbf{H_i}) / EE_{BS}(\mathbf{X}) > (2^{2R_{th}} + 1) \left(\frac{d_{RM} + d_{BR}}{d_{BM}} \right)^2 \qquad (19)$$

Triangle inequality tells us that $d_{RM} + d_{BR} > d_{BM}$, so $EE_{RS}(\mathbf{X}, \mathbf{H}) > EE_{BS}(\mathbf{X})$, which means BS should transmit data to MS directly. When $b_1 = b_2 = 4, EE_{RS}(\mathbf{X}, \mathbf{H}) / EE_{BS}(\mathbf{X}) > (2^{2R_{th}} + 1) \left(\frac{d_{RM}^2 + d_{BR}^2}{d_{BM}^2} \right)^2$. Law of cosines tells us that cell separation boundary between BS and RS must be behind the line which vertical to the connection of BS and RS and pass RS. When LOS exists between BS and RS, then $d_{BM} - (2_{th}^R + 1)^{1/b_1} d_{RM} = 0$,which is a parabola.

Cell separation boundary for AF strategy is shown in Fig. 3. Three different channel cases are provided, which conform to theoretic analysis.

3.3   Energy Efficient Center Searching

Energy efficient cell separation divides a cell into $N + 1$ regions. BS communicates with MS in S_i through RS_i, while BS transmits data to MS in region

S_{N+1} directly. In this section, we will optimize RS_i position to maximize energy efficiency in S_i, which can be formulated as

$$\min_{\mathbf{H_i}} \iint_{S_i} \frac{P_s(\mathbf{X}, \mathbf{H_i}) + P_r(\mathbf{X}, \mathbf{H_i})}{R} f(\mathbf{X}) d\mathbf{X}, i = 1, 2, \ldots, N \tag{20}$$

Owing to complex shape of S_i, and complex expression of traffic distribution, it is hard to get a theoretic solution of the optimal RS locations; however, numerical techniques can be used to find near-optimal relay positions. We quantize a cell region into grids. So (20) can be translated into

$$\min_{\mathbf{H_i}} \sum_{\mathbf{X_j} \in S_i} \frac{P_s(\mathbf{X_j}, \mathbf{H_i}) + P_r(\mathbf{X_j}, \mathbf{H_i})}{R} Prob(\mathbf{X_j}), i = 1, 2, \ldots, N \tag{21}$$

Where $Prob(\cdot)$ is the probability function. When grid is small enough we can get the near-optimal result. To make the calculation faster, two-dimensional FFT is utilized.

Expression (7) and(15) can both denote energy cost of RS and BS, because when $d_{BR_i}^{b_2} = 0$,(7)=(9),(15)=(9). And (7), (15) can be both expressed as $EE_{RS_i} = g(\mathbf{X} - \mathbf{H_i})$. So (17) can be transformed into

$$\min_{\mathbf{H_i}} \sum_{\mathbf{X_j} \in S_i} g(\mathbf{X_j} - \mathbf{H_i}) f(\mathbf{X_j}) \tag{22}$$

which is a convolution of $g(\mathbf{X})$ and $f(\mathbf{X})$. Using two-dimensional FFT can largely decrease the complexity of calculation.

After a few iterations of energy efficient cell separation and energy efficient center searching, the near-optimal locations for N RSs will be obtained.

4 Numerical Results for EERP Algorithm

The EERP algorithm was implemented for both AF and DF relays. Both uniform and random traffic distribution is examined. We suppose cell radius $R_{cell} = 1000m$. The channel model we adopted is Urban Macro Model in ITU-R M.2135 [12] with and without LOS as follows,

$$PL_{NLOS} = 39 \log_{10} d + 20 log_{10} d + 20 log_{10} f_c + 13.5$$
$$PL_{LOS} = 22 \log_{10} d + 20 log_{10} d + 20 log_{10} f_c + 28.0 \tag{23}$$

So we can get $a_1 = 10^{-2.1}$, $a_2 = 10^{-3.6}$, $b_1 = 3.9$, $b_2 = 2.2$. When traffic follows uniform distribution $f(\mathbf{X}) = c, c > 0$, the near-optimal RS locations are shown in Fig.4 and Fig.5, when $N = 3, 4, 6, 12$. The cross mark denotes the near-optimal RS locations. We find that channel fading factor b has a great effect on results. In uniform distribution, the near-optimal results show symmetric

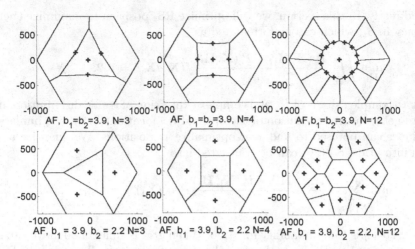

Fig. 4. Near-optimal RS locations for uniform traffic distribution(AF)

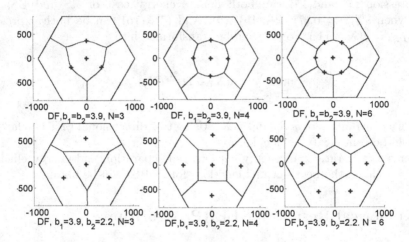

Fig. 5. Near-optimal RS locations for uniform traffic distribution(DF)

placement in a cell. And comparing DF and AF relay strategy, we find that RS locations are almost the same. However, the cell separation boundaries are different, especially when $b_1 \neq b_2$, which conform to the above theorems and corollaries. When traffic distribution $f(\mathbf{X})$ is not uniform, the nearoptimal RS locations are shown in Fig.6. The color shows the normalized traffic density. By comparing with uniform case Fig.5, we can see that energy efficient relay postion of each region tend to be near high traffic density areas. RS locations are not symmetric any more.

In a specific traffic distribution, as shown in Fig.7, nearoptimal RS locations are illustrated for different RS types,different channel conditions and different RS number. When LOS exists between BS and RS, AF and DF have almost the same near-optimal RS locations and similar cell separation diagram. Without LOS

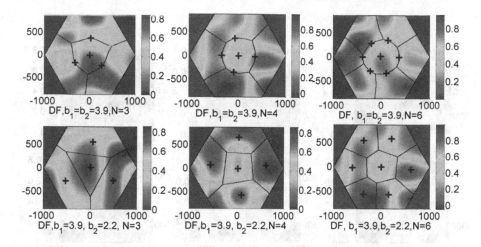

Fig. 6. Near-optimal RS locations under random traffic distribution in DF

between BS and RS, both cell separation boundary and RS locations are different for two kinds of relay strategies. Comparing with uniform traffic distribution, we find that both the RS locations and cell separation boundaries are affected by the distribution.

To evaluate the effectiveness of EERP algorithm, we repeat simulation for 1000 times with N=6 and the same traffic distribution as Fig.7. The red lines are CDF (cumulative distribution function) of cell energy consumption of EERP algorithm with random initial relay positions, while the blue lines are CDF of cell energy consumption when relays are randomly distributed in the cell. From Fig. 8, we can see that EERP algorithm can largely reduce cell energy consumption, and the red lines also prove stability of EERP algorithm.

5   Conclusion

In this work, we propose a traffic-aware energy-efficient relay position searching method for relay-assisted cellular network. We optimize multiple relay locations in a cell based on statistical traffic distribution to maximize energy efficiency. An algorithm named EERP is proposed to solve the problem, which contains an iteration of two steps, i.e. energy efficient cell division and energy efficient center searching. A cell is divided into small subregions covered by RSs and BS based on energy efficient power allocation. Close-form expressions of cell separation boundary are provided, and shapes of cell separation boundary are concluded under certain pathloss factors b. Energy efficient center searching is used to get the optimal RS positions according to cell division and traffic distribution. Two-dimensional FFT is used to reduce the complexity. Simulation results show near-optimal relay positions in different pathloss factors, relay scenarios and relay numbers.

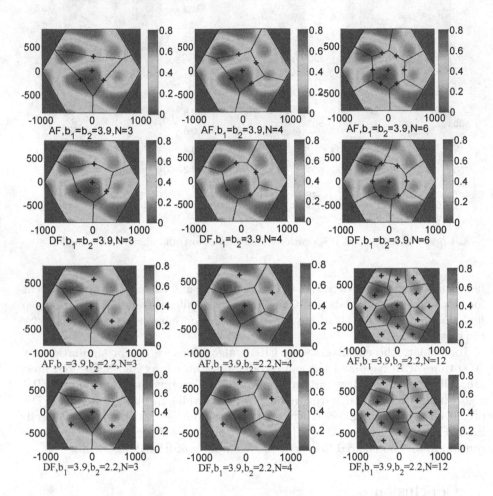

Fig. 7. Near-optimal RS location compare of AF and DF

The main contribution of this paper contains three aspects. First, an algorithm which can effectively obtain near-optimal positions for N RSs is provided. Second, close-form cell division boundary and its shape under some specific pathloss conditions are concluded, which can help placing or selecting relay nodes. Third, energy efficient center searching scheme is based on traffic distribution. Once network planning is proposed based on traffic distribution, less energy will be wasted because of low traffic. FFT is adopted to decrease the complexity from N2 to Nlog2N, which make EERP more practical.

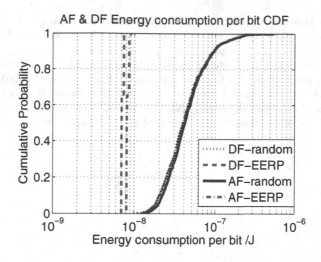

Fig. 8. Energy consumption CDF,when $N = 6$

Acknowledgment. This work is supported by National programs for High Technology Research and Development (SS2012AA011402) and NSFC(61172088).

References

1. Oh, E., Krishnamachari, B., Liu, X., Niu, Z.: Toward dynamic energy-efficient operation of cellular network infrastructure. IEEE Communication Magazine 49(6), 56–61 (2011)
2. Weng, X., Cao, D., Niu, Z.: Energy-Efficient Cellular Network Planning under Insufficient Cell Zooming. In: 73rd IEEE Vehicular Technology Conference (VTC Spring), pp. 1–5 (2011)
3. Niu, Z., Wu, Y., Gong, J., Yang, Z.: Cell zooming for cost-efficient green cellular network. IEEE Communication Magazine 48(11), 74–79 (2010)
4. Yin, R., Zhang, Y., Yu, J.Z.G., Zhang, Z., Optimal, Y.H.: relay location for fading relay channels. In: 72nd IEEE Vehicular Technology Conference (VTC Fall), pp. 1–5. IEEE Press, New York (2010)
5. Lu, H., Liao, W., Lin, F.Y.: Relay station placement strategy in IEEE 802.16j WiMAX Networks. IEEE Trans. on Communications 59(1), 151–158 (2011)
6. Lin, B., Ho, P., Xie, L., Shen, X., Tapolcai, J.: Optimal relay station placement in broadband wireless access networks. IEEE Trans. on Mobile Computing 9(2), 259–269 (2010)
7. Cannons, J., Milstein, L.B., Zeger, K.: An algorithm for wireless relay placement. IEEE Trans. on Wireless Communication 8(11), 5564–5574 (2009)
8. Zhou, Z., Zhou, S., Cui, J., Cui, S.: Energy-Efficient Cooperative Communication Based on Power Control and Selective Single-Relay in Wireless Sensor Networks. IEEE Trans. on Wireless Communication 7(8), 3066–3078 (2008)

9. Zhou, S., Goldsmith, A.J., Niu, Z.: On optimal relay placement and sleep control to improve energy efficiency in cellular networks. In: IEEE International Conference on Communications (ICC), pp. 1–6 (2011)
10. Sendonaris, A., Erkip, E., Aazhang, B.: User Cooperation Diversity–Part I: System Description. IEEE Trans. on Communications 51(11), 1927–1938 (2003)
11. Secord, A.: Weighted Voronoi stippling. In: 2nd International Symposion on Non-Realistic Animation and Rendering (NPAR), pp. 37–43. ACM Press (2002)
12. ITU-R, M.2135: Guidelines for evaluation of radio interface technologies for IMT advanced

Simulation and Analysis of EVDO Network for Mobile Internet Traffic Behavior

Zhou Tao, Liu Chen, Shao Zhen, and Pu Han

Shanghai Research Institute of China Telecom, South Pudong Road,
Shanghai 200122, P.R. China
{zhoutao,liuchen,shaozhen,puhan}@sttri.com.cn

Abstract. In recent years, the popularity of intelligent terminals and diversification of data applications become a great impetus for mobile internet. Undoubtedly, the success of mobile internet brings the benefits for operators, but it makes wireless networks encounter the unprecedented challenges and impacts. This article is based on the newly developed simulation platform which is oriented for mobile internet traffic behavior, and the problems about "signaling storm" and "mobile data bearing value" of EVDO network are studied.

Keywords: EVDO, signaling storm, control channel, access channel, simulation.

1 Introduction

In the EVDO PS domain, the problem about wireless resource occupation when no data is transferring is solved through introducing the dormant state, which makes a data transfer goes through following procedures: air interface connection establishment, data transferring, dormancy time and air interface connection release. With the mobile network development and the influx of internet applications, the traffic behavior such as small burst data and periodic heartbeat mechanism are more notable. Can those applications bring additional value for operators, and what is "mobile data bearing value". At the same time, it should be evaluated that whether it will cause more overload for control channel and access channel of the mobile network, leading to signaling storm. In the traditional simulation platform, only capability of traffic channels is considered, which cannot meet simulation need for mobile internet traffics. From the above, the new simulation platform development should be in first place.

2 Simulation Process of the New Platform

The new simulation platform is based on traditional timeslot-driven traffic channel simulation process. The simulation input will be single-user real test trace which fits for statistical characterisation of traffic scenarios defined by 3GPP. Reasonable separation of simulation process of forward link and reverse link is achieved by adding judgment

H. Qian and K. Kang (Eds.): WICON 2013, LNICST 121, pp. 137–144, 2013.

of state transition between forward link and reverse link. Then, simulation process of forward control channel and reverse access channel will be introduced.

In the simulation process of forward link, three channels are considered. Synchronous Control channel is used to send sync message, quick-config message, sector parameter message, paging message, etc. Sub-Synchronous Control channel is used to send paging message, etc. Asynchronous Control channel is used to send traffic channel assignment message、 UATI assignment message, etc.

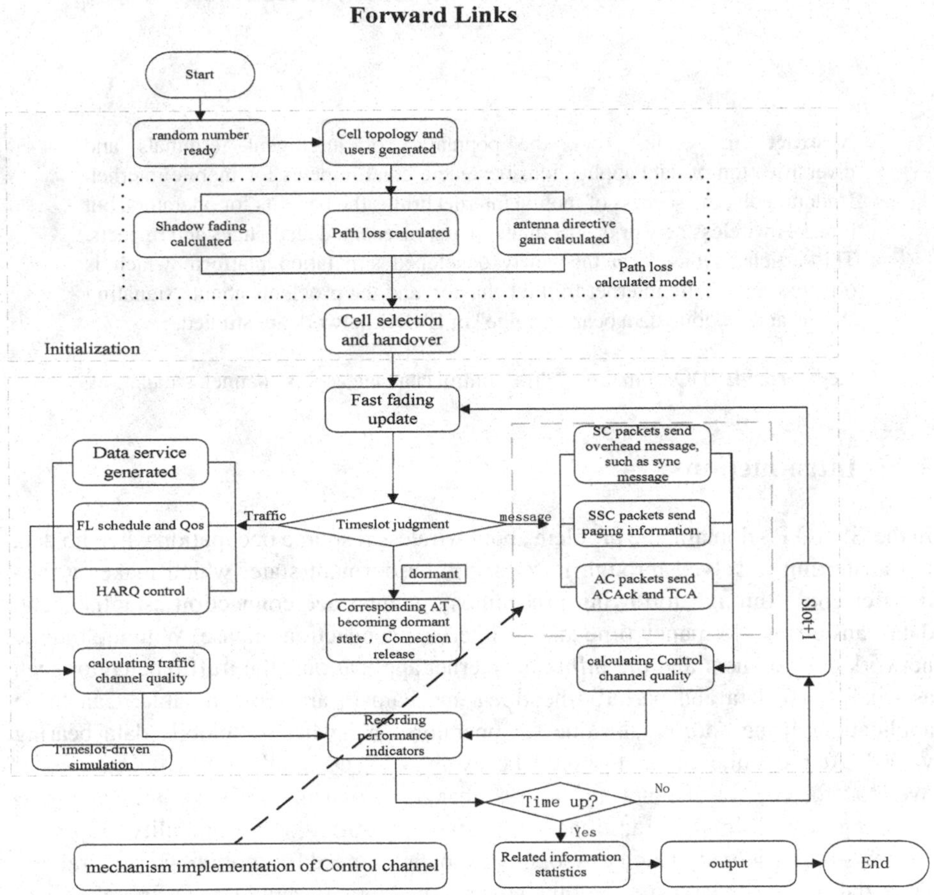

Forward Links

Fig. 1. Simulation procedure of forward link

In the simulation process of reverse link, access sequence, access probe, conformance testing and collision detection which are related with access process are introduced.

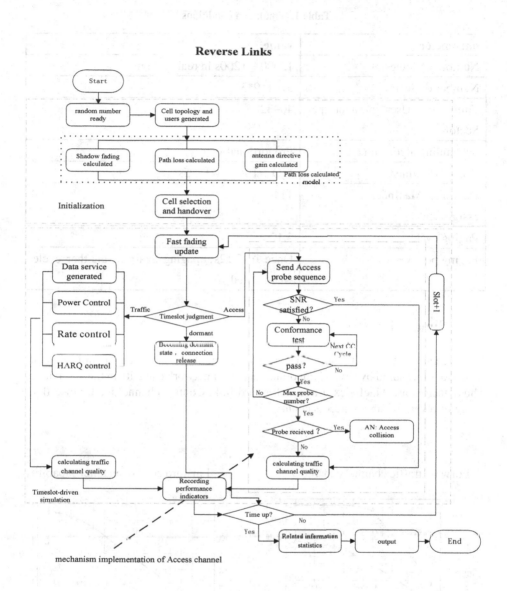

Fig. 2. Simulation procedure of reverse link

3   Simulation Conditions

Resource consumption of wireless network is evaluated for QQ and Microblog. Restricted factors of bearer capability for different traffic scenarios are estimated.

Table 1. Simulation conditions

parameter	value
Number of Timeslot	120000 （200s in real system）
Number of Sector	57 （19*3）
Equivalent User number per Sector	40~320
Scheduling algorithm	Proportional Fair
Dormancy timer	MO : 10s MT : 5s
Downlink MacIndex assignment	114
Paging cycle	5.12s
Paging policy	Once in 5.12s, paging again in another cycle when failed

4   Simulation Result

Bearing capability for QQ and Sina MicroBlog in single sector under multiple cells scenario is measured by several important factors of network capacity in the simulation. Those factors are MacIndex usage of forward link, Control channel load, noise floor rising of reverse channel, access count.

Forward traffic channel capability   Forward control channel capability

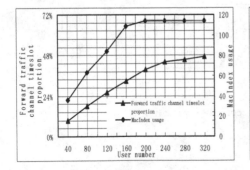
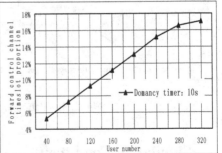

Fig. 3. Simulation results for QQ

Reverse ROT

Reverse access number

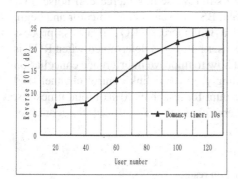

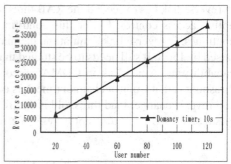

Fig. 3. *(Continued)*

Forward traffic channel capability

Forward control channel capability

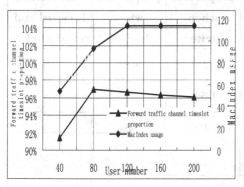

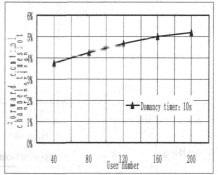

Reverse ROT

Reverse access number

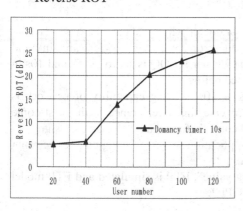

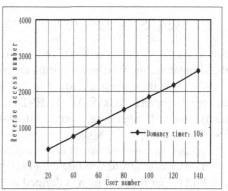

Fig. 4. Simulation results for Sina Microblog

By analyzing simulation results, bearing capability for QQ and Sina MicroBlog in EVDO is limited by reverse link. After the users in reverse link increase, if noise floor in reverse link has exceeded the RAB threshold, BS will send busy indicator and begin uplink access control. Under this condition, it will increase ROT if access process continues. In reverse link simulation, the max user number is determined when ROT is raised by 15dB. It still needs to be studied that how to improve interference cancellation capability in reverse link in CDMA. Accordingly, forward link control channel load threshold is that Control channel timeslots account for less than 20% of total timeslots, and reverse channel load threshold is that reverse channel access timeslots account for less than 40% of total timeslots in engineering.

Table 2. Simulation result

Application	direction	Max user number	Limitation	Control timeslot proportion when limited	Traffic timeslot proportion when limited	Bearer Capability（considering forward and reverse link）
QQ	forward	180	MacIndex	6.5%	80%	65
	reverse	65	ROT	1.5%		
Sina MicorBlog	forward	80	Traffic timeslot proportion	5.45%	94%	60
	reverse	60	ROT	1.15%		

In EVDO, the dormancy timer is a key parameter which balance the load between traffic channel and signaling channel(including control channel of forward link and access channel of reverse link). The dormancy timer for QQ is set to 2s, 5s and 10s in the simulation, the simulation results are listed below.

Whatever the dormancy timer is 2s, 5s or 10s, bearing capability of network is limited by reverse link ROT. In EVDO, reverse link interference is the first-come restriction and "signaling storm" will not come before that. Sometimes, "signaling storm" may happen for a short time when application servers of a popular service shut down causing many terminals keep connecting to the servers.

In order to evaluate "mobile data bearing value", FTP is simulated and FTP model use Full buffer model which is defined in 3GPP2.

Forward traffic channel capability

Forward control channel capability

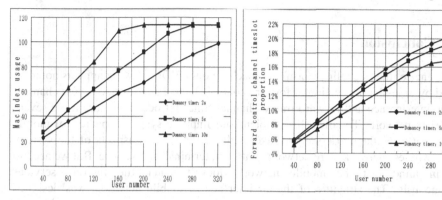

Reverse ROT index

Reverse access number

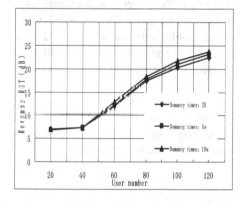

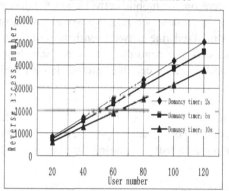

Fig. 5. Simulation results of different dormancy timer configuration (QQ)

Table 3. Throughput per sector when reaches their max capability for three services traffics

Application	Throughput per sector when reaches max capability
QQ	65 users, Forward 30kbps, Reverse 20kbps
Sina MicroBlog	60 users, Forward 300kbps, Reverse 96kbps
FTP	Forward 920kbps, Reverse 436kbps

Simulation results reveal that throughput of FTP is larger than that of QQ using the same bearing resources, which means FTP has a higher "mobile data bearing value". For operators, the bigger challenge than "signaling storm" is how to solve the problem of "mobile users increasing without corresponding profit" which mobile internet traffic brings.

5   Conclusion

The essence of the "signaling storm" approaching our EVDO network appears not to be limited by time-slot occupation of forward control channel and reverse access channel, reverse interference and forward traffic channel time-slot occupancy are more severe for EVDO network. To solve this problem and improve system capacity for mobile internet services, the carriers could take methods via various aspects of the system, such as wireless network, core network, platform, terminal, and service. But we need to bear in mind that the mobile network doesn't match the Internet services spontaneously. The structure of the air interface of mobile networks was designed about 10 years ago, when all today's popular mobile Internet services didn't exist. Therefore the mobile network was not designed to satisfy these services. And if we take a look at these services, we would find most of them are based on IP, a protocol come from fixed line network with no consideration of mobile network scenario. Mobile network use centralized resource scheduling because of the consideration of limited wireless resource, but internet is designed differently because they think every end point should have equal usage of bandwidth. To make things worse, both mobile communication technology and IP technology are too popular today to make any big change to fit with each other. Thus we could conclude that current solutions for mobile internet performance optimization can only temporarily relieve the network pressure, and the industry is waiting for a revolution to solve the problem completely.

References

[1] 3GPP2.C.S0024-A v3.0 CDMA2000 High Rate Packet Data Air Interface Specification. 3GPP2 (2006)
[2] 3GPP2.C.R1002-B CDMA2000 Evaluation Methodology Revision B.3GPP2 (2009)

A Novel Mobility Model for Mobile Ad Hoc Networks

Cheng Li, Zhangdui Zhong, Hao Wu, and Lei Xiong

State Key Laboratory of Rail Traffic Control and Safety,
Beijing Jiaotong University,
Shangyuancun 3, 100044, Beijing, China
licheng1988@gmail.com

Abstract. In this paper, we investigate mobility models in mobile ad hoc networks (MANETs) and propose a novel mobility model for mobile ad hoc nodes with intelligence. The proposed model named Attracting Group Mobility (AGM) Model means mobile node moving from one attracting point to another. Compared to the traditional mobility models, the proposed model has intelligent property. Once a reference point is full, mobile nodes can't enter even they are attracted and the mobile nodes already in the reference point may leave it with a probability. Besides, mobile nodes have inertia that moving speed and direction have only a small variation. Moreover, inhomogeneity is discussed in this paper. Simulation results show that the proposed mobility model can also be a method of generating inhomogeneity distribution.

Keywords: Mobile ad hoc networks, mobility model, inhomogeneity.

1   Introduction

Mobile ad hoc networks (MANETs) are growing at a very fast rate, and are likely to continue in the future. How to effectively mimic moving behaviors of mobile nodes in a real environment is a challenging issue. Besides, the evolution of improved designs and new systems will always depend on the ability to predict MANETs performance using simulation methods [1].

The challenging of building an effective mobility model has motivated many researchers to propose mobility models and use them in their simulation. For instance, random waypoint (RWP) model [2-3] and random direction (RD) model [4] are most commonly used mobility models. They all have sharp turn, and base on random distribution. Small world in motion (SWIM) [5] presents a small world in motion, a mobility model that can be set by setting just a few parameters. Semi-Markov Smooth (SMS) model [6] can avoid average speed decay problem and always maintains a uniform spatial node distribution.

Existing mobility models aimed at mobile nodes without life. However, nowadays many mobile nodes are set on people or animals such as cows and sheep. So, the social behavior should be taken into account. Existing random mobility models have their limitations such as totally random mobile nodes and no prediction which don't accord with life's law of motion. Our intelligent group mobility model just hits it.

H. Qian and K. Kang (Eds.): WICON 2013, LNICST 121, pp. 145–154, 2013.

Moreover, people and animals have intelligence; they can be attracted such as applicants being attracted by recruitment table, people on the square being attracted by performance, animals being attracted by food and drinking water. Even if there is no physical attraction source, people and animals may form some group by themselves. But if a group is too crowded, people and animals may feel ill and leave out. Thus, this paper proposes a novel group mobility model, named as Attracting Group Mobility Model, aimed at the characteristic of such mobile nodes.

The remainder of the paper is organized as follows: Section II briefly discusses the related work of mobility models. In Section III, we describe our group mobility model in details. Section IV describes the defined inhomogeneity measure with equations and derives the inhomogeneity's upper bound of the proposed mobility model. Section V shows a case study of using the model to simulate some properties such as inhomogeneity. And finally in Section VI, we summarize this work and point some issues for further research.

2   Related Work

There were already many models used to describe the movement of mobile nodes in MANETs [7]. In general, classic mobility models could be categorized into entity mobility models and group mobility models. The two most commonly used entity models were the RWP model and the RD model.

According to the RWP model, the movement of a mobile node can be described by a stochastic process. At first, the initial position (x, y) of a mobile node was chosen uniformly over the simulation area, that is x and y were uniformly distributed over $[0, X_{max}]$ and $[0, Y_{max}]$, respectively. For each time state, a node selected a destination inside the simulation area and moved at a constant speed v toward the destination, in which v was uniformly chosen over $[V_{min}, V_{max}]$. When the destination was reached, the node stayed there for a pause time. Later, the node chose the new destination and speed, and started the new movement. The shortcoming of RWP model were that it had sharp turn and based on random distribution.

According to the RD model [8], a mobile node moved with a certain speed which was chosen from a uniform distribution for a selected direction. After certain time which was selected, it paused for a certain period and then started over.

SWIM [5] presented small world in motion, a mobility model for MANETs. SWIM was relatively simple, was easily set by just setting a few parameters. SWIM was proved to generate traces that look real, and it could provide an accurate estimation of forwarding protocols in real mobile ad hoc networks.

Semi-Markov Smooth model [6] presented a mobility model that had characters such as evenly speed acceleration/deceleration and temporal correlation of velocity. The entire moving process in SMS model was smooth just as in real scenarios. SMS model had no average speed decay problem and could appropriately and flexibly mimic widespread real motion. Besides, SMS model could maintain a uniform spatial node distribution.

In Charge Vector Group mobility model [9], mobile nodes could carry a kind of charge and transit among three states named individual movement, tracking and group movement. And reference point could carry another kind of charge and generate force field to attract mobile nodes. The Charge Vector Group mobility model could simulate motions such as grouping in proposed, individual random movement, aggregating and disaggregating. The model had shown characters in real moving behaviors such as randomness and some orderliness.

3   Proposed Attracting Group Mobility Model

3.1   Mobiles in Real Life

In this section, we propose our group mobility model. There are two mobile states in mobility model. One is individual state; the other is group mobile state. Once captured by a reference point (RP), mobile node begins group mobile state. For instance, recruitment table are put in order and motionless in the recruitment hall. Applicants wander outside the recruitment table. When an applicant is attracted by a recruitment table, and the table is not full, he or she could enter the recruitment table. If a recruitment table is not full, everyone could not leave; on the contrary, if the table is full, everyone's leaving probability is equal. Meanwhile, mobiles in real life also have their inertia. People often move at a certain range of speed and ahead to a certain range of angle. Even they would like to change, they may not change sharply.

3.2   Model Description

In the following, we describe the model's basic characteristics. Consider a scenario of nodes moving in a square area with section blocks. RPs are randomly distributed on lattice points, which are uniformly distributed in the area. The space between lattice points Δ is twice larger than the radius of RP's coverage R. We consider a set of mobiles moving around in a given domain. Each mobile node has two mobile states. One is individual state, mobile nodes wandering in the simulation area, we regard it as state 0; the other is group mobile state, mobile nodes moving around RP, we regard it as state 1. Then we get a state transition diagram as Fig.1.

Fig. 1. Markov state transition diagram

The speed and direction of the proposed model are different from RWP model. We get,

$$v_{t+1} = (1-\alpha)v_t + \alpha\Delta v$$

where, v_t denotes the velocity of current time, v_{t+1} denotes the velocity of next time, v_0 denotes the velocity of initial time, $v_0 \sim U(0, V_{max})$. Δv denotes the increment of velocity, $\Delta v \sim U(0, V_{max})$. α is a parameter.

$$\theta_{t+1} = \theta_t + \alpha \Delta \theta$$

where θ_t denotes the direction of current time, θ_{t+1} denotes the direction of next time, θ_0 denotes the direction of initial time, $\theta_0 \sim U(-\pi, \pi)$. $\Delta \theta$ denotes the increment of direction, $\Delta \theta \sim U(-\pi, \pi)$.

Regard mobile nodes' mobile state at k time as $T_k \in \{0,1\}$, $k=0,1,2,....$ Regard the maximum number of mobile node that a RP could tolerance as N_{max}. If a mobile node moves ahead to a RP, and the RP is not full, mobile node transits from state 0 to state 1. Otherwise, mobile node maintains at state 0. If RP's mobile nodes equals to the maximum number of mobile nodes that a RP could tolerance, mobile node is selected according to a departure probability $p_1 = 1/N_{max}$ to transit from state 1 to state 0. Otherwise, mobile node maintains at state 1.

4   Defined Inhomogeneity Measure

An objective measure for the inhomogeneity of spatial distributions has defined in the literature [10]. The computation of the inhomogeneity is shown as follow.

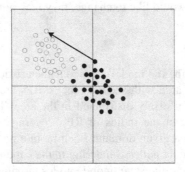

Fig. 2. Offset for a moved cluster

1) Divide the simulation area A into s^2 subareas with the same proportion.

2) Count the numbers of the nodes in each subarea.

3) Compute the expected number of the nodes in each subarea with uniform distribution.

4) Compare the actual numbers of the nodes to the expected number of the nodes, and accumulate the absolute deviation.

5) The weighted sum over all segmentations is calculated yielding the final inhomogeneity value.

6) Consider all possible offsets (x, y) as shown in Fig.2. So that we can achieve the same inhomogeneity value h for distributions which only differ in mirroring, movement and so on.

7) All nodes are moved x length units in horizontal direction and y length units vertically. Offset is picked that maximizes the local deviation for each subdivision. The number of nodes in the ith subarea for a given offset (x, y) is called $m_{i, (x, y)}$.

The measure is normalized on the interval [0,1]. While 0 signifies a optimal grid distribution and 1 signifies absolute inhomogeneity with all nodes at the same position.

$$h(s) = \max_{(x,y)} h_{(x,y)}(s) \tag{1}$$

where,

$$h_{(x,y)}(s) = \frac{1}{2n} \sum_{i=1}^{s^2} \left| m_{i,(x,y)} - \bar{m}(s) \right| \tag{2}$$

The average mobile nodes in each subarea is $\bar{m}(s) = n/s^2$. The subareas can be categorized into those with RP and without RP. So, let S_0 denotes the set of the indexes of the subareas without RPs, and S_1 denotes the set of the indexes of the subareas with RPs.

Assumption 1:

The subarea with RP has N_{max} mobile nodes at most. That is, $m_{i, (x, y)} = N_{max}$.

Assumption 2:

The number of mobile nodes in the subarea without RP is less than the average values. That is, $m_{i, (x, y)} < \bar{m}(s), i \in S_0$.

According to equation 1, clearly, the inhomogeneity reaches the maximum value when all the RP located in the center of subareas. Thus, the upper bound of inhomogeneity is as follows:

$$h_u(s) = \frac{1}{2n} \left[\sum_{i \in S_0} \left| m_{i,(x,y)} - \bar{m}(s) \right| + \sum_{i \in S_1} \left| m_{i,(x,y)} - \bar{m}(s) \right| \right]$$

$$= \frac{1}{2n} \left[\sum_{i \in S_0} \left(-m_{i,(x,y)} + \bar{m}(s) \right) + \sum_{i \in S_1} \left(N_{max} - \bar{m}(s) \right) \right] \tag{3}$$

$$= N_{RP} \left(\frac{N_{max}}{n} - \frac{1}{s^2} \right)$$

Due to the above two assumptions, the upper bound is only a loose bound. However, the following simulation will show that the upper bound has a good approximation.

5   Simulation

Upon above description of the proposed model, in this section, we set up a scenario and simulate it as a case study. Consider a scenario of nodes moving in 100m×100m area with 20×20 section blocks as Fig.3. Circles represent RPs, red stars represent mobile nodes. Such scenario is to simulate mobiles' individual and group mobility in a recruitment hall. There are 20 RPs in the simulation area. They are stationary, as if fixed recruitment table. The RPs are randomly distributed on lattice points, which are uniformly distributed in the simulation area. The space between lattice points is twice larger than the radius of RP's coverage. The radius of RP's coverage is $R=2.5m$. The maximum number of mobile nodes that a RP can tolerance is $N_{max}=20$. The parameter $\alpha=0.05$. The upper bound of inhomogeneity is calculated as 0.75.

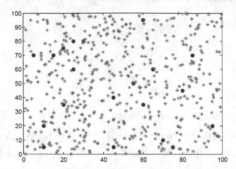

Fig. 3. Initial spatial node distribution of mobile nodes

5.1   Distribution of Mobile Nodes

In the simulation area, there distributed many mobile nodes. We first analyze the impact of the moving parameters on the node distribution. Many parameters affect the node distribution such as the number of mobile nodes, the number of RPs, the velocity of mobile nodes, mobile times of mobile nodes, the coverage of the RP, maximum number of mobile nodes in RP's coverage and so on. In the experiments, it is performed with a varying maximum speed of mobile nodes. For the number of nodes $n=500$, Fig.4a, Fig. 4b and Fig. 4c show how the node distribution changes if we increase maximum speed of mobile nodes from 0.5m/s (Fig.4a) over 1m/s (Fig.4b) to 2m/s (Fig.4c). In the recruitment hall, someone moves fast like running; someone moves slowly like watching advertisement while walking. From the process of simulation, we know that the higher the maximum speed of mobile nodes is, the more clustered the simulation picture is.

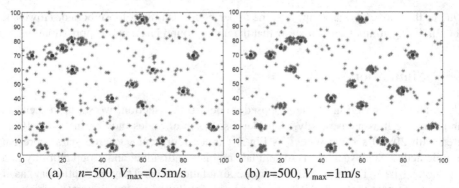

(a) $n=500$, $V_{max}=0.5m/s$ (b) $n=500$, $V_{max}=1m/s$

Fig. 4. Spatial node distribution after 300 seconds simulation

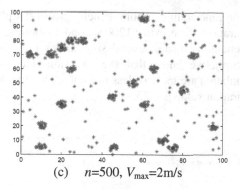

(c) n=500, V_{max}=2m/s

Fig. 4. *(Continued)*

5.2   The Moving Trace of a Single Mobile Node

Single mobile node has two mobile states in the simulation. One is cruise state outside RP, the other is captured state inside RP. A mobile node may be captured by a RP, and then leave it. After moving for a while, it may be captured by another RP. Fig.5 shows the moving trace of a single mobile node with V_{max}=1m/s. From the figure, we can see that the node begins moving in cruise state. Then it encounters boundary and rebounds to the simulation area at once. Afterward, it is captured by a RP located in (85,70) and then it releases from the RP. It encounters boundary again, and rebounds to the simulation area. After rebounding, the mobile node moves in cruise state for a while and is finally captured by another RP located in (30,80). Clearly, the trace of the proposed model is more accord with the law of life's motion than that of RWP model.

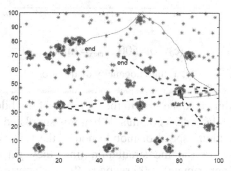

Fig. 5. The moving trace of a single mobile node (solid line denotes the trace of AGM, dot line denotes the trace of RWP)

5.3   Measuring Inhomogeneity in Spatial Distribution

In the following simulation, we measure inhomogeneity of mobile nodes using equations. As Fig.6, x axis means simulation time, y axis stands for inhomogeneity.

In Fig.6a, as simulation time adding, inhomogeneity grows sharply until 1200 seconds when it reaches a saturation value. After 1200 seconds, inhomogeneity keeps a steady value with small fluctuations. From several simulations in Fig.6a (each line means one time of simulation), we know that the variation rules of inhomogeneity in different times of simulation are more or less the same wherever RP and mobile nodes are, and the final saturation value is 0.75.

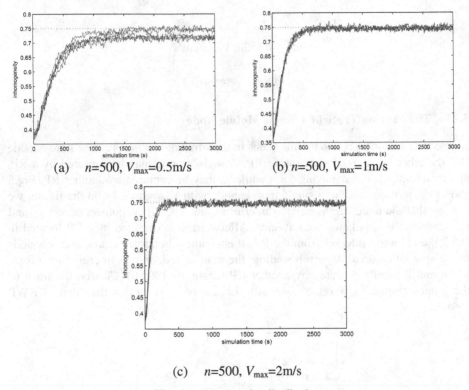

(a) $n=500$, $V_{max}=0.5$m/s   (b) $n=500$, $V_{max}=1$m/s

(c) $n=500$, $V_{max}=2$m/s

Fig. 6. Inhomogeneity distribution

The above simulation is done when the number of mobile nodes is 500 and maximum speed of mobile nodes is 0.5m/s. When it is simulated at 1m/s (Fig.6b), and 2m/s (Fig. 6c) for maximum speed of mobile nodes, the variation rules are more or less the same. Except for the the simulation time they get saturation value are different, for 1m/s is approximately 600 seconds, 2m/s is approximately 300 seconds. From the result, we know that the mobile time reaching saturation value is inversely proportional to the maximum speed of mobile nodes. On the other hand, the saturation values are the same for different maximum speed of mobile nodes. From this, we know that the saturation value has no matter with the maximum speed of mobile nodes. Besides, this mobility model can be a method of generating inhomogeneity distribution.

6   Conclusion

In this paper, we propose a novel mobility model for mobile ad hoc nodes with intelligence named Attracting Group Mobility Model. The proposed model takes the social behavior into account. The inhomogeneity's upper bound is derived. What's more, the variation rules of inhomogeneity in different times of simulation are more or less the same wherever RP and mobile nodes are. Meanwhile, we know that the mobile time reaching saturation value is inversely proportional to the maximum speed of mobile nodes. And the saturation value has no matter with the maximum speed of mobile nodes. This paper has just given a novel idea for modeling mobile node with intelligence. However, the performances evaluation of network protocols and routing with the proposed mobility model should be studied deeply in the future.

Acknowledgment. This work is supported by the National Natural Science Foundation of China under Grant(No.61222105), the Key grant Project of Chinese Ministry of Education(No.313006), the Program for Changjiang Scholars and Innovative Research Team in University under Grant (IRT0949), the Coal Joint Fund of National Natural Science Foundation of China and the Shenhua Group (Grant No. U1261109), and the Fundamental Research Funds for the Central Universities(2010JBZ008 and 2012JBZ017), the State Key Laboratory of Rail Traffic Control and Safety (RCS2011ZZ002).

References

[1] Bansal, N., Liu, Z.: Capacity, delay and mobility in wireless ad-hoc networks. In: 22th Conference of the IEEE Computer and Communications, pp. 1553–1563 (2003)

[2] Yoon, J., Liu, M., Noble, B.: Random waypoint considered harmful. In: 22th Annual Joint Conference of the IEEE Computer and Communications, pp. 1312–1321 (2003)

[3] Bettstetter, C., Resta, G., Santi, P.: The node distribution of the random waypoint mobility model for wireless ad hoc networks. IEEE Transactions on Mobile Computing 2(3), 257–269 (2003)

[4] Nain, P., Towsley, D., Liu, B., Liu, Z.: Properties of random direction models. In: 24th Conference of the IEEE Computer and Communications, pp. 1897–1907 (2005)

[5] Mei, A., Stefa, J.: Swim: A simple model to generate small mobile worlds. In: 28th Conference of the IEEE Computer and Communications, pp. 2106–2113 (2009)

[6] Zhao, M., Wang, W.: Wsn03-4: A novel semi-markov smooth mobility model for mobile ad hoc networks. In: IEEE Global Telecommunications Conference, pp. 1–5 (2006)

[7] Le Boudec, J.-Y., Vojnovic, M.: Perfect simulation and stationarity of a class of mobility models. In: 24th Conference of the IEEE Computer and Communications, pp. 2743–2754 (2005)

[8] Royer, E., Melliar-Smith, P., Moser, L.: An analysis of the optimum node density for ad hoc mobile networks. In: IEEE International Conference on Communications, pp. 857–861 (2001)

[9] Tu, L., Zhang, F., Wang, F., Wang, X.: A random group mobility model for mobile networks. In: Symposia and Workshops on Ubiquitous, Autonomic and Trusted Computing, pp. 551–556 (2009)
[10] Schilcher, U., Gyarmati, M., Bettstetter, C., Chung, Y.W., Kim, Y.H.: Measuring inhomogeneity in spatial distributions. In: IEEE International Conference on Vehicular Technology Conference, pp. 2690–2694 (2008)

Two-Hop Geographic Multipath Routing in Duty-cycled Wireless Sensor Networks

Yuhui Dong[1,4], Guangjie Han[1,2], Lei Shu[3],
Hui Guo[1], and Chuan Zhu[1,2]

[1] Department of Information & Communication Systems,
Hohai University, Changzhou, China
[2] Changzhou Key Laboratory of Sensor Networks
and Environmental Sensing, Changzhou, China
[3] College of Electronic Information and Computer,
Guangdong University of Petrochemical Technology, China
[4] The Patent Examination Cooperation Center of SIPO, Jiangsu, China
{titiyaya09,hanguangjie,guohuiqz,dr.river.zhu}@gmail.com, lei.shu@live.ie

Abstract. As an extension of our previous designed Two-Phase geographic Greedy Forwarding (TPGF) routing algorithm in wireless sensor networks (WSNs), this paper proposes a new 2-hop geographic greedy forwarding algorithm called TPGFPlus, which uses 2-hop neighborhood information for geographic routing. In our TPGFPlus, a forwarding node selects its next-hop node which is closest to the based station among all its 1-hop and 2-hop neighbor nodes. Moreover, to prolong network lifetime, not all the nodes are awake for working in our work since the EC-CKN algorithm is applied to make the network be duty-cycled. We evaluate the performance of our algorithm versus running existing TPGF algorithm on the same duty-cycled WSNs. Simulations show that our proposed algorithm outperforms previous work TPGF on finding more average paths and shorter average length of paths, yet without causing additional energy consumption.

Keywords: Duty-cycle, Wireless sensor networks, 2-hop neighborhood, Geographic routing.

1   Introduction

Geographic routing is considered to be an efficient and scalable data delivery scheme and is quite commonly adopted for information delivery in large scale WSNs . The basic idea for geographic routing is greedily forwarding data packets to the neighbor geographically closest to the destination. Sensors need only maintain local knowledge on the locations of their one-hop neighbors to select their next forwarders [2,8].

TPGF routing algorithm [9] is one of the earliest geographical multipath routing algorithms designed for multimedia transmission in static & always-on WSNs. In TPGF, packets are expected to proceed in such a greedy manner: they are always forwarded to a node closest to the based station among all

H. Qian and K. Kang (Eds.): WICON 2013, LNICST 121, pp. 155–166, 2013.
© Institute for Computer Sciences, Social Informatics and Telecommunications Engineering 2013

1-hop neighbors. Such a greedy strategy, were it to succeed, can explore the maximum number of near shortest node-disjoint multipaths. Early studies (e.g., [1,2,3,4]) assume all sensors are always on during forwarding. However, several recent studies [5], [8], [11], [12] have stressed that such assumption of previous works is unrealistic, for sensors in practical deployment are duty-cycled to save energy. There have also been a few works addressed the problem of geographic forwarding on duty-cycled wireless sensor networks [14], [16], [17], e.g., GeRaF [17] considers geographical forwarding in a wireless mesh network in which sensors know their locations, and are sleep-wake cycling. HM Ammari [8] proposes the first design of a geographic forwarding protocol for duty-cycled k-covered WSNs with data aggregation.

Moreover, the knowledge of the 2-hop neighborhood has been assumed in many distributed algorithm and protocols such as constructing structures, improved routing, broadcasting, and channel assignment [6]. Stojmenovic and Lin [10] have previously proposed GEDIR-2 extending existing geographic routing schemes to two-hop neighbors. It has shown 2-hop GEDIR increases the success rates compared with the 1-hop variant, nevertheless, is also implemented in static & always-on WSNs. It is expected that higher performance improvement will be achieved even if taking the duty-cycle schedule into consideration. Duty-cycling, this important characteristic seems to be ignored in [9,10] and insufficiently studied in [12].

In this work, we address the research of a novel geographic routing combining both characteristics of 2-hop neighborhood and duty-cycling. Specifically, we design a geographic routing protocol using 2-hop neighborhood information on EC-CKN [13] based duty-cycled WSNs.

The rest of the paper is organized as follows: Section 2 reviews related work. Section 3 introduces the network model of our research work. Section 4 describes the design of our algorithm. Section 5 shows the simulation results. Finally, we conclude this paper in section 6.

2   Related Work

2.1   CKN and EC-CKN

The Connected K-Neighborhood sleep scheduling algorithm CKN [14] allows a portion of sensor nodes going to sleep but still keeps all awoken sensor nodes k-connected to elongate the lifetime of a WSN. Then it carries on geographic routing duty-cycled nodes. This algorithm provides the first formal analysis of the performance of geographic routing on duty-cycled WSNs, where every sensor has k awake neighbors.

A variant of this method called EC-CKN [13] prolongs network lifetime further. Different from CKN, EC-CKN takes nodes' residual energy information as the parameter to decide a node to be active or sleep, not only can achieve the k-connected neighborhoods problem, but also can assure the k awake neighbor nodes have more residual energy than other neighbor nodes at the current epoch.

2.2 Geographic Routing with 2-Hop Neighbors

Geographic routing uses position information to forward a message to its destination. Sensor nodes are not required to maintain global and detailed information on the entire network topology. They only need to maintain local knowledge on their one-hop neighborhood information with respect to their final destination. Although most geographic routing protocols use one-hop information, generalization to two-hop neighborhood is also possible [10]. Extending geographic routing schemes to two-hop neighborhood increases success delivery rate, referring to 2-hop GEDIR. Another algorithm called NADV [17] also considers a geographic routing scheme that uses two-hop neighborhood information. Not surprisingly, utilizing two-hop neighborhood information leads to higher-quality paths than the one-hop case.

However, these schemes still cannot guarantee that packets are delivered in an energy-efficient manner. In real networks, nodes commonly employ low duty-cycling and are asleep at most time to get a long battery life [15]. This important feature is ignored in previous work.

2.3 Geographic Multipath Routing in Duty-Cycled WSNs

Although many multipath routing protocols have been studied [18], most of them focus on reducing delay, providing reliability, reducing overhead, maximizing network lifetime or supporting hybrid routing, and are extended versions of DSR [19] and AODV [20]. These routing protocols cannot provide a powerful searching mechanism for the maximum number of shortest paths, as well as bypassing holes [21], not to mention in duty-cycled WSNs. For such drawbacks, we propose TPGFPlus, which is a geographic node-disjoint multipath routing algorithm in duty-cycled WSNs.

To the best of our knowledge, there is no existing multipath routing researching on exploring geographic multipath routing in duty-cycled WSNs.

2.4 TPGF Geographic Multipath Routing

TPGF [9] does not require the computation and preservation of the planar graph in WSNs. This point allows more links to be available for TPGF to explore more node-disjoint routing paths, since using the planarization algorithms actually limits the useable links for exploring possible routing paths. GDSTR [1] is another geographic routing approach that does not apply the planar graph, but maintains two or more hull trees. However, GDSTR does not support multipath routing, since the number of available links in the hull trees topology is limited.

Our TPGF algorithm includes two phases:

- Phase 1 is responsible for exploring a delivery guaranteed routing path while bypassing holes.
- Phase 2 is responsible for optimizing the found routing path with the least number of hops.

TPGF algorithm finds one path per execution and can be executed repeatedly to find more node-disjoint routing paths with the guarantee that any node will not be used twice. At the same time, TPGF algorithm has been well implemented on duty-cycled WSNs based on CKN algorithm through our previous research work [12].

2.5   Our Novelty in TPGFPlus

In conclusion, existing researches either are concerned with duty-cycling or 2-hop forwarding. In this paper, TPGFPlus first tries to consider both duty-cycling and 2-hop geographic forwarding for shortest node-disjoint muli-path routing.

3   Network Model

We model a network with N sensors randomly deployed. The locations of sensor nodes and the base station are fixed and can be obtained by using GPS. Each node knows its own location and the locations of its 1-hop and 2-hop neighbors. r is the communication range of each node.

Definition 1. 2-hop neighbors. Let $N(v_i)$ and $N(v_i)'$ be respectively the sets of node v_i's 1-hop and 2-hop neighbor nodes, that is, v_i's 2-hop neighbors are the neighbors of v_i's 1-hop neighbors after removing the duplicated ones.

We assume all nodes are operated with EC-CKN based wake/sleep duty-cycling. 2-hop neighbors are gathered when executing EC-CKN for sleep scheduling in WSNs. Each sensor dynamically turns on and off the radio in turn based on the 2-hop neighbors' remaining energy information. Time is divided into epochs, and each epoch is T. In each epoch, the node will first transmit packets, and then run the EC-CKN sleep/awake scheduling algorithm to decide the state of the next epoch: sleep or awake. Sensor nodes depend on their current energy levels to adjust power consumption accordingly. Each wireless sensor node is only equipped with a single radio interface, and has the same initial energy E_{init}.

Note that, the impact of MAC layer is ignored in our model. In other words, if the network is collision-free and connected, then each message is delivered.

4   The TPGFPlus Algorithm

We combine 2-hop geographic forwarding and the characteristic of duty-cycled WSNs for a novel multipath routing. *The gathering of 2-hop neighbors is not an additional overhead for TPGFPlus algorithm, since the 2-hop neighborhood information is obligatorily gathered when executing EC-CKN.* But extending to 3-hop or even more will incur extra broadcasting, which is not included in EC-CKN any more. In summary, TPGFPlus algorithm consists of two phases: A) 2-hop geographic forwarding; B) Path optimization.

4.1   2-Hop Geographic Forwarding

This phase consists of two courses: *greedy forwarding* and *step back & mark*.

The *greedy forwarding* policy is: Suppose a current forwarding node always chooses its next-hop node which is closest to the based station among all its 1-hop and 2-hop neighbor nodes and the next-hop node can be further to the base station than itself. Once the forwarding node chooses its next-hop node among its 2-hop neighbor nodes that have not been labeled, it will have to find an intermediate 1-hop direct neighbor that has not been labeled according to some selecting policy. A digressive number-based label is given to the chosen sensor node along with a path number. This greedy forwarding principle is different from the greedy forwarding principle in [2]: a forwarding node always chooses the 1-hop neighbor node that is closer to the base station than itself. And, the Local Minimum Problem does not exist.

Supposing candidate nodes with similar progress to the destination, the one with higher residual energy will first be chosen. In this point, our work is significantly different from the previous TPGF [9] of which the strategy is forwarding the packets to the direct 1-hop neighbor which is nearest to the sink. Fig. 2 and Fig. 1 briefly describe the geographic forwarding process of TPGF and TPGF-Plus respectively.

Fig. 1. 1-hop geographic forwarding example: Node *a* always forwards packets to node *b* since it has the shortest distance to the sink

Though such a method does not have well-known Local Maximum Problem, there may be *block situations* [9]. During the discovering of a path, if any forwarding node has no 1-hop neighbors except its previous-hop node, we will mark this node as a *block node* and this situation as a *block situation*. In this situation, the *step back & mark* course will start. The *block node* will step back to its previous-hop node, which will attempt to find another available neighbor as next-hop node. This course will be repeatedly executed until a node successfully finds a next-hop node to convert back to the *greedy forwarding* course.

4.2   Path Optimization

Though our work use 2-hop neighborhood, path circles also appears. To eliminate the path circles and optimize the found routing path with the least number of hops, we introduce the *label based optimization*. The principle of the *label based*

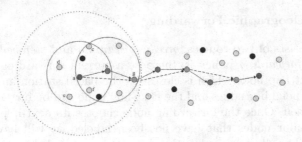

Fig. 2. 2-hop geographic forwarding example: Node a choose 2-hop neighbor g as its next-hop which is closest to the sink among all a's 1-hop and 2-hop neighbors. Once choose g, we have to select b as an intermediate 1-hop direct neighbor.

optimization is: Any node in a path only relays the acknowledgement to its one-hop neighbor node that has the same path number and the largest node number. A release command is sent to all other nodes in the path that are not used for transmission. These released nodes can be reused for exploring additional paths. After receiving the successful acknowledgement, the source node then starts to send out data to the successful path with the pre-assigned path number.

5   Simulation Results

To evaluate the performance of TPGFPlus algorithm, we conduct extensive simulations in NetTopo [22]. The studied WSN has the network size: 800 m * 600 m. The number of deployed sensor nodes are increased from 100 to 1000 (each time increased by 100). The value of k in EC-CKN algorithm is changed from 1 to 10 (each time increased by 1), letting more nodes awake. For every number of deployed sensor nodes, we use 100 different seeds to generate 100 different network deployments, in which ordinary nodes are random distributed. A source node is deployed at the location of (50, 50), and a sink node is deployed at the location of (750, 550). The transmission radius for each node is 60 m. Each node is initialized with a certain amount of energy (100 Units) before deployment. The energy consumption is simulated to be 1 Unit for executing EC-CKN one time in each node. The following performance metrics are evaluated during the simulations:

5.1   The Average Number of Paths of TPGFPlus Algorithm

Fig. 3 shows the comparison of explored average number of paths by TPGF-Plus and TPGF algorithms when the value of k changes for different number of deployed nodes. We can see that TPGFPlus algorithm finds more transmission paths than TPGF. In addition, as shown in Fig. 3, when k exceeds 6, waking up more sensor nodes cannot always increase the number of found paths.

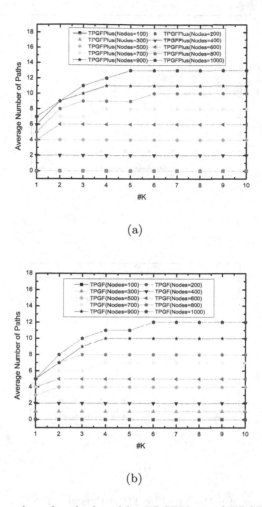

(a)

(b)

Fig. 3. Average number of paths found by TPGFPlus and TPGF vs. the value of k

5.2 The Optimized Average Hops of Paths of TPGFPlus Algorithm

Fig. 4 shows the optimized average hops of paths obtained by TPGFPlus and TPGF algorithms. Both algorithms are not dramatically affected by the changing value of k. But our TPGFPlus utilizes 2-hop neighborhood information and performs better.

5.3 The Comparison of Network Lifetime of TPGFPlus and TPGF Under EC-CKN and CKN Algorithms

The network lifetime in both EC-CKN and CKN based WSNs are represented by the number of epochs. By executing TPGFPlus and TPGF under the same

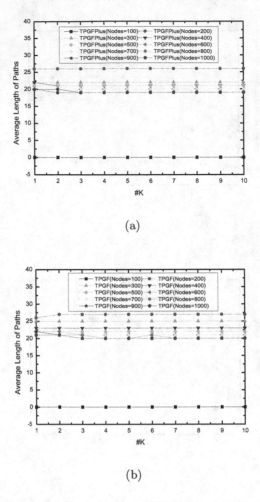

(a)

(b)

Fig. 4. Average hops of paths found by TPGFPlus and TPGF vs. the value of k

situation, simulation results in Fig. 5 reveals that our algorithm incurs no additional energy consumption, while achieving better routing performance in terms of both average number and average hops of paths, but somewhat prolong network lifetime. In addition, Fig. 5 and Fig. 6 reflect that implementing EC-CKN sleep scheduling algorithm prolongs network lifetime over CKN algorithm. Furthermore, it confirms that decreasing the value of k, letting more nodes sleep can definitely prolong the network lifetime, particularly when network nodes are densely deployed.

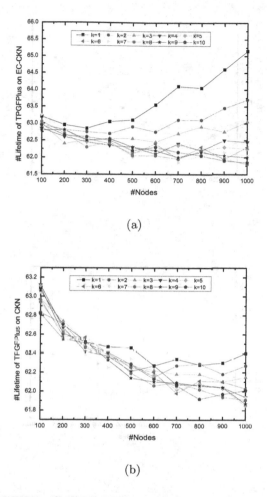

(a)

(b)

Fig. 5. Lifetime of WSNs while TPGFPlus based on EC-CKN and CKN algorithms are executed

6   Conclusions

In this paper, TPGFPlus researches on 2-hop neighborhood information for geographic routing in EC-CKN applied duty-cycled WSNs. In summary, the major contributions of our work can be summarized as follows:

- To the best of our knowledge, few previous works consider utilizing 2-hop neighborhood information for geographic routing and solve the problem of dynamically finding or updating multipath in duty-cycled WSNs,
- Through extensive simulations we evaluate the performance of TPGFPlus and show that it achieves better routing performance in terms of both

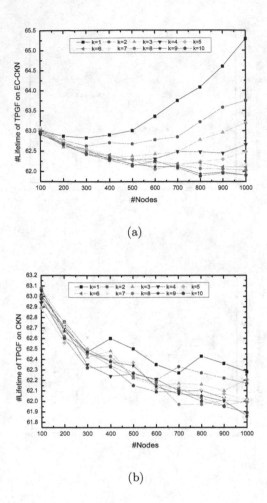

Fig. 6. Lifetime of WSNs while TPGF based on EC-CKN and CKN algorithms are executed

average number and average hops of paths. Moreover, in EC-CKN based WSNs, 2-hop based geographic routing can prolong network, allowing more nodes to sleep while achieving the same desired average number of paths, compared with that of 1-hop based algorithm,

– Geographic routing in duty-cycled WSNs should be 2-hop based, but not 1-hop based, and it is mandatory for gathering 2-hop neighborhood information in most existing sleep-scheduling algorithms.

7 Future Work

As mentioned in previous subsection 4.1, there are several different policies for selecting the intermediate node in TPGFPlus. Particularly, our interests fall into the following three policies:

- Finding an intermediate 1-hop direct neighbor node which is closest to the 2-hop neighbor node. For the first forwarding policy, it will find a neighbor closest to the 2-hop neighbor node and make the maximum progress to the destination.
- Finding an intermediate 1-hop direct neighbor node which forwards packet from current node to its 2-hop neighbor node with the shortest distance. The second forwarding policy attempts to minimize total geographical distance between the source node and the sink.
- Finding an intermediate 1-hop direct neighbor node with the most remaining energy, or the best link quality (interference-minimized), or even the optimal multi-factor weighted cost function value, and so on.

In this paper, due to space limitation, we research on the first policy and provide its simulation results. For future works, we will study other policies and provide comparison among the different policies.

Acknowledgment. The work is supported by "the Applied Basic Research Program of Changzhou Science and Technology Bureau, No.CJ20120028", "the research fund of Jiangsu Key Laboratory of Power Transmission & Distribution Equipment Technology, No.2010JSSPD04" , "the Scientific Research Foundation for the Returned Overseas Chinese Scholars, State Education Ministry" and "the Innovative Research Program for Graduates of Hohai Univ, No.CGB014-09".

References

1. Leong, B., Liskov, B., Morris, R.: Geographic routing without planarization. In: Proceedings of NSDI (2006)
2. Karp, B., Kung, H.T.: GPSR: greedy perimeter stateless routing for wireless networks. In: ACM MobiCom, pp. 243–254 (2000)
3. Kim, Y.J., Govindan, R., Karp, B., Shenker, S.: Geographic routing made practical. In: Proc. NSDI, pp. 217–230 (2005)
4. Bisnik, N., Abouzeid, A.A.: Capacity deficit in mobile wireless ad hoc networks due to geographic routing overheads. In: Proceedings IEEE INFOCOM, pp. 517–525 (2007)
5. Lai, S., Ravindran, B.: On Multihop Broadcast over Adaptively Duty-Cycled Wireless Sensor Networks. In: Rajaraman, R., Moscibroda, T., Dunkels, A., Scaglione, A. (eds.) DCOSS 2010. LNCS, vol. 6131, pp. 158–171. Springer, Heidelberg (2010)
6. Calinescu, G.: Computing 2-hop neighborhoods in ad hoc wireless networks. In: Pierre, S., Barbeau, M., An, H.-C. (eds.) ADHOC-NOW 2003. LNCS, vol. 2865, pp. 175–186. Springer, Heidelberg (2003)

7. Lee, S., Bhattacharjee, B., Banerjee, S.: Efficient geographic routing in multihop wireless networks. In: Proc. ACM MobiHoc, pp. 230–241 (2005)
8. Ammari, H.M., Das, S.K.: Joint k-coverage, duty-cycling, and geographic forwarding in wireless sensor networks. In: IEEE Symposium on Computers and Communications, Sousse, Tunisia, July 5-8, pp. 487–492 (2009)
9. Shu, L., Zhang, Y., Yang, L.T., Wang, Y., Hauswirth, M., Xiong, N.: Tpgf: geographic routing in wireless multimedia sensor networks. Telecommunication Systems 44(1-2), 79–95 (2009)
10. Stojmenovic, I., Lin, X.: Loop-free hybrid single-path/flooding routing algorithms with guaranteed delivery for wireless networks. IEEE Transactions on Parallel and Distributed Systems 12, 1023–1032 (2001)
11. Dutta, P., Grimmer, M., Arora, A., Bibyk, S., Culler, D.: Design of a wireless sensor network platform for detecting rare, random, and ephemeral events. In: ACM/IEEE IPSN (2005)
12. Shu, L., Yuan, Z., Hara, T., Wang, L., Zhang, Y.: Impacts of duty-cycle on TPGF geographical multipath routing in wireless sensor networks. In: The 18th International Workshop on Quality of Service (IWQoS 2010), Beijing, China, June 16-18 (2010)
13. Yuan, Z., Wang, L., Shu, L., Hara, T., Qin, Z.: A Balanced Energy Consumption Sleep Scheduling Algorithm in Wireless Sensor Networks. In: Proceedings of the 7th International Wireless Communications & Mobile Computing Conference (IWCMC 2011), Istanbul, Turkey, July 5-8 (2011)
14. Nath, S., Gibbons, P.B.: Communicating via fireflies: geographic routing on duty-cycled sensors. In: Proceedings of the International Conference on Information Processing in Sensor Networks (IPSN 2007), Cambridge, Massachusetts, USA, April 25-27 (2007)
15. Wang, X., Zhang, X., Zhang, Q., Chen, G.: An Energy-Efficient Integrated MAC and Routing Protocol for Wireless Sensor Networks. In: Proceedings of the 2009 IEEE international Conference on Communications, June 14-18, pp. 1–6 (2009)
16. Biswas, S., Morris, R.: ExOR: Opportunistic multi-hop routing for wireless networks. In: Proc ACM SIGCOMM 2005 Conf. on Applications, Technologies, Architectures, and Protocols for Computer Communication, pp. 133–143 (2005)
17. Zorzi, M., Member, S., Rao, R.R., Member, S.: Geographic Random Forwarding (GeRaF) for Ad Hoc and Sensor Networks: Multi-hop Performance. IEEE Transactions on Mobile Computing 2, 337–348 (2003)
18. Tarique, M., Tepe, K.E., Adibi, S., Erfani, S.: Survey of multipath routing protocols for mobile ad hoc networks. Journal of Network and Computer Applications (2009)
19. Johnson, D.B., Maltz, D.A.: Dynamic source routing in ad hoc wireless networks. In: Mobile Computing. Kluwer Academic Publishers, Dordrecht (1996)
20. Perkins, C.E., Belding-Royer, E.M., Das, S.: Ad hoc on demand distance vector (AODV) routing. IETF RFC 3561
21. Shu, L., Zhang, Y., Yu, Z., Yang, L.T., Hauswirth, M., Xiong, N.: Context-aware cross-layer optimized video streaming in wireless multimedia sensor networks. Supercomput., 94–121 (2010)
22. Shu, L., Wu, C., Zhang, Y., Chen, J., Wang, L., Hauswirth, M.: NetTopo: beyond simulator and visualizer for wireless sensor networks. ACM SIGBED Review 5(3) (October 2008)

Impacts of Network Parameters on Data Collection in Duty-cycled Wireless Sensor Networks

Hui Guo[1], Guangjie Han[1,2], Chenyu Zhang[1], Jia Chao[1], and Lei Shu[3]

[1] Department of Information & Communication Systems,
Hohai University, Changzhou, China
[2] Changzhou Key Laboratory of Sensor Networks
and Environmental Sensing, Changzhou, China
[3] College of Electronic Information and Computer,
Guangdong University of Petrochemical Technology, China
{guohuiqz,hanguangjie,zhangchenyu,chaojia.chj}@gmail.com, lei.shu@live.ie

Abstract. In wireless sensor works (WSNs), data collection is the most important evaluating criterion as well as network lifetime. This paper proposes a novel approach to investigate the most easily adjustable factors, these factors have an influence on network data collection both in coordinated and randomized duty-cycled sleep schedule networks. By analyzing and calculating the energy consumption, expected network lifetime and three major parameters are recognized as the indexes for evaluating the data collection. In addition, since most current WSNs adopt coordinated duty-cycled sleep schedule to reduce energy consumption and prolong network lifetime, we put forward a method to find the most optimal network parameters to guarantee the superiority of this kind of sleep schedule. We choose Connected k-Neighborhood (CKN) as the model of the coordinated sleep schedule. Simulation results show the most optimal network parameters can be found under expected network lifetime.

Keywords: WSNs, network parameters, duty-cycled.

1 Introduction

Recent technological advances have enabled the emergence of tiny, battery-powered sensors with limited on-board signal processing and wireless communication capabilities. WSNs may be deployed for a wide variety of applications [1]. In many applications of WSNs, the amount of data collection is critically essential, it can help to provide more information about real-time environment to a base station, thus help the base station make a proper decision. There are too many factors in WSNs that have impacts on data collection. These factors are inspired from the sensor nodes characteristics (nodes' limited power and cache capacity, etc.), the physical deployment of the WSNs (node density, sleep schedule and nodes' transmission radius, etc.), and the WSNs' information functions

H. Qian and K. Kang (Eds.): WICON 2013, LNICST 121, pp. 167–177, 2013.
© Institute for Computer Sciences, Social Informatics and Telecommunications Engineering 2013

(transmission power, the signal to noise ratio and the radio coverage, etc.). In addition, network lifetime is another key factor of WSNs [2].

It is well known that node power is precious, therefore improving energy efficiency is critical to WSNs. Hence, many research has been done for duty-cycled sleep schedule to save energy. Duty-cycled mechanism can be classified into two basic categories: 1) *Randomized duty−cycled sleep schedule*, individual sensor node performs sleeping and waking up operations independently without checking their neighbor nodes' current status, 2) *Coordinated duty − cycled sleep schedule*, each sensor node performs sleeping and waking up operations according to their neighbor nodes' current status. The major difference between randomized duty-cycled sleep schedule WSNs and coordinated duty-cycle sleep schedule WSNs is the time-varying network connectivity: 1) In randomized duty-cycled WSNs, the network-wide connectivity is not guaranteed, 2) In coordinated duty-cycled WSNs, the network-wide connectivity is guaranteed.

In this paper, we assume nodes in WSNs operating with Connected k-Neighborhood (CKN) based sleep scheduling [3]. Compared to Randomized Sleep (RS) schedule [4], CKN algorithm is more energy balanced and energy consumption is lesser during the same network lifetime. We further investigate the most important and easily regulated network parameters in RS networks and CKN networks, respectively. Based on the results of extensive calculation and simulations, we can find the most superior parameters in CKN based networks to gain the most data collection.

The rest of this paper is organized as follows. In the next section, we summarize the related work, Section 3 we describe our method in details. The simulation along with results is done in Section 4. Finally, the paper is concluded in Section 5.

2 Related Work

2.1 Duty-Cycled Sleep Schedule

Duty-cycled sleep schedule has become a critical mechanism to minimize the energy consumption in WSNs. The basic idea of this mechanism is to put a part of sensor nodes in a low power sleep state instead of idle state. Previous literatures have proposed various duty-cycled sleep schedule for WSNs. In [5], Michael et al. present a low power MAC protocol X-MAC. X-MAC proposes solutions to problems like high energy consumption, excess energy consumption at nontarget receivers by employing a shortened preamble approach that retains the advantages of low power listening, namely low power communication, simplicity and a decoupling of transmitter and receiver sleep schedules.

Ghadimi et al. introduce a novel opportunistic routing metric that takes duty-cycled into account[6]. The method is based on a new metric named Estimated Duty Cycled wake-ups (EDC) that reflects the expected number of duty-cycled waken nodes that are required to successfully deliver a packet from source to destination.

In [7], Yanjun Sun et al. present a new asynchronous duty-cycled MAC protocol, called Receiver-Initiated MAC (RI-MAC), which uses receiver-initiated data transmission in order to efficiently and effectively operate over a wide range of traffic loads. RI-MAC attempts to minimize the time a sender and its intended receiver occupy the wireless medium to find a rendezvous time for exchanging data, while still decoupling the sender and receiver's duty cycle schedules.

In [8], an asynchronous duty cycle adjustment MAC protocol ADCA is proposed. ADCA is a sleep/wake protocol to reduce power consumption without lowering network throughput or lengthening transmission delay. It is asynchronous; it allows each node in the WSN to set its own sleep/wake schedule independently. The media access is thus staggered and collisions are reduced. According to the statuses of previous transmission, ADCA adjusts the duty cycle length for shortening transmission delay and increasing throughput.

2.2 Expected Network Lifetime

In [9], Lei Shu et al. focus on the efficient gathering of multimedia data in WSNs within an expected lifetime. An adaptive scheme to dynamically adjust the transmission Radius and data generation Rate Adjustment (RRA) is proposed based on a cross layer designed by considering the interaction among physical, network and transport layers.

Lei shu et al. also propose a situation where applications generally expect that WSNs can provide continuous streaming data during a relatively short expected network lifetime. Then they solve two basic problems: 1) gathering as much data as possible within an expected network lifetime, 2) minimizing transmission delay within an expected network lifetime [10].

2.3 The RS and CKN Sleep Schedule Algorithm

In RS sleep schedule networks, each sensor keeps an active-sleep schedule independent of another, thus the network is essentially a collection of independent active or sleep process. Hereby we assume the sleep ratio as 1-β (0 <β <1).

CKN sleep schedule is adopted for duty-cycled WSNs. It allows a portion of sensor nodes going to sleep but still keeps all awoken sensor nodes k-connected to elongate the lifetime of a WSN, i.e. every node has k awake neighbors. In terms of that, the following conditions should be guaranteed.

– Each node in the WSN has at least $m=min(k; |Nu|)$ awake neighbors.
– All awake nodes are connected.

2.4 Our Novelty

As a conclusion, while above literatures either concern with expected network lifetime or duty-cycled sleep schedule, or neglect the amount of data collection. We propose a way to find most superior parameters to collect the most amount of data in a specific CKN based network. We make a comparison of energy consumption between CKN and RS sleep schedule, then we further show the results after simulation.

3 Our Approach

3.1 Assumptions and Notations

We consider a set of N wireless sensor nodes (hereafter refers to nodes) uniformly distributed in a square area A. Thus node density is ρ. Each node u has same transmission radius R. As long as an awake node u is in the transmission area of another awake node v, we consider they can communicate with each other, and a number of nodes s form a communication graph called G_s. N_u and N_u' is the set of node u's 1-hop neighbor nodes, C_u and C_u' is the subset of N_u and N_u' under special condition in CKN algorithm. The expected network lifetime until the first node drained of its energy is defined as ELT. ELT is divided into many epochs, which also can be call round. In each round, nodes execute sleep schedule once. Thus the timespan of each round is defined as T, and we use R_d to denote the number of T. We assume all above parameters are the same in RS networks and CKN networks. Let DC be the total amount of data collection by all nodes. Parameters and the initial values are listed in Table 1.

3.2 RTS/CTS Model and First Order Radio Model

As mentioned in [11], under RTS/CTS interference, we get the probability that a node sends a packet P_S equals to the probability that a node receives a packet P_R is

$$P = P_S = P_R = \frac{2AC_1}{N\pi R^2} \tag{1}$$

and the probability that a node keeps idle P_I is

$$P_I = 1 - 2P \tag{2}$$

where C_1 subjects to (3) which is related to the specific network.

$$C_\varepsilon \leq (6\varepsilon + 1)^2 + 11 \tag{3}$$

Each node is equipped with single interface, and has the same initial energy available. Our energy model for nodes is based on the first order radio model [12] where the radio dissipates to power the transmitter or receiver circuitry, and for the transmit amplifier. E_{elec} is the energy required for transceiver circuity to process one bit of data, E_{amp} is the energy required per bit of data for transmitter amplifier, d is the communication radius of node u. Energy consumption to send a l-bit message over distance R is

$$E_S(l, R) = E_{elec}l + E_{amp}ld^2 \tag{4}$$

While transmitter amplifier is not needed by node u to receive data and the energy consumed by node u to receive a l-bit data packet is

$$E_R = E_{elec} * l \tag{5}$$

while E_I, the energy consumed by nodes with the radio in the idle model, is approximately the same with the radio in the receiving mode, i.e.,

$$E_I = E_R \tag{6}$$

Table 1. Parameter definition

Parameter	Definition
$|.|$	The number of network elements in a set
N	Number of sensor nodes in the network
U	Set of sensor nodes
R	Node transmission radius
A	Network area
ρ	Node density
M	Number of packets
T	The unit epoch of time
R_u	Set of node u's neighbors' ranks
k	The determining value in CKN algorithm
$1 - \beta$	Sleep ratio in RS schedule
$rank_u$	Random rank of node u
E_S	Consumed energy to transmit a packet represented by l bits over distance d
E_R	Consumed energy to receive a packet represented by l bits over distance d
E_I	Consumed energy to keep idle
P_{asleep}	Probability of sleep state with CKN
P_{awake}	Probability of awake state with CKN
P_{idle}	Probability of idle state with CKN
N_u/N_u'	The set of node u's 1-hop neighbors and 2-hop neighbors
C_u/C_u'	The sub set of N_u/N_u' whose $rank \leq rank_u$
DC	Data collection of the whole network

3.3 Some Probabilities in CKN Schedule

As mentioned above, CKN algorithm can be described as following two phases.

- Graph $G_{C_u+C_u'}$ is connected.
- Graph G_{N_u} is k-connected by nodes in C_u.

The probabilities of two phases are P_{rob1} and P_{rob2}, respectively. With ρ is node density

$$\rho = \frac{N}{A} \qquad (7)$$

Moreover, the probability that the communication graph G is k-connected can be calculated as the probability that there exists at least k different paths connecting any two different vertices in the graph which is

$$P_{(G_{k-connected})} = (1 - \sum_{n=0}^{k-1} \frac{(\rho \pi R^2)^n}{n!} e^{-\rho \pi R^2})^N \qquad (8)$$

here

$$\rho' = \frac{|U'|}{A} \qquad (9)$$

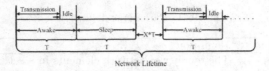

Fig. 1. Node's sleep schedule in RS networks

then we can get that the probability that graph $G_{C_u+C_u'}$ is connected is

$$P_{rob1} = (1 - e^{\rho'\pi R^2})^{(|C_u|+|C_u'|)} \tag{10}$$

and the probability that graph G_{N_u} is k-connected by nodes in C_u is

$$P_{rob2} = (1 - \sum_{n=0}^{k-1} \frac{(\rho'\pi R^2)^n}{n!} e^{-\rho'\pi R^2})^{|C_u|} \tag{11}$$

Thus the sleep probability and awake probability of node u is

$$P_{awake} = 1 - P_{rob1} * P_{rob2} \tag{12}$$

$$P_{asleep} = P_{rob1} * P_{rob2} \tag{13}$$

3.4   Energy Consumption of RS Networks

As aforementioned, in RS networks, nodes sleep ratio is 1-β, β is a random value between 0 and 1. It is well known that nodes energy is mainly consumed in their active epoch, while the energy consumption in sleep epoch can be neglected.

Fig. 1 shows a nodes' sleep schedule in a single epoch in RS networks. In an awake state, nodes turn on their transmit unit, keep transmitting or keep idle, both consumed a lot of energy. But with a certain probability β, nodes transfer into sleep state and save energy. Thus the energy consumption of RS networks is equal to

$$E_T = T\beta M[P_S E_S - P_R E_R + E_R]{=}T\beta M E_1 \tag{14}$$

3.5   Energy Consumption of CKN Networks

Fig. 2 depicts a node's sleep schedule adopting CKN. At the beginning of each single epoch, it costs node T_1 to execute CKN algorithm automatically, we assume T_1 is bound to ω, which is related to the specific network.

$$T_1{=}\omega T(0 < \omega < 1) \tag{15}$$

Then node's state in the rest time of epoch depends on the executive results. Thus time and energy consumption can be calculated if other parameters are fixed.

Therefore, the energy consumption of CKN network can be caculated by

$$
\begin{aligned}
E_{ckn-T} ={}& P_{awake}\{E_{ckn} + T_1[P_S E_S + P_R E_R + \\
& (1 - 2P)E_I]M\} + P_{asleep}E_{ckn}
\end{aligned}
\tag{16}
$$

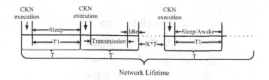

Fig. 2. Node's sleep schedule in CKN networks

3.6   Key Parameters

For the sake of clarity, we denote DC as

$$DC = R_d * N_{act} = \frac{ELT}{T} * N_{act} \tag{17}$$

In (17), N_{act} is the number of nodes which worked or is awaking. With this condition satisfied, DC can be determined by ELT, T and N_{act}. We need to guarantee that CKN networks is more energy efficient, i.e. $E_{ckn-T} < E_T$. Thus (14) and (16) allow us to have a lower bound of T to satisfy this condition

$$T > \frac{E_{ckn}}{ME_1(\beta - \omega P_{awake})} \tag{18}$$

As aforementioned, k is a specific value in CKN algorithm, N is the number of nodes which is changeable with specific WSNs applications, R is transmission radius that varying according to node's power level. Based on those previously analysis, we define k, N, and R is the three regulable parameters as well as expected network lifetime ELT.

The pseudo code of our approach is showed as follows.

Require:

E_T ⇐the energy consumption of WSNs under RS sleep schedule
E_{ckn-T} ⇐the energy consumption of WSNs under CKN sleep schedule
if $E_T > E_{ckn-T}$ **then**
    Find the determine T
else
    return
end if
Determine the datacollection with different values
while datacollection reaches maximum **do**
    return most optimal parameter values.

4   Simulation and Results

4.1   Simulation Settings

All the simulations are implemented with MATLAB. Table 1 shows the simulation parameters.

Table 2. Simulation parameters

Parameters	values
Network size(m^2)	600*800
N	500-1000
k	1-20
$R(m)$	50,60,70
$LT(h)$	40,80,120,160
C1	60
$E_{elec}(J)$	50e-9
$E_{amp}(J)$	0.1e-9
$l(bit)$	1024
M	100
ω	0.8
β	0.5

4.2   Simulation Results

The variation trend of DC with different k, N and ELT as well as R is shown from Fig. 3 to Fig. 5. The x-axis denotes the total node number N in the sensing area, the y-axis represents k, and z-axis stands for DC. The four different colors stand for different ELT as shown in each figure. Since A is fixed, we can regulate node density ρ by changing the number of nodes N.

Fig. 3 shows the variation of DC from different angles when R is 50m, 60m, 70m and 80m. Four curved surfaces of different colors refer to 40h, 80h, 120h and 160h expected network lifetime respectively. The variation tendency of DC is like a shape of saddle. Four curved surfaces in each figure gets their maximum values of DC at the same k when N is fixed. For instance, in Fig. 3(a) when N is fixed to 500, four curves achieve their maximum values of DC when k is equal to 4, while N is fixed 800, the maximum value of DC can be found at k equals 6. Fig. 3 (b),(c) and (d) reflect that the longer network lifetime is, the more DC achieved, but not proportional. This can be explained as follows. When k reaches a certain point, under CKN algorithm, most nodes are awake to insure that there is at least k awake neighbors during network lifetime. DC and T can be calculated by (17) and (18) respectively. Equation (18) reflects the fact that T increases rapidly as P_{asleep} increases consistently, and P_{asleep} is closely related to k. As a result, DC decreases gradually. The more awake nodes, the more energy consumed. If the energy consumption in CKN network becomes larger than a certain threshold value and even larger than the energy consumption of RS algorithm, CKN algorithm will lose its superiority. This simulation results show that we can realize the maximum data collection in CKN networks when preseted N and k under expected network lifetime. When ω and N are fixed to 0.5 and 600 respectively which means node density is fixed, while other parameters are identical to Table I, the variation of DC with different transmission radiuses (from 10m to 150m) is shown in Fig. 4. It is clear that R, k and ELT have a significant influence on the data collection. In Fig. 4(a) and Fig. 4(b), the

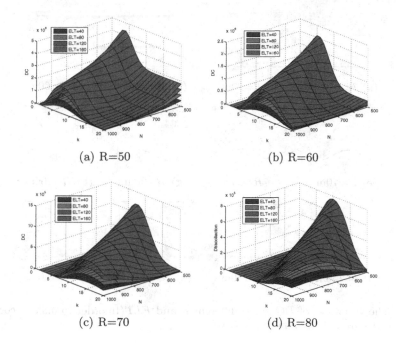

(a) R=50   (b) R=60

(c) R=70   (d) R=80

Fig. 3. The variations of DC when R is $50m$, $60m$, $70m$ and $80m$, respectively

value of DC is much larger than others. It is mainly due to the fact that the shorter transmission radius is, the less energy consumed during the transmission period. While in Fig. 4(c) to Fig. 4(h), the relationship between k and DC is an approximate quadratic curve. That is to say, when R varies from $50m$ to $100m$, there always exists an optimal value of k to achieve maximum DC. When R is equal to $130m$ or $150m$, it seems that the variation tendency of curves is different from previous as shown in Fig. 4(i) and (j). However, Fig. 4(k) and (l) reflect that an approximate quadratic equation also can be found to express parts of the curve when k is large enough. In real applications, k should have appropriate boundaries, neither too large nor too small. In this paper, we do not discuss the boundaries of k, just try to find the relationships among these parameters. These results give a straight solution of finding the most appropriate k to achieve maximum data collection under CKN algorithm.

5   Conclusions

This paper proposes a CKN based energy saving approach to optimize network parameters. In the proposed approach, we assume nodes in WSNs is working according to Connected k-Neighborhood sleep schedule. We provide a theoretical analysis on the energy consumption of networks adopting CKN sleep schedule and RS schedule, then find a bound value to insure the superiority of CKN

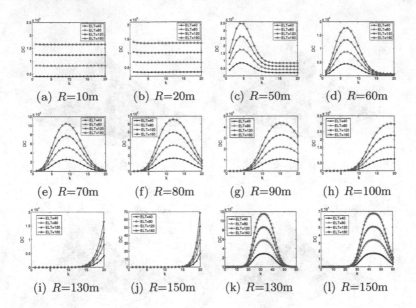

Fig. 4. The variations of DC under different R and ELT(In order to make a comparison, k varies from 1 to 60 in (k) and (l)).

algorithm. Simulation results depict the relationship between data collection and other three different network parameters. Performance analysis can help to select the most appropriate network parameters under expected network lifetime.

Acknowledgment. The work is supported by "the Applied Basic Research Program of Changzhou Science and Technology Bureau, No.CJ20120028", "the research fund of Jiangsu Key Laboratory of Power Transmission & Distribution Equipment Technology, No.2010JSSPD04" , "the Scientific Research Foundation for the Returned Overseas Chinese Scholars, State Education Ministry" and "the Innovative Research Program for Graduates of Hohai Univ, No.CGB014-09".

References

1. Deng, J., Han, Y.S., Heinzelmanc, W.B., Varshney, P.K.: Balanced-energy sleep scheduling scheme for high-density cluster-based sensor network. Applications and Services in Wireless Networks 28(14), 1631–1642 (2005)
2. Mansouri, M., Sardouk, A., Merghem-Boulahia, L.: Factors that may influence the performance of wireless sensor networks. Journal of Software, 29–48 (2010)
3. Nath, S., Gibbons, P.B.: Communicating via Fireflies: Geographic Routing on Duty-Cycled Sensors. In: Proceedings of the 6th International Conference on Information Processing in Sensor Networks (IPSN 2007), pp. 440–449 (2007)
4. Hsin, C.-F., Liu, M.: Network Coverage Using Low Duty-Cycled Sensors: & Coordinated Sleep Algorithms. In: Proceedings of the 3rd International Symposium on Information Processing in Sensor Networks (IPSN 2004), pp. 433–442 (2004)

5. Buettner, M., Yee, G.V., Anderson, E., Han, R.: X-MAC: a short preamble MAC protocol for duty-cycled wireless sensor networks. In: Proceedings of the 4th International Conference on Embedded Networked Sensor Systems (SenSys 2006), pp. 307–320 (2006)

6. Ghadimi, E., Landsiedel, O., Soldati, P., Johansson, M.: A metric for opportunistic routing in duty-cycled wireless sensor networks. In: Proceedings of 9th Annual IEEE Communications Society Conference on Sensor, Mesh and Ad Hoc Communications and Networks, pp. 335–343 (2012)

7. Sun, Y., Gurewitz, O., Johnson, D.B.: RI-MAC: a receiver-initiated asynchronous duty cycle MAC protocol for dynamic traffic loads in wireless sensor networks. In: Proceedings of the 6th ACM Conference on Embedded Network Sensor Systems (SenSys 2008), pp. 1–14 (2008)

8. Yu, C.C., Jehn, R.J., Jang, P.S.: An Asynchronous Duty Cycle Adjustment MAC Protocol for Wireless Sensor Networks. Journal of International Technology 13(3), 395–404 (2012)

9. Shu, L., Hauswirth, M., Zhang, Y., Ma, J., Min, G., Wang, Y.: Cross Layer Optimization for Data Gathering in Wireless Multimedia Sensor Networks within Expected Network. Journal of Universal Computer Science 16(10), 1343–1367 (2010)

10. Shu, L., Zhang, Y., Zhou, Z., Hauswirth, M., Yu, Z., Hynes, G.: Transmitting and Gathering Streaming Data in Wireless Multimedia Sensor Networks within Expected Network Lifetime. In: ACM/Springer Mobile Networks and Applications (MONET), vol. 13, pp. 306–322 (2008)

11. Wang, W., Wang, Y., Li, H.X.-Y., Song, W.-Z.: Ophir Frieder: Efficient interference-aware TDMA link scheduling for static wireless networks. In: Proceedings of the 12th Annual International Conference on Mobile Computing and Networking (MobiCom 2006), pp. 262–273 (2006)

12. Heinzelman, W.R., Chandrakasan, A., Balakrishnan, H.: Energy-Efficient Communication Protocol for Wireless Microsensor Networks. In: Proceedings of the 33rd Annual Hawaii International Conference on System Sciences, January 4-7 (2002)

Innovating R Tree to Create Summary Filter for Message Forwarding Technique in Service-Based Routing

Nguyen Thanh Long[1], Nguyen Duc Thuy[2], Pham Huy Hoang[3], and Tran Dinh Chien[1]

[1] Informatic Center of Ha noi Telecommunications
75 Dinh Tien Hoang, Hoan Kiem, Ha Noi, Viet Nam
{longptpm,chientd}@vnpt-hanoi.com.vn
[2] Research Institute of Posts and Telecommunications
122 Hoang Quoc Viet, Nghia Tan, Cau Giay, Hanoi, Viet Nam
thuynd@ptit.edu.vn
[3] Hanoi University of Science and Technology
1 Dai Co Viet Road, Hanoi, Viet Nam
hoangph@soict.hut.edu.vn

Abstract. In service-oriented routing [5], the problem for storing routing table of filters includes search predicates received from subscribers through subscription messages is an important job. When a content request happens, subscriber will create one subscription message, the subscription message stores several kinds of information, the most important content is filter that is a conjunction of some constraints [5]. One filter is denoted by F character, that has mathematical formula: $F = P_1 \wedge P_2 \wedge \ldots \wedge P_n$ (1), in which P_1 is service request, has format: P_1 = 'Service_name = requested_service_name'. Every P_i (in which $i = \overline{2..n}$) is a constraint that is formed by three components: (Key, op, Value), Key is a keyword for searching, op is an operator, Value is searching condition. Key belongs to the set of name of properties of content that the requested service supplies. Op is operator that depends on the type of data of the Key. Therefore the routing table of the service based routing is a set of filters which are received from all subscribers on networks. The algorithms for inserting, updating, deleting and finding filters that match content messages have been published by service providers are very important. In this paper, We mention the technique on filter summary for storing and searching filter quickly that based on some previous researches and cluster routing [6] based on root's summary filter.

Keywords: Service based routing, filter, constraint, service, routing, tree, split, summary, R, cluster, head.

1 Overview Summary Filter Technique

Considering the overarching concept, assume that there are two filters F_1 and F_2 are requirements of one service that arising from one subscriber. We suppose that F_1 covers F_2 by the notation: $F_1 \ni F_2$ (2), if all messages satisfy conditions of F_2 then they satisfy F_1.

H. Qian and K. Kang (Eds.): WICON 2013, LNICST 121, pp. 178–188, 2013.

Symbol by: $F_1 = P_{12} \wedge P_{13} \wedge \ldots \wedge P_{1n}$, $F_2 = P_{22} \wedge P_{23} \wedge \ldots \wedge P_{2m}$ (3).
In that: $P_{12} = K_{12} op_{12} V_{12}$, $P_{13} = K_{13} op_{13} V_{13}$, ..., $P_{1n} = K_{1n} op_{1n} V_{1n}$,
$P_{22} = K_{22} op_{22} V_{22}$, $P_{23} = K_{23} op_{23} V_{23}$, ..., $P_{2m} = K_{2m} op_{2m} V_{2m}$.
For (2) we must have: $\{K_{12}, K_{13}, \ldots, K_{1n}\} \subseteq \{K_{22}, K_{23}, \ldots, K_{2m}\}$.
Suppose the predicate: $P = K$ op V, called X is the value domain of the constraint, that means the values V are belonged to X that will satisfy the constraint.

If (2) is true, at the same time with conditions: $n \leq m$ and $K_{12} \equiv K_{22}$, $K_{13} \equiv K_{23}$, ..., $K_{1n} \equiv K_{2n}$, and $op_{12} \equiv op_{22}$, $op_{13} \equiv op_{23}$, ..., $op_{1n} \equiv op_{2n}$:
Must have: $X_{12} \supseteq X_{22}$, $X_{13} \supseteq X_{23}$, ..., $X_{1n} \supseteq X_{2n}$.

That means all the keysand operators are contained in F_1 that are also contained in F_2, domain value of each of constraintof F_1coversdomain value of each constraintof F_2.

We suppose that F_1 and F_2 overlap each other if the following terms are satisfied:
$$X_{12} \cap X_{22} \not\equiv \emptyset, X_{13} \cap X_{23} \not\equiv \emptyset, \ldots, X_{1n} \cap X_{2n} \not\equiv \emptyset \ (5).$$
Assume specific domain of each constrainthasmagnitude of $|X|$, so that specific domain of the filter has magnitude of $\prod_{i=1}^{n} |X_i|$ (6).

When receiving a new subscription message from network interface (I) which requests service S, it has a filter is denoted by formula: $F = P_{12} \wedge P_{13} \wedge \ldots \wedge P_{1n}$. We have to check whether F is covered by an existing filter. If there is no filter, have to check whether it has any common constraints with existing filter emitted from an node interface I. For doing this task efficiently We have to apply and innovate R tree, in this paper it is called R^+, this tree nowadays is used in many different fields. For example R tree is applied for storing space objects in Google MAP, digital Map, System Paging file with high efficiently in storing and searching.

2 Improving R^+Tree to Store and Search Filter

2.1 Structure of R^+ Tree

Structure of leaf node: it is a set S that consists of n elements, each element consists of two items P and FS: P is a pointer that points to a filter F that is indexed in this R^+ tree and FS is a filter summary that covers filter F: $FS \supseteq F$.

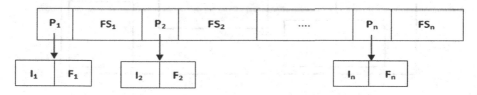

Fig. 1. The structure of a leaf node of R^+ tree

The filters are added by the algorithm that will be presented in the following section.

a) The leaf node stores the set of summary filters of some filters in routing table that are indexed in the R^+ tree that are received from routers on networks.

b) Each filter is indexed in R^+ tree consists of two components: I and F, in which I is address of router that have sent subscription message, F is a filter including of some constraints.

c) The inner nodes of tree that are not the leaf nodes, each node stores a set of summary filters of its child nodes. Similarly leaf node, the structure of an inner node is as follows:

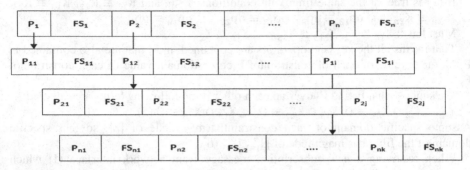

Fig. 2. The structure of an inner node in R^+ tree

d) Thus, each inner node stores a set of n elements in which each element consists of two components: P and FS, P is a pointer that points to an inner node or leaf node of the R^+ Tree. FS is a summary filter that covers the whole set of n summary filters of the node pointed by P. This means: $FS = \bigcup_{i=1}^{n} FS_i$. The following diagram describes the covering relationship with n=6:

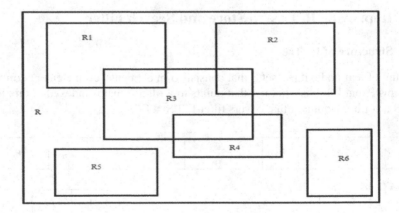

Fig. 3. The covering model with R filter covers its six child filters R_1 to R_6

Thus We have:

a) The Root node stores a set of the highest level summary filters of its child nodes that form the routing table. Therefore the summary filter of root node covers the whole routing table. So that when checking if a filter belongs to routing table, at first examine whether it is covered by summary filter of the root node. If it is not covered, We conclude this filter doesn't belong to the routing table.

b) Each leaf node or inner node has a number of child nodes which is bound by a lower bound m and a upper bound M: $Amount_{child} \in [m, n]$, m and $M \in N$. Usually We choose $m = \lfloor \frac{M}{2} \rfloor$ or $m = \lfloor \frac{M}{3} \rfloor$ because when number of child nodes of one node reaches M+1, We have to split this node into two nodes so that each node has a approximately equal number of child nodes.

c) R^+ tree is a balance tree, this means that the height from any leaf node to root node of tree is equal. The proving is based on building tree with new filter is only added to some leaf node. At the beginning, the tree has only one node which is both root and leaf node simultaneously. When number of filters are added to node is greater than M, create a new leaf node, split its child nodes into 2 leaf nodes. Then create a new root node, it is parent of these two leaf nodes. Assume that at some time, all inner nodes and leaf nodes and root are having M child nodes. The problem is to insert one filter to some leaf node (L), the solution is to create a new leaf node (L_1), and split the set of filters of current node into two subsets of leaf nodes of L and L_1. At this time parent node (N) of current leaf node L has (M+1) child nodes, so have to create new node N_1 with the same level of N, split child nodes of N into two nodes N and N_1. Gradually applying the same procedure getting to the root node (R), at root node, create new node (R_1), divide the set of child nodes of root node into two nodes R and R_1. Create new root node R' points to R and R_1. At this moment the height of all leaf nodes is increased by one. So that R^+ tree is balance tree.

d) Thus the height of the tree from a leaf node to the root node is satisfied the following un-equation system: $\log_M(N) - 1 \leq Height_{R^+} \leq \log_m(N)$, in which N is number of nodes of tree. Prove: i) At level 0, We have one node that is root node (equal to M^0), at level 1, We have maximum number of M^1 nodes, minimum number of m^1 nodes,..., at level n, We have maximum number of M^n nodes and minimum number of m^n nodes. ii) Consequently, with R^+ tree with high is n We have nodes of n+1 levels: 0, 1, 2, ..., n, total of nodes R^+ tree is N which has to satisfy un-equation system: $N \leq \sum_{i=0}^{n} M^i = \frac{M^{n+1}-1}{M-1}$ and $N \geq \sum_{i=0}^{n} m^i = \frac{m^{n+1}-1}{m-1}$ $=> m^n \leq N \leq M^{n+1}$ $=> [\log_M(N) - 1] \leq n \leq \log_m(N)$.

2.2   Establishing and Searching Algorithms

2.2.1   The Establishing Algorithm

At first R^+ tree has only one node, this is both leaf and root of tree, this node points to a filter is created to store the filter of new subscription message that has been received at current router. When adding new filter F to R^+ tree, We have to find a leaf node N, add F to N. The process for finding node N begins from root node R:

a) If R has no child node then: N=R;

b) If R has some child nodes, that means R^+ tree has some inner nodes, assume that R consists of n components: $C_1, C_2, ..., C_n$, denote by $S = \{C_1, C_2, ..., C_n\}$. In which each C_i has two items: P_i and FS_i, P_i points to its child node and FS_i is summary filter of its child node filters.

For each component C_i in S: *i)* Find minimum filter F_{min} satisfies: $(FS_i \cup F_{min}) \supseteq F$, it means FS_i is extended by minimum filter to cover filter F. *ii)* After this loop finished We will find out $F_{min_{final}} = min\{F_{min_i}\}$ it is respective to C_{min}. *iii)* If there are many C_i satisfy this condition, choose the component that has $|FS_i|$ is minimum.

c) Assume finding out C_{final} that has pointer points to its child node R_{child}. Assign temporary node $N_{temp} = R_{child}$.

d) Apply the step (b) for N_{temp} continuously until N_{temp} is leaf node.

e) Assign: $N = N_{temp}$.

f) Top up the set of filters that are stored by N with F.

2.2.2   Searching Algorithm

a) The searching algorithm finds a leaf node N that has a filter that conforms most to a given filter F. Starting from the root of tree, assume that R has n components: $S = \{C_1, C_2, ..., C_n\}$. Assign R to $N_{current}$ and execute step (b).

b) Execute for each component C_i of $N_{current}$: C_i consists of two items P_i and FS_i, P_i points to $N_{current}$'s i^{th} child node denoted by $Child_i$, FS_i is summary filter of all filters that are stored by $Child_i$.

Check condition FS_i and F have common part, if it's true then continue to check if $Child_i$ is leaf node then execute (c) else assign $Child_i$ to $N_{current}$ and execute (b) recursively;

c) We calculate FS_{common} is common part of FS of $Child_i$ and F. Denote S_F is a set of some FS_{common} found. Add FS_{common} to S_F. Go to (b) for next component of $N_{current}$.

d) Find some maximum items (FS) from S_F, that belong to some leaf nodes $\{N_{max}\}$. Thus the set $\{N_{max}\}$ is result of algorithm.

2.2.3   Algorithm for Adding a Filter to R^+ Tree

This algorithm adds a new filter F to a R^+ tree: First, establish R^+ tree if it does not exist. Secondly,check if this filter exists in this R^+ tree. If it's true then exit the algorithm, otherwise find a leaf node in tree to store this filter. In this section introduce the algorithm to insert a filter to a leaf node:

a) Create a filter node to store filterF and I, I is interface address of the route has emitted the subscription message which containedthe filter F, *i)* create a filter node FN, *ii)* add filter F to FN and assign interface address I to FN: FN.filter=F; FN.Interface=I;

b) Assume current node is N, if number of components of N is lower than M then *i)* create new component C_{new} of N, it has two elements P and FS; *ii)* Calculate filter summary of F and assign to FS, P points to FN: N.FS=Summary(F); N.P=FN. Otherwise go to step (c).

c) Have to do *i)* create new node N_1, *ii)* split the set of all components of N in addition C_{new} into two subsets fairly, each of which contains components of one node N or N_1. Check the condition, whether N has no parent node, if it's true new node $P_N$iscreated, this node has two components C_1 and C_2. Assign $C_1.FS = Summary(N_1)$, $C_1.P = N_1$, $C_2.FS = Summary(N_2)$ and $C_2.P = N_2$. Now P_N is the root of R^+ tree, finish algorithm (the root of tree has at least two children). Otherwise, go to step (d).

d) N has a parent node, this node is denoted by P_N, P_N stores component C_N, C_N has two elements FS and P, P points to N, *i)* if N_1 hasn't been created in (c) then recalculate filter summary for N, assign to FS then go to step (f), *ii)* otherwise go to step (e).

e) Create a new component C_{new} of P_N, C_{new} has two elements P, FS, *i)* calculate filter summary of N_1, assign to FS: $C_{new}.FS=Summary(N_1)$; *ii)* assign P to N_1: $C_{new}.P=N_1$. Go to step (g).

f) Check filter summary of P_N, if it has changed, have to assign $N=P_N$, then go to step(d). Continue until N is root node.

g) Check number of components of P_N, if this number more than M, assign $N=P_N$, go to step (c). Continue until go to the root node then finish algorithm.

2.2.4   Algorithm for Deleting a Filter from R⁺ Tree

Assume need to remove a filter F from R^+ tree. First, leaf node N has been found which is leaf node and may store F. Secondly check whether N really stores F. The purpose of this algorithm is to find N by some following steps:

a) If R^+ tree have only one node R this is both leaf and root of tree then: N=R;

b) Denote N_{temp} is current processing node: $N_{temp}=R$; N_{temp} has n components: {C_1, C_2, ..., C_n}, for each component C_i of N_{temp} has two elements P_i and FS_i:

c) If FS_i and F have common part then assign $N_{temp}=C_i.P_i$, if N_{temp} isn't leaf node then continue step (b); otherwise: $N= N_{temp}$, assume N stores a set of n filters {F_i}, check each filter F_i of N to see whether F_i and F are equal, *i)* if this condition is true then remove F_i from N, recalculate R^+ by following regulating algorithm, this algorithm is finished; *ii)* if no filter satisfies then continue step (c) for next component of N_{temp}.

d) Continue until F is found or all tree's nodes are scanned.

2.2.5   Algorithm for Regulating R⁺ Tree

a) Starting from the leafnode S from which a filter is removed.

b) If the number of components of S isn't satisfied the condition (3) then remove S from R^+, add S to a set Q which stores temporarilyall nodes have removed of R^+ and go to step (c). If it is satisfied then finish algorithm.

c) If S has parent node then assign S=S.parent, *i)* if S is not root of the tree then go to step (b); *ii)* otherwiseadd root of the tree to Q.

d) Get last node S has just been put to set Q, scan this subtreefor adding its filters to original R^+ tree.

3   Algorithm for Splitting One Node of R⁺Tree into Two Nodes

3.1   Processing Steps of the Algorithm

When number of components of one node is more than upper bound M, thus having to split this node into two nodes with each node has about $\left\lceil \frac{M+1}{2} \right\rceil$ components. Assume current processing node is N:

a) Create new node N_1, get $\left\lceil \frac{M+1}{2} \right\rceil$ components from N to N_1 by one of two algorithms that are described morespecific below.

b) *i)* If parent of N exists then add N_1 to the set of children of N and continue step (c); *ii)* otherwise create new node that will be new root of tree R. Add N and N_1 to the set of children of R, finish the algorithm.

c) Assign N=N.Parent, *i)* if number of child nodes of N is more than M then go to step (a); *ii)* otherwise finish the algorithm.

3.2   Algorithm Evaluation

The algorithm has maximum complexity in case of regulating tree from one leaf node to the root node of the tree. This is $O[\log_m(N)*K]$, in which N is number nodes of the tree, K is complexity of the splitting algorithm.

4   Algorithm for Splitting Components of a Node into Two Subsets

4.1   Quadratic Algorithm

4.1.1   Algorithm Specification

Assume S is a set of summary filters of current processing node that needs to be splited: $S=\{F_1, F_2, ..., F_n\}$ satisfies equation: n=M+1. The requirement of algorithm is: splitting S into two subsets S_1 and S_2 with almost the same size. Require to choose two beginning elements for these two subsetsby the following algorithm:

Algorithm 1:

a) Give filter $F_{temp}$is temporary filter, id_1, id_2 are two integers for storing two indexes of choosen filters, assign filter $F_{temp} = \emptyset$, id_1=-1, id_2=-1;

b) For each filter F_i in theset S of filters execute (c);

c) For each filter F_j in the set S execute (d);

d) Calculate filter F_{ij} that covers both filter F_i and F_j; calculate: $F_i' = F_{ij} \setminus F_i$, $F_j' = F_{ij} \setminus F_j$, if $|F_i' \setminus F_j'| > |F_{temp}|$ (in which $\setminus$ is filter subtract operator) then assign: id_1=i, id_2=j and $F_{temp}= |F_i' \setminus F_j'|$.

When this algorithm finished, gain id_1 and id_2 are indexes of two filters (FI_1 and FI_2) for beginning filters of two sets S_1 and S_2.

Choose next elements for each setS_i and $S_j$according to following algorithm:

Algorithm 2:

a)Assume$F_1$and$F_2$are summary filters of S_1 and S_2respectively, assign $F_1=\emptyset$, $F_2=\emptyset$.

b) For each filter $F_i$of the set S except FI_1 and FI_2 execute (c).

c)CalculateF_1'=$(F_1 UF_i) \setminus F_i$, F_2'=$(F_2 UF_i) \setminus F_i$,in which denote $(F_1 UF_2)$is filter that is result of extending$F_1$to cover F_2. Go to step (d).

d) If $F_1'> F_2'$then put F_i into S_2 and assign $F_2=F_2 UF_i$ (4).

e) If $F_1'< F_2'$ then put F_i into S_1 and assign $F_1=F_1 UF_i$ (5).

g) If $F_1'= F_2'$ then put F_i into what set depends on the set that has number of elements isless than other set, if two sets have equal number of elements then put $F_i$into a random set, recalculate (4) or (5) respectively. Go to (b) for the next item of S.

4.1.2. Evaluating Algorithm

The algorithm 1 has complexity of $O(n^2)$, the algorithm 2 has complexity of $O(n)$. Therefore the complexity of Quadratic algorithm is $O(n^2)$.

4.2   Linear Algorithm

4.2.1. Algorithm Specification

We have to split the set S of summary filters of the current processing node into two approximate equal sets S_1 and S_2.

Some assumptions:

a)Each filter of S has a set of predicates, each predicate has a value domain D.

b) Each value domainDhas lower boundD_{min} and upper boundD_{max}, so that $D=[D_{min}, D_{max}]$.

The algorithm for finding two first elements of two subsets S_1 and S_2

a) For each key K, find maximum lower bound L_{max} and minimum upper bound $U_{min}$of all predicates of Swhich have key K. These bounds are belonged to two filters FL_{max}, FU_{min} respectively.

b) For each K, also find the minimum lower bound L_{min} and maximum upper bound U_{max} of all predicates of S that have key K. These bounds are belonged to two filters FL_{min} and FU_{max} respectively.

c) Calculate for each key: $V_m = \frac{U_{min}-L_{max}}{U_{max}-L_{min}}$ (6).

d) Choose two first elements of two subsets S_1 and S_2 froma pair of filters (FL_{min}, FU_{max}) which has V_m that is maximum on all their keys.

e) With (n-2) remaining filters, put each filter to one of two sets S_1 and S_2 in turn.

4.2.2   Evaluating Algorithm

The complexity of algorithm to choose two first filters of two sets S_1 and S_2 is rated by formula ($|F|*|S|$), $|F|$ is number of predicates of filter F, $|S|$ is number of filters of S.

The complexity of algorithm to put (n-2) remaining filters to two sets S_1 and S_2 is $O(n)$, n is number of filters of the set of filters S.

5   Cluster Routing Based on Filter Summary [6]

5.1   Cluster Routing Concept

Each node builds it's own R^+ tree when it receives subscription filter from network. The root of each tree will store filter summary of it's routing table. Define a point (P) is centroid of the rectangle that is established from each filter summary. To cluster network based on centroid of subscription filter, assume that: i) the space of all filter is S, ii) S consists of some sub-spaces $\{S_1, S_2, ..., S_n\}$. So when a node on a cluster receives one filter, it will forward this filter to appropriate cluster head based on point P of this filter.

5.2   Cluster Routing Performance

Use this cluster routing that will reduce time required to find matched subscriptions with each received content message. When a node receives a content message, this content message is a point on space S. It checks to find sub-space S_i that P belongs to and S_i has cluster head (CH_i) respectively. Then the node forwards this content message to CH_i. In CH_i all matched subscriptions will be found using above search algorithm. This cluster algorithm has complexity is $O(n*m)$, n is number of sub-spaces and m is number of predcates of each filter, it is nearly a constant.

6   Evaluating Results and Future Development

6.1   The Results of Executing above Mentioned Algorithms

a)   Build a R^+ tree from a set of filters entered from keyboard or read from disk file.

All classes and modules to simulate presented algorithms have been written by C#.NET. Besides there are some algorithms for following purposes:

*i,*Check if one filter covers or overlaps other filter.

*ii,*Extend one filter to cover other filter.

*iii,*Calculate subtractionof two filters.

b)   Build R^+ with number of filters changes from 100000 to 290000, measure the time in ms required to execute for each number of filters to draw the diagram based on these results as below:

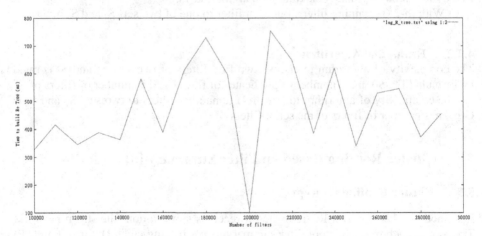

Fig. 4. Execution time in ms to build R^+ tree

As the diagram shows that the time required to build R^+ does not increase continuously when number of filters increases.

c)   Build a R^+tree and use theQuadratic algorithm for splitting node with the number of filters changes from 100000 to 290000 and delete filters, measure the time required in mili second to delete filters and regulate the tree to draw diagram based on the measured results:

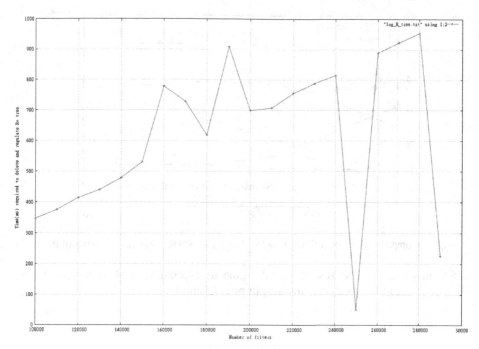

Fig. 5. Execution time in ms to delete filters and regulate R⁺ tree

As the diagram shows that the time required to delete filters and regulate R⁺ does not increase continuously when number of filters increases.

  d)   Search a filter from R⁺ tree, measure searching time when number of filters is gradually changed. See following diagram, conclude that when number of filters is increased, required time is reduced.

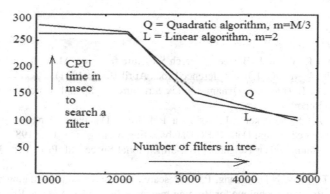

Fig. 6. Compare execution time to search filter with number of filters changed

  e) Update, delete filters from R⁺ tree, with concurrently regulating tree to satisfy the constraint on number of child nodes of each inner node. Draw diagram to evaluate operational time based on two splitting node algorithms and variable number of nodes of R⁺ tree[2].

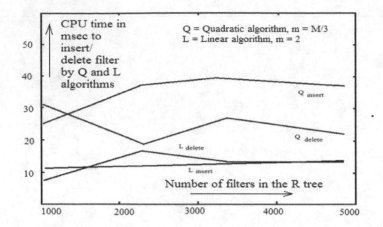

Fig. 7. Compare operational time to insert/ delete filters with change in number of filters

See this figure to get results that the time to execute is stable when number of filters increases for two algorithms to split node Q and L.

6.2 Future Developing

At the current time above algorithms have been simulated to get above operational results are on numeric value type of predicate, in the future applying above algorithms for value type of string.

Acknowledgements. I would like to thank the dedicated instructors, teachers for help and support. My office, family, brothers and friends have made many favorable conditions for studying and researchingto complete this research paper.

References

[1] Robmson, J.T.: The K-D-B Tree A Search Structure for Large Multldimenslonal Dynarmc Indexes. In: 4CM-SIGMOD Conference Proc., April 10-18 (1981)
[2] Guttman, A.: R-Trees - A Dynamic Index Structure for Spatial Searching, University of California Berkeley
[3] Guttman, A., Stonebraker, M.: Using a Relational Database Management System for Computer Added Design Data. IEEE Database Engineering 5(2) (June 1982)
[4] Yuval, G.: Finding Near Neighbors in k-dimensional Space. Inf. Proc. Lett. 3(4), 113–114 (1975)
[5] Long, N.T., Thuy, N.D., Hoang, P.H.: Research on Innovating, Evaluating and Applying Multicast Routing Technique for Routing messages in Service-oriented Routing. In: Vinh, P.C., Hung, N.M., Tung, N.T., Suzuki, J. (eds.) ICCASA 2012. LNICST, vol. 109, pp. 212–228. Springer, Heidelberg (2013)
[6] Wang, Y.-M., Qiu, L., Verbowski, C., Achlioptas, D., Das, G., Larson, P.: Summary-based Routing for Content-based Event Distribution Networks, Microsoft Research, Redmond, WA, USA (2004)

Research on Improving, Evaluating and Applying the Ternary Search Tree and Binary Search for Storing and Searching Content - Based Address for Forwarding Technique in Service-Oriented Routing

Nguyen Thanh Long, Nguyen Duc Thuy, Pham Huy Hoang, and Tran Dinh Chien

[1] Informatics Center of Ha noi Telecommunications
75 Dinh Tien Hoang, Hoan Kiem, Ha Noi, Viet Nam
{longptpm,chientd}@vnpt-hanoi.com.vn
[2] Research Institute of Posts and Telecommunications
122 Hoang Quoc Viet, Nghia Tan, Cau Giay, Hanoi, Viet Nam
thuynd@ptit.edu.vn
[3] Hanoi University of Science and Technology
1 Dai Co Viet Road, Hanoi, Viet Nam
hoangph@soict.hut.edu.vn

Abstract. Service-based network infrastructure is a new network interface in which the flow of messages is controlled by class of services that generated it. Next is its content, improved shipping address specified by the sender and attached to the message. Networks based on services complement for networks based on traditional unicast and multicast addresses, which provides support for communication patterns based on the service class of large-scale applications, loose connections, multiple partitions and scattered like auctions, information sharing, distributed according to personal information.

With Service Based Routing (SBR), the sender does not indicate message receiver by the unicast or multicast use. Instead it simply pushes messages to the network. It defines the routing based on the messages it cares. It determines the appropriate message class based on message content based on its key-value pairs or regular expressions. Therefore, in SBR routing the receiver determines the transmission of messages, not the sender. Communication based on content services increases the independence, flexibility in the distributed architecture. In SBR the routing table consist of content based addresses, We have to find the structure to store and organize routing table efficiently and save memory and time to search all its items match a content message. In this paper We introduce and improve *Ternary Search Tree* structure to use for storing and process the SBR routing table.

Keywords: Ad hoc network, MANET, TST, ternary search tree, binary, forwarding, service, content.

H. Qian and K. Kang (Eds.): WICON 2013, LNICST 121, pp. 189–202, 2013.
© Institute for Computer Sciences, Social Informatics and Telecommunications Engineering 2013

1   Introduction of Service-Oriented Routing

1.1   Service-Oriented Routing Protocol Model

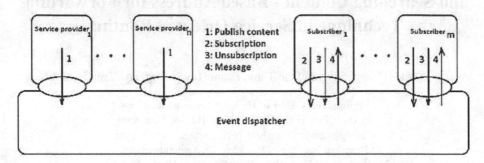

Fig. 1. Model of service-oriented routing network

Interaction model of service delivery or content publishing and content subscription (abbreviated by P / S) is the interaction model is done asynchronously in the service based routing (SBR)system.

Most of the SBR routing system is based on the P / S model.

1.2   Overview of Service Oriented Architecture

Service Oriented Architecture is the architecture based on the patterns.

There are three types of Pattern:

    a)   Architecture;

    b)   Design;

    c)   Enforcement;

In Pattern-oriented software, schema structured platform is shown for software systems. It provides a set of subsystems defined, indicating the ability to perform, including the rules and guidelines for organizing the relationship between them.

Overlaying the traditional point - to - point: modern communication based on Virtual Endpoint / Message Broker.

To allow flexible communication, the ability to provide location transparency for the transmission of information between applications. Position transparency is defined as to avoid the point - to - point connection because the application is separated with the data transmission services below, will undertake the implementation when the applications require communicating with each other.

1.3   Characteristics of Service-Oriented Routing

Service-based network infrastructure is a new network interface in which the flow of messages is controlled by class of service that generated it. Next is its content, improved shipping address specified by the sender and attached to the message.

Networks based on services complement for networks based on traditional unicast and multicast addresses, which provides support for communication patterns based on the service class of large-scale applications, loose connections, multiple partitions and scattered like auctions, information sharing, combined, distributed, sensor networks, distributed according to personal information, service discovery, multi-player game.

In the SBR routing, the sender does not indicate message receiver by the unicast or multicast use. Instead it simply pushing messages to the network. It defines the routing based on the messages it cares. It determines the appropriate message class based on message content based on its key-value pairs or regular expressions. Therefore, in SBR routing the receiver determines the transmission of messages, not the sender. Communication based on content services increases the independence, flexibility in the distributed architecture.

2   Organization of the Message Types in SBR Network [7]

2.1   The Subscription / Unsubscription Message

Subscription / unsubscription message is emitted from the application service classes to subscribe / unsubscribe content requests. The message is structured: the address of the subscriber and binding on the list of services and content requirements (constraints). In particular, each constraint is a set of 3 components, has the form: (key, operator, value). For example, the contents of the registration message: [service_class = "Network monitor" $\land$ alert-type = "instrusion" $\land$ severity> 2] or [service_class = "Network monitor" $\land$ class = "alert" $\land$ device-type = "web-server"], these are 2 request messages of Network monitor service class.

2.2   The Content Message

Content messages are transmitted from the host service provider. These messages will be transmitted to the network, it will be transmitted to the machine based on the subscription request message received from that machine.

2.3   The Advertisement Message

Advertisement message is the message advertises the basic content that certain services provide for applications. To direct the subscription requests to the right offer places. Prevents spread the subscription messages throughout the network.

Advertisement message is very useful for establishing multicast tree from the root that is destination node to a group of matched content providing nodes. Then matched content will be sent simultaneously from leaf nodes to root node by this multicast tree.

Establish multicast tree by a pair of messages Route Request (RREQ) and Route Reply (RREP): i) the node has subscription request will make RREQ, broadcasts it to network; ii) any node that has advertisement messages that are matched this subscription message, will make RREP that stores the path from the content publishing node to the content requesting node and forward back to this node; iii) after a time interval, all paths from received RREP messages will make the multicast tree from requesting node to content publishing nodes.

The advertising message is passed under the minimum spanning tree from source node.

Advertisement message is also structurally similar content message, including a set of attributes. So the content message is to expand the content of advertising messages.

Advertisement message is transmitted from the service delivery system.

2.4   The Message Pair of Update Request and Reply Sender

Use this pair of messages to update source node routing table on demand. Sender request: request from the router, the structure includes 3 fields. Two fields: sender address and request number determine the uniqueness of the message. Timeout determines the longest time the sender waits for an answer. This message is transmitted by the minimum spanning tree (Broadcast) starting from the source router (formed by Prim algorithm) to the other routers in the network.

When the leaf router nodes of Broadcast tree receive the sender request message, it will respond by reply update (UR) message. The message consists of three fields, two fields from the sender request, the field no.3 contains its content based address. The UR message spreads back the sender router.

On the way to the sender router, the intermediate router will incorporate its content based address and of the message then push it to the sender router.

When the sender router receives UR message, it updates its routing table. End of the implementation process.

2.5   Route Request and Route Reply Message Pair

This pair of messages is used to detect routes on the network to a set of destination addresses from a source node for building multicast trees with root is source node and leaf nodes are this set of destination nodes.

Route request message is used to make a request from the source router, the message structure consists of eight fields. Two fields: 1) Source Address and 2) Request Number determine the uniqueness of the message. 3) The Type field identifies of the kind of message, is set to 1; 4) the Timeout field determines the longest time the sender node waits for a response. 5) The Time To Live (TTL) field determines the maximum number of HOPs of the route that message is passed on. 6) The Route field records addresses of the hops on the route the message passes through. 7) The Free Time Slots field records free bandwidth at the nodes of the route that message is transmitted on. 8) The Destination List field saves address list that contains addresses of the set of destination nodes that are the leaf nodes of multicast trees that we need to build. The message is transmitted by broadcast protocol to other routers in the MANET. When a node receives RREQ, it checks whether it's address is in destination field, if it is true, this node makes Route Reply message and forwards back it to the source node on the detected route. RREQ message contains all fields as RREQ message except the destination field.

3   The Concepts and Terminology

3.1   Service Based Forwarding Table Concept

Each service has a separate forwarding table.

The table includes predicates, also called content-based addresses.

Forwarding table is mapping 1-1 between content-based address and the identity of the subscriber.

Predicate is logical disjunction of filters are received from the subscriber.

Forwarding algorithm is the algorithm finding in the forwarding table the filters match message content received.

Filter is required content (subscription) from a subscriber. Each filter is a combination of subscriber identification and conjunction of the constraints.

3.2   Routing Technology in Service Oriented Routing

A. Find relevant content and communications

Upon receiving a content message from certain application services on the network. The router compares the received data with predicate list to determine compliance Predicates. If found, the message will be pushed to the requested nodes respectively.

The algorithm finds out set of routers have predicates   match message received.

How to find the shortest path from source node to the nodes with compliance requirements:

Option 1: Find the shortest path from source node to the appropriate node on the request graph is weighted according to **Dijkstra**'s algorithm. Synthesis of the routes forms the tree for transmitting messages from the source node.

Option 2: Find the minimum spanning tree by **Prim**'s algorithm, using the nearest neighbor method. The tree is found to satisfy the conditions of having root is the original source node, the leave nodes are the requesting nodes.

At each router has appropriate request, when receiving a message, it sends the message to the request nodes in its own network.

3.3   Messages Forwarding Technique in Service-Oriented Routing

A. Concepts and terminology:

Forward algorithm is finding algorithm in the forwarding table the filter matches message content received.

The transition Table is the 1-1 relation between Predicate and the identity of the subscriber.

Filter is required content subscription from the subscriber. Each filter is a combination of subscriber identification and conjunction of the constraints.

Predicate is disjunction of filters is received from the subscriber.

Forwarding table includes predicates also called content-based addresses.

B. Find relevant content and communications

1. Find matched predicates

Upon receiving a content message from certain application services of the network. Router will compare the received data with stored Predicate list on it to see which predicate matches. If found, the message will be pushed to the requested node.

The algorithm will find all routers have matched predicates with the message received. Divide the set of all constraints into two subsets: i) the first subset includes constraints which have value component of string type; ii) the second subset includes constraints which have value component of number type. Build improved ternary search tree from the first subset of constraints. Build a dynamic array with each element for each separated key, an element of the array is the root of a multi branches tree, a branch for one of operators that stores all values of all constraints with this key and operator.

2. Routing requested content to the nodes that have matched subscription

How to find the shortest path from source node to the node with compliance requirements:

a)   *Method 1:*

Find the shortest path from source router to other routers in the network by **Dijkstra**'s algorithm.

The algorithm ends when finding the shortest path to all routers have consistent requirements. So we find the tree of transmitting messages from the source router to routers with the matched requirements by removing the leaf nodes don't have matched requests.

On the paths from the source router, the intermediate routers don't have matched requests will relay the message to the next routers on the tree.

When the message has reaches the leaf routers, will pass the message to its child nodes in their own network and don't relay message to other routers on the network.

b)   *Method 2:*

Find the minimum spanning tree by **Prim** algorithm, using the nearest neighbor method. The tree found to satisfy the conditions of having root is the original source node, the leave nodes are the request nodes.

Description of algorithm: The graph consists of n vertices or routers form the network, the weights of links between routers is given by the weighted matrix C. Conventional weighting of the link between not directly connected routers is a very large number.

At the tree T and a node v, called the minimum distance from v to T is the smallest weights of the edges connecting v to a vertex point in T: $d[v] = \min \{c[u, v] \mid u \in T\}$.

1. Initially started skeleton tree T consisting of the source node s: $T = \{(s,)\}$.

2. Then just select from the set of nodes outside of the tree T a node v has link e with the smallest weight, admitting it to T, simultaneously admitting that link e into skeleton tree T: $T = T \cup \{(v, e)\}$.

3. Perform step 2 until:

Or has admitted all of the requested nodes, we have T is the smallest skeleton tree from source node to all the request nodes.

Or not admit all of the request nodes when the node outside T have links to any node of T has extreme large weight. When it will only transmit the message to a subset of request nodes.

At each router has appropriate request, when receiving the message it sends to the nodes have appropriate requests on its own network.

4   Storing Predicates Having String Values in Ternary Search Tree

4.1   Overview Ternary Search Tree

In computer science, ternary search tree (TST) is a tree data structure in which the child nodes of a tree are arranged as a standard binary search tree. Denote TST by recursive formula:

$$TST = \{TST_{left}, Root, TST_{right}\} \tag{1}$$

In which Root stores the first character X of the first string, it has left and right pointers that point to left and right child TSTs denoted by TST_{left} and TST_{right} respectively. TST_{left} has root stores a character which stands before X in Alphabet table. TST_{right} has root stores a character which stands after X in Alphabet table. Root has middle child that store next character in current string. End of string is detected by storing a special character for example '#'.

The search for a string in a Ternary Search Tree consists of a series of binary search steps, each step for finding a character in a string. Current character in the string value compares with the character of the current node, one of the three options can happen:

i) If character in string value is less than then continues the search with the left child node.

ii) If character in string value is more than then continues the search with the right child node.

iii) If equal, the search continued with the middle node and move to the next character in the string value.

The image below illustrates a ternary search tree with the strings "as", "at", "cup", "cute", "he", "i" and "us":

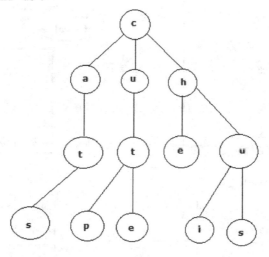

Fig. 2. Ternary Search Tree stores "as", "at", "cup", "cute", "he", "i" and "us"

As with the structure of another ternary data, each node in a ternary search tree represents a prefix of the string is stored. All the strings are in the middle of a tree that begin with that prefix.

Unlike a binary search tree, a ternary search tree can be balanced or unbalanced, based on the order of strings are added to the tree. The search for a string length m in a balanced ternary search tree is to use: $[m + \log_2(n)]$ character comparisons. In particular, each of a comparison or a character is found in the tree or the search area is divided into 2 parts.

A ternary search tree can store data in compressed format to save storage space in which the redundant nodes are removed.

4.2   Improve Ternary Search Tree to Store the Predicates (Content - Based Addresses)

For data of string type has more data comparisons, use the modified Ternary Search Tree structure (Ternary Search Tree: TST).

The end node of string value in TST has a pointer to the dynamic list of pointers, each pointer points to the dynamic list of operators, which are described in the diagram below:

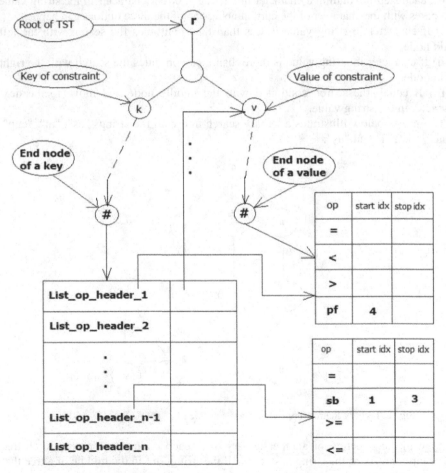

Fig. 3. Improved Ternary Search Tree stores predicates in Routing Table

Assuming the value domain of each key of the constraints is independent.

In case of a key is associated with multiple constraints will be organized into groups. In which the operators associated with a given value are put into a dynamic array, a pointer to the first element is List_op_header_i. The pointers that consist of List_op_header_1, List_op_header_2, …, List_op_header_n are stored in a dynamic array.

The set of the operators that are belonged to a group of constraints related to one key by the way: (denote a constraint by: (key, op, value)).

Archive list of operators associated with a value in a dynamic array:

With each list of the operators, maintain a pointer to the head of this list: List_op_header.

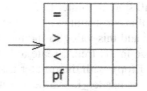

Fig. 4. Dynamic array of the operators of a group by a pair of a value and a key

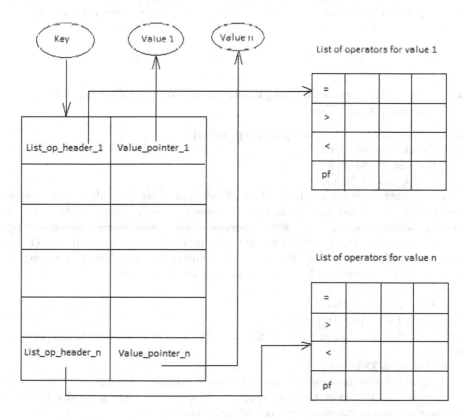

Fig. 5. Linked list of operators of a group of constraints have a same key

A set of pointers that point to head of the lists are put into a dynamic array.

The end node of a key in the ternary search tree will store a pointer that point to this dynamic array.

The dynamic array stores a list of pointers, each pointer points to the first element of the dynamic list of corresponding operators of the constraints of a value.

The algorithm checks existence and adds a constraint to a Ternary Search Tree, the constraint has the form of (**key, op, value**) has the following steps:

1, Check whether the key exists in the ternary search tree or not.

2, If it doesn't already exist, add the key in the ternary search tree. We create a list of pointers (List_of_operator) that has one pointer List_op_header. The List_op_header point to the list of storage components for storing the constraint operators (at first having op). The leaf node in the Ternary Search Tree is belonged to a part of Tree stores key that will store a pointer to List_of_operator.

3, Check if the value part of this constraint exists in the Tree.

4, If it doesn't already exist: add this value to the tree with Value_pointer_i points to the starting node of this value in the tree. Create a dynamic list, at first with only one item for storing the operator (op), with the pointer List_op_header_i points to this list. Two components (List_op_header_i, Value_pointer_i) belong to an item Key_group_i. Add Key_group_i to the list of pointers.

5, If exists, get the pointer to the list of operators corresponding value. Update this list of operators so that this list contains the operator op of the current constraint.

6, Check if the operator op has been stored in the dynamic list pointed by List_op_header_i.

If it doesn't exist, add an item to store op at the end of the list.

4.3   The Algorithm for Checking Existence and Adding a Constraint to Ternary Search Tree

Assume a constraint is denoted by **{key, op, value}**:

1. Check ∃ key in TST.

2. If ∄ key in TST then

a. TST = TST ∪ {key};

b. Create operator list: List_of_operator with only one item: List_of_operator_item={List_op_header, Pointer_to_node_value}. In which List_op_header points to the operator list with one element op, Pointer_to_Node_value points to entrance node in TST belongs to a part of TST that stores value of this constraint. We have to set a pointer in leaf node of TST belongs to a part of TST that stores the key which points to List_of_operator.

3. Check ∃ value in TST:

4. If ∄ value in TST then:

a. TST = TST ∪ {value}

b. Create dynamic list with one element op, and set List_op_headerpoints to this list.

5. If value in TST then:

a. Set: List_op_header points to the list of operators of value.

b. Check ∃ op in the list of operators is pointed by List_op_header. If ∄ then add new element stores op and relative information to this list.

4.4   The Algorithm for Finding All Nodes That Have Suitable Subscriptions with a Content Message

1) Build TST tree   from all constraints in routing table if this tree doesn't exist.

2) Use SBR_Couting algorithm to find all constraints are suitable with every property of content message and finally get list of nodes to transfer content message to depending on addresses (predicates) of content based routing table:

a) For each key that exists in current content message: find List_of_operator which is pointed by a pointer of leaf node in TST which belongs to a part of TST that stores key of current property as indicated in above algorithm. For each item in List_of_operator, get List_op_headerelement from List_of_operator_itemthat is the pointer to list of operators relating to the value of current property. Associate this list of operators and other information such as key and value of constraints, replace key with the value from content message. Evaluate the given expressions, We can get all constraints that accommodate current property.

```
public List<cContraint> find_constraint(_message msg)
{
    List<cContraint> kq = new List<cContraint>();
    foreach (_property pt in msg.msgcontent)
    {
        op_1 = Contains(pt.ten);
        if (op_1 != null)
        {
                kq.AddRange(cCommon.find_constraint_match(pt,
op_1.List_op_header, msg.service_name));
        }
    }
    return kq;
}
```

b) Check condition 1: For each constraint found We check if all constraints of the filter accommodate the content message. If this condition is true, add this filter to result list simultaneously add address of node that emit the filter to list of nodes to transfer content message to.

c) Check condition 2: if list of nodes contain all nodes of the network or loop all executions of operations then stop the algorithm.

5   How To Use Binary Search to Store and Search Constraints with Values of Number Type

5.1   How to Implement

Each constraint is a set of 3 components: {key, operator, value}, the set of constraints are divided into 2 types of constraints are: number or string depend on the type of component value.

With type of number:

Step 1: key-based indexing;

Step 2: set up sub-index based on values of each key.

For example, to index the values of the constraints that all have key is name: {name, <, k_1}, {name, <, k_2}, ..., {name, <, k_n}, we sort array of values {k_1, k_2, ..., k_n} in increasing order. Then find all the relevant constraints by the modified binary search to find out range [k_i, k_{i+1}] which attribute value x belongs to. So all the constraints have value from the k_i value backwards satisfied.

5.2   Algorithm Diagram

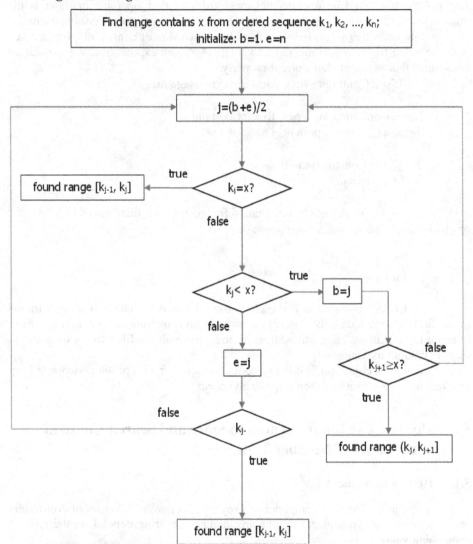

Fig. 6. Algorithm diagram finds out constraints satisfy an attribute of a content message with type of its value is number

6   Simulate the Techniques Presented

Write an application in C# on .NET 4.0 to implement the following tasks:

1) Create subscription message.

2) Create content message.

3) Transmit subscription message to the network using the broadcast method of transmission.

4) Transmit content messages to the network using broadcast method of transmission.

5) When a router receives subscription messages will update the forwarding table.

6) Making ternary search tree based on the transition table for constraints have string type values.

7) Make a list of binary search for constraints have number type values.

8) When a router receives a content message will look in the ternary search trees and binary search list to get a list of constraints have matched this content message.

9) We measure time to find routers by SBR_Couting Algorithm that accommodate a content message when it is happened on network. Transmit to each router in the list using unicast transmission or optimized transmission method. With the amount of predicates change over time We can draw a diagram that represent all results of the test. Following is the diagram that show that results are rather change evenly.

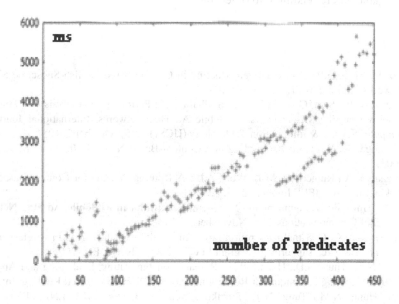

Fig. 7. CBR_Couting Algorithm result diagram

7   Conclusions and Further Research

Ternary search tree has been used in many fields especially in computer science for searching quickly and saving memory. For example, in dictionary searching, because it can be used for approximately search. In one searching time, it can get all items in TST tree that have approximate values with condition value. In association with dynamic arrays and pointers to improve standard TST tree for storing and searching content based addresses in service oriented routing effectively and reliably. Because of using dynamic data structures, so the memory resources are easily to allocate and suppress so that according with computation in MANET. According to simulation results, the time is increased non-linearly when the number of predicates increases.

The use of ternary search trees and binary search list is very effective in the storage, making quick and accurate search.

1) Ternary search tree has the computational complexity is $O[l*(log2(N) + l)] + l$ **result** l, where l is the length of input data, N is the number of strings in TST, result is the result set returned.

2) Binary search on a list of numbers has computational complexity is $O[log2(N)*log2(K)]$, where N is the number of attributes (key), K is the number of corresponding values of the attribute (value).

In near future will research and apply some techniques such as technique to find route that satisfy some quality of service requirements. Search techniques to organize MANET network for SBR routing effectively and safely.

Search a number of other techniques for storing and looking up predicates, such as using hash function. For example, use hash function for hashing all predicates in Routing Table before sending it to other routers.

References

[1] Cao, F., Singh, J.P.: Efficient Event Routing in Content-based Publish-Subscribe Service Networks. In: Proc. IEEE Infocom (2004)
[2] Kalaiarasi, R., Sara, G.S., Pari, S.N., Sridharan, D.: Performance Analysis of Contention Window Cheating Misbehaviors in Mobile Ad Hoc Networks. International Journal of Computer Science & Information Technology (IJCSIT) 2(5) (October 2010)
[3] Carzaniga, A., Wolf, A.: Forwarding in a Content-Based Network. In: Proc. SIGCOMM (2003)
[4] Carzaniga, A., Rutherford, M.J., Wolf, A.L.: A Routing Scheme for Content-Based Networking. In: Proc. IEEE Infocom 2004 (2004)
[5] Li, J.: Time Slot Assignment for Maximum Bandwidth in a Mobile Ad Hoc Network. Journal of Communications 2(6) (November 2007)
[6] Wu, H., Jia, X.: QoS multicast routing by using multiple paths / trees in wireless ad hoc networks, Research supported by a grant FFCSA 2006. Elsevier BV (2006)
[7] Long, N.T., Thuy, N.D., Hoang, P.H.: Research on Innovating, Evaluating and Applying Multicast Routing Technique for Routing messages in Service-oriented Routing. In: Vinh, P.C., Hung, N.M., Tung, N.T., Suzuki, J. (eds.) ICCASA 2012. LNICST, vol. 109, pp. 212–228. Springer, Heidelberg (2013)

Author Index